## DATE DUE

| | | |
|---|---|---|
| | | |
| | | |
| | | |
| | | |
| | | |
| | | |
| | | |
| | | |
| | | |
| | | |
| | | |
| | | |
| | | |
| | | |
| | | |
| | | |
| | | |
| | | |
| GAYLORD | | PRINTED IN U.S.A. |

# Cemetery John

# Cemetery John

## The Undiscovered Mastermind of the Lindbergh Kidnapping

## Robert Zorn

*Foreword by John Douglas and Mark Olshaker*

THE OVERLOOK PRESS

NEW YORK, NY

This edition first published in hardcover in the United States in 2012 by
The Overlook Press, Peter Mayer Publishers, Inc.
141 Wooster Street
New York, NY 10012
www.overlookpress.com
For bulk and special sales, please contact sales@overlookny.com

Photographs appearing on pages 21, 25, 67, 69, 87, 92, 118, and 168 are
courtesy of the New Jersey State Police Museum. Photographs appearing on
pages 33, 45, and 188 are courtesy of the Library of Congress. The map on pages
18-19 furnished by the New York Public Library. The map on page 147 furnished
by the University of Texas at Austin Library, merged the findings of Dr. Kim Rossmo
and reprinted with his permission. Wood grain comparison on page 256 provided
by Kelvin Keraga and reprinted with permission. Original drawing of the Lindbergh
estate on page 263 by George H. Jones. Photographs of John Knoll on pages 21, 121,
and 175 provided by his family members and reprinted with their permission.
Images on pages 62 and 117 are from the author's personal collection.

Cataloging-in-Publication Data is available from the Library of Congress

*Book design and typeformatting by Bernard Schleifer*
Manufactured in the United States of America
2 4 6 8 10 9 7 5 3 1

ISBN 978-1-59020-856-4

*To the memory of my father, Eugene C. Zorn, Jr.*

"When you have eliminated the impossible, whatever remains, however improbable, must be the truth."
—SIR ARTHUR CONAN DOYLE

# Contents

# Foreword

Criminal investigation is a collaborative process, and behavioral profiling is one aspect of that investigation. We stress that regardless of the Hollywood image attached to profilers in recent years, they are not the ones who catch the criminals.

What a good profiler can do—and we note that, like every other profession, they come in all degrees of competence—is either to refocus or redirect an investigation. We do this by studying the crime scene photographs, detective and evidence reports, medical examiner protocols, interviews with victims or their survivors and friends, and any other relevant data that can be supplied. What we try to come back with is a description of the unknown subject, or UNSUB in police jargon, including sex (generally male); age; race; marital, educational and socioeconomic status; whether he is a local or from somewhere else, and if local, where he might live; likely triggers or inciting factors for the crime; the types of behaviors we would expect to see post-offense; and strategies that might help lead to his identification and arrest.

Depending on the nature of the crime and how it was perpetrated, one or another of these factors may be emphasized. But what we can't offer, despite the joking request we're often handed by local law enforcement agencies, is his name, address and phone number. We'll describe the offender, we tell them, but it is up to you to identify him from your own suspect list, or go out and find new suspects based on what we tell you.

Some years ago, when we set out to write our book *The Cases That Haunt Us*, we wanted to take a fresh and objective look at murder cases that for one reason or another had captured the public imagination and that, for one reason or another, either remained unsolved or the subjects of ongoing and passionate controversy. We intended to do this by applying everything we had learned about behavioral profiling and modern criminal investigative analysis as practiced by the FBI's National Center for the Analysis of Violent Crime at the Bureau's academy in Quantico, Virginia. We took on cases from the 1888 Whitechapel Murders of Jack the Ripper in Victorian London up through the 1996 killing of six-year-old JonBenet Ramsey in modern-day Boulder, Colorado.

One of the most intriguing, perplexing, and poignantly tragic cases we analyzed was the 1932 kidnapping and murder of little Charlie Lindbergh, the twenty-month-old firstborn of the Lone Eagle and his wife Anne Morrow, the most famous couple in the world. It was not for nothing it was dubbed the "Crime of the Century."

Pressure to solve the case was intense. Police investigators initially focused on their belief in a small group of co-conspirators. But after a trace of one of the ten-dollar ransom bills led to Bruno Richard Hauptmann, a German immigrant carpenter living in the Bronx, evidence seemed to begin falling into place. So once they had their man and were able to put him on trial, most talk of a conspiracy silenced. And since Hauptmann's 1936 execution in the New Jersey electric chair without ever having admitted involvement, the focus of the controversy has been primarily on the question of whether he did it or was framed by a law enforcement establishment more concerned with closing a notorious case than seeing justice done.

In our own investigation and analysis, we ended up on a somewhat middle, but no less controversial, ground. Going back to some of the original police suppositions, we concluded that Hauptmann was unquestionably involved with the crime but could not possibly have acted alone. We profiled as accomplices at least two other members of the German immigrant community, contemporaries of Hauptmann, living in the South Bronx, one of whom would have been the ringleader or idea man, and the other a compliant follower.

That was where the matter stood until the summer of 2011, when a man named Robert Zorn contacted us to say he had read *The Cases That Haunt Us*, believed we were correct in our conclusions and, what's more, thought he had the names and identities to fill in our profile of the Lindbergh kidnappers.

This kind of thing actually happens more often than one might think. Over the years we have been presented with alternative theories to Jack the Ripper, the Green River killer, the Unabomber, the BTK strangler, the Black Dahlia slayer, and the Zodiac, among others, and none of them has ever panned out. But Mr. Zorn's story about his father Gene and his own years-long transatlantic investigation after his dad's passing sounded at least plausible, so we invited him to come present his findings and evidence to us in person.

Over the course of six or seven hours Bob walked us through the background, the physical indicators, photographs, handwriting samples, temporal and geographical links, firsthand accounts of people who had known the subjects and opinions from various experts he had consulted. In sum, he connected more dots than we had ever seen connected in this most baffling of all contemporary murders.

Bob's quest began with his father Gene's reconstructed belief that as a teenager living in the South Bronx he had known men who might have been involved with the crime, so he set off to determine whether his dad's analysis held up to close scrutiny. While we had done the profiling, Bob did the work a modern police detective squad would do in qualifying a suspect. He was meticulous, thorough, and always healthily skeptical.

When he finished his presentation, we said that while we could not be one hundred percent certain of his conclusion without direct comparisons of fingerprints, handwriting exemplars and/or DNA sequencing, should any of these be available, we were certain of our own profile and his subjects were the best fit that anyone had ever come up with. They made logical sense, and if this had been an actual police investigation, this is where we would advise them to concentrate their investigative efforts.

So now we leave it to each reader to confront and evaluate Robert Zorn's evidence and argument for him or herself. We think you will be as intrigued as we were in this important addition to the literature of criminal justice and the annals of the "Crime of the Century."

—John Douglas and Mark Olshaker

# Introduction

Settling in for a wait at the Day-N-Nite barbershop in Dallas, Texas, Gene Zorn reached for a magazine. It was December of 1963, and from the stack my father pulled a recent issue of *True*, "a man's magazine" of the day which featured a story and new theory about the kidnapping and murder of the infant son of world famous aviator Charles A. Lindbergh.[1] My father remembered the case well. It had happened in 1932, when he was a boy in the South Bronx. As he turned the pages, he started to remember more.

The author contended that Bruno Richard Hauptmann, the man who went to the electric chair for the crime, did not accomplish it alone. Because of Hauptmann's grim silence to the very end, however, his accomplices, including a man with a German accent who called himself John, were never found. The article mentioned the Bronx and one of its landmarks, Woodlawn Cemetery, as well as nearby Englewood, New Jersey, where Charles and Anne Morrow Lindbergh had lived early in their marriage.

Because these were familiar names and places, my father's mind rolled back to the days of his boyhood and Jackson Avenue. He thought about Woodlawn Cemetery, where he had watched his own father laid to rest just four months earlier, and about the apartment where his family of eight had shared a single bathroom. He recalled a German immigrant named John Knoll, a delicatessen clerk who had lived three doors down the block. Having been encouraged by Knoll to take up stamp collecting, he would visit his neighbor's ten-dollar-a-month rented room and sort their stamps into albums. "I got no talent for that," John had said.

After reading the *True* piece, my father began to research the kidnapper who had received the ransom money at a Bronx cemetery—the man known in the case as "Cemetery John." In an investigation of the crime, the identity of Cemetery John is the missing linchpin. Like Hauptmann, he spoke English with a German accent, but there were marked differences in appearance that no one has ever been able to explain. If Cemetery John was in truth Hauptmann, that raises the question: Who were the lookouts observed near the two cemeteries while he was seeking to collect the ransom? If someone else identified himself as "John," it is certain that at least two men participated in the kidnapping, only one of whom ever answered for the crime. And if this was the case, although Hauptmann had been put to death in 1936, at least one other man escaped justice entirely and may have lived safely to old age.

My father's thoughts kept returning to John Knoll, the German deli clerk who used to hang around my grandparents' apartment in the early 1930s, and to one incident in particular. On a summer day in 1931, John, then twenty-seven, invited my fifteen-year-old father to go for a swim at Palisades Amusement Park in New Jersey. During the Great Depression, a time when every nickel counted, the outing was a rare treat. Because John did not own a car, they rode the subway from Jackson Avenue Station into the City. "I can still hear how John pronounced *subway* in his German accent," my father once told me. "He called it the *supway*."

From the number 1 line's stop at 125th Street in Manhattan, they walked past Riverside Park and Grant's Tomb. It would have been impossible not to notice the contrast between the elegant apartment buildings that lined Riverside Drive—one of which housed William Randolph Hearst's thirty-thousand-square-foot palace in the sky—and the wooden row houses containing the long, narrow "railroad" flats in the South Bronx. On Riverside Drive the newspaper mogul and his affluent neighbors enjoyed commanding views of the Hudson. On Jackson Avenue the street offered the sights and sounds of boys playing stickball and of the clip-clopping of dray horses pulling the wagons of immigrant peddlers. "Rabbits I shoot myself! Rabbits I shoot myself!" my father recalled one man shouting.

John Knoll and Gene Zorn boarded the Fort Lee Ferry in Manhattan and crossed the Hudson. Under construction in the distance, the George Washington Bridge,[2] with its two colossal steel towers and the long, graceful arc of its river span, gleamed in the sky. My father's first glimpse of the great bridge would have remained his most enduring memory of that afternoon—but for what happened later.

With its Ferris wheel visible from Manhattan, Palisades Amusement Park lay two hundred feet above the river at the top of New Jersey's Palisades Cliffs. A city block wide and three times as long, the pool had a circular island in the deep end where swimmers could lounge in the sunshine and dangle their feet in the cool salt water. Hundreds of tons of sand hauled in from the coast created the effect of a beach. A boardwalk with umbrellas and a wave-making machine hidden below a waterfall at the deep end completed the illusion of leisure at the Jersey shore.

Knoll and my father climbed the stairs that ascended from the ferry landing to the top of the cliffs, from which the sweeping panorama of the Hudson and the expanse of New York City were breathtaking. The view of the recently completed Empire State Building alone would have been reason enough for a boy to make the trip from the Bronx. Next came a short hike to Lovers Lane, a twisting path through a wooded area to the entrance gates.

John enjoyed swimming, especially in the East River, but he did not go into the pool that day. "Those are not toes on your feet," he said as my father pulled off his shoes. "Those are fingers." The remark hurt my father's feelings. Because he did not learn to swim until his college days, he lolled on the beach, watched girls run to and fro, and splashed around at the shallow end. Later, after he'd showered and changed in the two-story bathhouse, he exited the park and rejoined his neighbor at the top of the stairs that descended to the ferry dock.

Talking with his brother Walter and a man my father did not recognize, Knoll spoke in German. He knew that the boy did not speak the language and could not understand what they were saying. Yet my father clearly heard Knoll call the third man *Bruno* and also recognized another word from the conversation—*Englewood*.

*Palisades Park was located a short walk away from the dock on the New Jersey side of the 125th Street Ferry. Englewood was four miles to the north.*

The amusement park was located four miles south of the upscale New Jersey city, home to some of the most influential titans on Wall Street. After a few minutes, John instructed my father to return to the Bronx by himself. Shocked that Knoll had abandoned him, the boy watched the three men walk away together. On the ferry ride back to Manhattan, he leaned over the railing of the deck, feeling bewildered.

It was a moment my father was never to forget, a sharp memory even in his later years. And after he had read that *True* magazine article about the Lindbergh kidnapping more than thirty years later, what he had seen and heard that day in 1931 started adding up to much more than a minor childhood trauma.

Although hardly conclusive in itself, that meeting among the three German immigrants—just a short distance from the Lindberghs' residence in Englewood—was surely no casual chat among friends. Was it possible

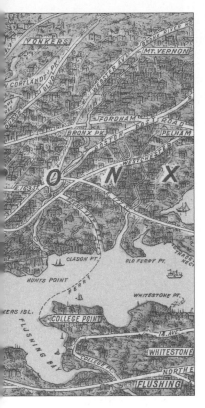

that the New Jersey State Police, the New York Police Department, J. Edgar Hoover's Bureau of Investigation, and the investigative unit of the U.S. Department of the Treasury—the "T-men" who had just outfoxed Al Capone—had all missed something? Might the man who planned it all have avoided not only capture and punishment, but even the mere mention of his name anywhere in the quarter-million case files? Was John Knoll "Cemetery John," a man who committed the "Crime of the Century" and escaped justice?

In time, it would become evident that John Knoll had invited my father to accompany him to Palisades Park that day for a reason a boy his age could not possibly understand. Knoll could be brusque, crude, and obnoxious in his day-to-day treatment of others. At times, however, he also seemed to be kind and generous to his young neighbor down the block, taking him places and favoring him with gifts that would soon include some quite rare and expensive stamps for a man of simple means. But perhaps this outing had been intended as a more sinister kind of keepsake for the boy to hold onto, a glimpse of the crime on the first day of issue when the conspirators met. If that was the case, Knoll guessed right. Gene Zorn at the time was just a kid busy with school, a paper route, and a devotion to Lou Gehrig and the Yankees who didn't make much of some guy named Bruno and two other Germans talking about the city in New Jersey where the Lindberghs lived. It would be many years before it all came back, an experience stamped in memory, and at last Gene Zorn grasped the enormity of what he had seen and heard as a boy of fifteen.

My father first told me his story while we were vacationing together during my spring break from graduate school in March of 1980.[3] At the time, and in all the years that we discussed the Lindbergh case, he relied entirely on his memory of Knoll's appearance. He never, at least in adulthood, saw a picture of the man he believed had led the kidnapping plot.

It would be nearly three decades before I saw for myself what my father's former neighbor looked like. And when I came across a clear image of John Knoll's face, the first thing I did was to set it beside the original police sketch of Cemetery John. The drawing was based on a detailed description by Dr. John F. Condon, the intermediary authorized by Lindbergh to meet with Cemetery John and pay him the ransom money. When Condon faced Bruno Hauptmann in a police lineup, he refused, despite prodding from detectives, to identify Hauptmann as the same person he had met in the cemetery, perhaps because he remembered the man pictured on the opposite page instead.

Since my father's death in 2006, I've made it my mission to establish whether this was the face that Condon described to a police sketch artist in 1932. Starting with my father's recollections about his former South Bronx neighbor, I cast off on my own research odyssey, which crisscrossed the United States, continued in the Old World, and ended in a quest for connections between John Knoll and the abduction and death of Charles A. Lindbergh, Jr. Although we began "Project Jackson" together, it fell to me to carry it through, and the book offers evidence my father never lived to see. The discoveries included a link between Hauptmann and Knoll in the form of the German immigrant who rented that very apartment in the Bronx to my grandparents, Eugene C. Zorn, Sr., and his wife, Charlotte; a photograph showing that Knoll, unlike Hauptmann, possessed an unusual physical feature that Condon had noticed on the left hand of the man who collected the ransom money; and a souvenir picture and a ship manifest proving, respectively, that Knoll departed America for Germany shortly before the trial of Hauptmann and left Europe on the day of his conviction—traveling both ways in the manner of a newly wealthy man. Individually, these and other pieces of evidence provide grounds for suspicion that would have attracted the interest of police investigators at the time had they not ceased in their pursuit of the kidnappers with the arrest of Hauptmann. Taken together, this book attempts to finally draw Cemetery John out of the shadows and reveal him as Johannes "John" Knoll of Herxheimweyher, Germany.

We start by examining the scene of the crime, with special attention to what has struck many students of the case and detectives assigned to the investigation as clear evidence that it was the work of more than one man. Once it is established that Hauptmann had accomplices, we

*On the left is a photograph of John Knoll taken around the time of the kidnapping. On the right is a police sketch of the suspect known as Cemetery John.*

proceed to the likelihood that John Knoll participated in the crime. Next the book turns to Charles Lindbergh and the intense adulation that, as he came to see it, brought him only grief. Familiar as the Lindbergh story might be to some, it is the historical context for an essential insight into a man who would want to kidnap the infant son of America's greatest hero, not just another crime but "a world-affair," as the ransom notes described it, a high-risk enterprise requiring such enormous audacity. From there, attention turns to John Knoll, tracing as much as can still be known of his early life in Germany, his path to the Bronx, and the curious circumstances of his life at the time when my father saw him in the company of Bruno Hauptmann.

Much of the book follows the developing investigation of the kidnapping and the trial of Hauptmann, departing appropriately to Knoll and the evidence, and in due course setting forth a summation of the case against him and a reconstruction of what likely happened on the night of the kidnapping. Not only is such physical evidence as photographs, handwriting samples, and studies to identify the source of the ransom notes included, but also evidence yielded by investigative methodologies unavailable in the 1930s.

To fill in the large gaps in my own knowledge of criminology and science, I sought the opinions of a wide-ranging collection of authorities—prosecutors, FBI profilers, geographic profilers, forensic psychiatrists and anthropologists, researchers of personality disorders and experts in optical handwriting recognition, forensic linguistics, child abduction, and pediatric head trauma. Drawn simply by the accumulation of evidence and a desire to see the matter proven one way or the other, they studied John Knoll through the lens of modern criminal investigative analysis. The closer they got, even across eighty years, the more familiar he seemed, especially to the profilers. They recognized a type. Clues about his behavior and personality, combined with the "victimology," as John Douglas calls it, reveal a man capable of committing such a crime. The facts of the case were set against the pattern of a life, and each time they coincided.

For my part, I had to prepare at every stage for the possibility that my father's theory was in error, that for all the clues seeming to point in John Knoll's direction I would one day come upon some definitive piece of evidence that simply ruled him out. At every point, faithfulness to my father did not demand proving that John Knoll kidnapped the Lindbergh baby. Faithfulness demanded only that I pursue the truth, establishing to the best of my ability what had really happened, and whether this neighbor from Gene Zorn's boyhood days was the same man who first appeared that night in Woodlawn Cemetery to collect the ransom money, calling himself John.

Over years of research, as one piece of evidence after another fell into place—to a degree that often amazed me and would have astonished my father—I tried to maintain this attitude of objective inquiry, if only to keep asking the right questions and anticipate the objections by critics who would dismiss his story about "Bruno" and "Englewood" as nothing more than the beginning of a series of coincidences, proving nothing to a certainty. Yet if John Knoll was not Cemetery John, I kept wondering, what was the likelihood of so much incriminating evidence—including the stamps he had given to my father, along with the envelopes bearing his own handwriting—leading directly to him? As retired FBI Special Agent Ed Sulzbach remarked, you can only go on for so long calling coincidence after coincidence a coincidence.[4] Life is just not that coincidental.

# 1

# The Crime

On the night of Tuesday, March 1, 1932, as the temperature dipped into the high thirties, a howling wind blew across the Lindbergh estate outside Hopewell, New Jersey.[1] Fed up with the ubiquity of reporters and wearied by public intrusions, Charles and Anne Morrow Lindbergh had built their dream home, Highfields, on 425 acres in the remote Sourland Mountains.[2] Five years earlier, the aviator's nonstop solo flight from New York to Paris in the *Spirit of St. Louis* had brought him unequaled acclaim across the globe. As one German observer put it, Lindbergh was *Der Name in aller Munde*—"the name in every mouth." It would be hard to exaggerate the level and reach of his fame.

Their move to Highfields incomplete, the family often spent weekends there but resided during the week at Next Day Hill, the Englewood mansion of Anne's recently widowed mother, Betty Morrow. The Lindberghs had not been to their new home in three weeks. On Saturday, February 27, a chauffeur had driven Anne and her baby, Charlie, to Highfields. That evening, as his mother would recall, the child "sneezed a good deal and was apparently coming down with a cold."[3] Two days later, on Monday, February 29, he was still "quite miserable with his cold," and with the weather damp and dreary, Anne wanted to keep him inside. She called Next Day Hill and told her twenty-eight-year-old Scottish nursemaid, Betty Gow, that she would not be coming back to Englewood with the baby. It was the first time the Lindberghs would spend a Monday night at Highfields.

At 10:30 a.m. on Tuesday, Anne phoned Betty and asked her to come down from Englewood and help with the baby. His cold was much better, and he had "no temperature."[4] After she received the call, Betty canceled her evening plans with her boyfriend, Henry "Red" Johnson, a Norwegian sailor in the country illegally. A pretty and petite brunette with deep-set blue eyes, Betty had been working for the Lindberghs just over a year. A chauffeur on the Morrow staff drove Betty to Highfields and dropped her off about 1:30 p.m.

Late in the afternoon after the baby's nap, Anne let him run around downstairs. He liked to "swing and dance" to the tunes of his music box and sway back and forth to the pendulum of the grandfather clock at Next Day Hill. He also enjoyed scampering around the house with the family's black-and-white fox terrier, Wahgoosh, named after one of Charles's boyhood dogs. As Charlie played on the floor with his Hansel and Gretel set, he was far too young to understand how a child-devouring witch could seize the lad in the German fairy tale and throw him into a cage—and far too innocent to imagine evildoers wicked enough to snatch little boys.

At 5:30 p.m., Charlie was running in circles around the kitchen table when Betty took his hand and led him upstairs to the nursery, which sat at the top of the stairs on the southeast corner of the home. The wallpaper in the room displayed stick figure images of a hunter with his dog, a deer, a rising sun, a man walking hand-in-hand with a toddler, a castle, and a fox. Betty, who had taken care of the baby for three months during his parents' celebrated survey flight to the Orient via the "Great Circle route," had grown to love him deeply.[5] The family joked that he learned to say "Gow" long before he ever tried to say "Mummy." With his blue eyes, blond, curly hair, and a cleft in his chin to match his father's, the twenty-month-old was adorable in looks and personality.

It was about six-fifteen when Anne came into the nursery just as Charlie was finishing his cereal. For a little more than an hour, she stayed with the baby, helped prepare him for bed, and straightened the room. His usual bedtime was seven o'clock. At Anne's request, Betty used a remnant of "a flannel petticoat for an infant" and some blue Sylko cotton thread to cut and sew a high-necked shirt for him to wear underneath his Dr. Denton's sleeping suit. The nursemaid rubbed the baby's

*Charlie Lindbergh on his first birthday*

chest with Vicks VapoRub, put on his nightclothes, and affixed a "Baby Alice Thumb Guard" to each hand to prevent him from sucking his thumbs. At half past seven, Anne went downstairs and sat at her desk in the living room. Meanwhile, Betty put Charlie into his crib and used two large safety pins to fasten his bedcovers to the mattress.[6] A folding screen with drawings of country folks, horses and buggies, and farm animals provided a cheery view as well as protection from drafts.

Along the eastern wall of the nursery sat a fireplace with a red, brick hearth trimmed with wood. Figurines of a rooster and two small birds stood on the mantle. The Lindberghs had installed blue-and-white Delft tiles imported from Holland for the fireplace surround. The tiles were hand decorated with a windmill, a sailboat, a milkmaid, a big ocean fish, a puppy, a turtle, an owl, and an elephant—"elepunt," as Charlie called it. The baby could identify the animals in his Noah's ark set, having learned them over weeks of quizzing by his father.

The nursery, fifteen feet by thirteen feet, eleven inches, had a French window facing south and a narrow, thirty-inch-wide window at each side of the fireplace. The window ledges sat thirteen feet, seven inches above the ground.[7] The shutters on the corner window were warped and would not close. "The house had been photographed for the press from every angle and the position of the child's quarters was publicly known," the *New York Times* would report. "Light in the windows would show when the child was alone and asleep."[8]

At eight o'clock, Betty stopped on her way to the kitchen and told Anne that she had just checked on the baby. He had fallen asleep unusually quickly and was breathing easily. Anne listened for the sound of her husband's car. Outside, she would recall, "the wind howled around the house."[9] Fifteen minutes before her husband arrived, Anne thought she heard the sound of car wheels on gravel.

Lindbergh had spent the day in the City. The newspapers had reported that he would be speaking that evening at a banquet given by New York University at the Waldorf-Astoria. Lindbergh missed the function, however, because of "a secretarial mix-up on his calendar."[10] At 8:25 p.m., he honked his horn as he pulled up the drive. Then he parked in the garage, came inside, and washed up in the master bathroom upstairs. The bathroom and the nursery were connected. After supper, he and Anne sat down on the living room sofa in front of a fire. Measuring fifteen by twenty-four feet, the simply furnished room with built-in bookshelves was paneled in mahogany. Tiny brass doorknobs were fitted into the interior doors of the home.

The butler, Olly Whateley, took the dishes to the kitchen and washed them with his wife, Elsie, the housekeeper and cook.[11] The Whateleys, whom Lindbergh considered "both absolutely honest and trustworthy in every particular,"[12] had lived at Highfields for four months. The couple had come to America from London in March 1930 and found work on Long Island. Lindbergh considered references unnecessary and relied on his gut feelings to size people up. He also trusted his instincts about the safety of living in a rural area.

Her kitchen chores finished, Elsie invited Betty Gow to come upstairs to look at a new dress. The Whateleys' bedroom on the northwest corner of the second floor was located farthest from the nursery. Olly lounged back in a chair in the servants' sitting room downstairs and leafed through a nickel copy of *The Saturday Evening Post*. On the cover was a drawing of a middle-aged doorman hailing a taxi for a handsome young man in a tuxedo and top hat with a bored-looking woman in a fur-trimmed coat.[13]

It was a few minutes past nine when Lindbergh heard a strange noise. His wife didn't hear anything. Nor did Wahgoosh, who lay asleep in his bed in the kitchen.[14] The Lindberghs resumed their conversation for a few minutes, then went upstairs to their bedroom at 9:15 p.m. and chatted for a few more. At nine-thirty, Charles came back downstairs to read in the library, which sat directly below the nursery. From his desk by the window, he could look out into the darkness.

As Elsie and Betty continued to visit in the Whateleys' bedroom, Anne started getting ready for bed. At 9:57 p.m., Betty excused herself to tend to the baby.[15] A household rule dictated that no one, not even the nurse-maid, was to disturb Charlie between eight and ten o'clock. Lindbergh, who sought to instill self-reliance in his boy, did not believe in having some-one check on the baby every time he started crying; sometimes he would put Charlie in his playpen outside and allow him to go on crying.

Betty entered the nursery and left the door ajar to allow a little light to seep in from the hallway. She felt a chill and plugged in the electric heater. The crib was strangely quiet. Reaching inside, she could not find the baby.[16]

Betty dashed into the master bedroom and saw that Anne was alone. "Did the Colonel take the baby, Mrs. Lindbergh?"

"I don't know," said Anne, looking puzzled. "He might have."

As Anne went into the nursery, Betty ran downstairs to find Lindbergh, who had a penchant for practical jokes. He was sitting at his desk in the library. "Colonel, do you have the baby? Please don't fool me."

"Isn't he in his crib?"

Lindbergh raced up the stairs to the nursery and looked inside the crib. Then, after he had rushed into the master bedroom, Anne asked him, "Do you have the baby?"

He didn't answer. He walked into his closet and took out his rifle. Anne ran back into the nursery and looked at the bedclothes, then opened the closets. By this point Elsie Whateley was following her from room to room. Anne rushed back into the master bedroom, threw open a window, and leaned way out. She heard "what sounded like a cry" outside.

Elsie had heard the same sound. "It was a cat, Mrs. Lindbergh."

Moments later, Lindbergh turned to his wife and looked her in the eye. "Anne," he said, "they have stolen our baby." For both of them, all happiness had vanished in an instant.[17]

*They*—the people who refused to leave him alone to pursue his ambitions and allow the members of his family to lead normal lives. *They* stalked him and pried into every aspect of his personal life. *They* exploded flash bulbs in his face and photographed his every move. *They* stole up behind him with hidden microphones. *They* used his name without permission to peddle their products. *They* spread wild, hurtful rumors about the baby—how he was deformed! And now, in a blinding flash, *they* had just delivered a grievous blow that would cast a shadow over the Lindberghs for the rest of their lives.

# 2

# Citizen of the World

One day, as we shared a wait at Boston's Logan International Airport, I fell into conversation with two students from Amherst College. One of them asked what I do. "I'm working on a book," I replied. They were curious about the subject, and when I told them about it I was amazed that neither had ever heard of the Lindbergh kidnapping—or even of Charles Lindbergh himself. I tried to explain just how famous a name Lindbergh had once been, but it was difficult to know where to begin.

Recalling the unmatched renown of Lindbergh is essential to understanding the kind of man who would target his infant son. The crime was "a world-affair," just as the author of the ransom letters described it, and indeed it would be hard to think of any potential targets in that era—even movie stars or heads of state—whose lives were more closely watched in the press than Charles Lindbergh. A key to understanding the mind of the kidnapper is that he wouldn't commit such a crime in spite of Lindbergh's fame and the certainty of intense publicity that would follow; he would commit the crime because of these factors, seeking what criminal profilers call the "anonymous fame" that would come with the deed.

Unlike other fliers of the time, Lindbergh seemed uniquely immune to the allure of fame. He was a highly rational, focused, and disciplined man, and in his preparations for the transatlantic flight allowed nothing to distract him. The competition had begun in 1919, when Raymond

Orteig conceived the Trans-Atlantic Air Race. The French-born Manhattan hotelier offered $25,000 for the first nonstop flight between New York and Paris, inspiring some of the world's most illustrious aviators to attempt, in some cases a little too hastily, this death-defying mission. Seven years later, René Fonck, the French "Ace of Aces," set out to capture the elusive Orteig Prize. On September 21, 1926, however, his trimotor Sikorsky S-35 crashed into a gully upon takeoff, spun around, and exploded at Roosevelt Field on Long Island. Two crewmembers perished. After he learned of the tragedy, Lindbergh lay in bed thinking about the large, overmanned plane. The key to flying the Atlantic, he was convinced, was a clear, simple strategy. One engine, one set of wings, one pilot. And he was that pilot.

As a boy, Lindbergh recalled, he lay on the grass at his family's Minnesota farm on the west bank of the Mississippi, gazed up at the clouds, and thought, "How wonderful it would be if I had an airplane! . . . I would ride on the wind and be part of the sky."[1] In a school notebook, he sketched a drawing of a plane and scribbled above it the names of Balboa and other explorers. The twenties were a time perfectly suited to such an adventurous spirit, a man who in adulthood carried himself with a modest manner that easily concealed a boundless confidence in his own abilities. "Oh, yes," a young Charles Lindbergh said to himself, "this is the dawn of a new life, a life in which I'm going to fly across the ocean to Europe!"[2]

In February of 1922, Lindbergh had failed out of the engineering program at the University of Wisconsin. Two months later, at age twenty, he took flying lessons in Lincoln, Nebraska. The following year, the War Department accepted his application for admission to the army flying cadet school, which he entered at Brooks Field, Texas, in the spring of 1924. During training maneuvers one day, he and a student officer bailed out after a mid-air collision caused their SE5s to lock together. The pilots were back in the air within an hour. In 1925, Lindbergh finished first in a class of nineteen cadets and received his commission as second lieutenant in the Air Force Reserve Corps.

Because the military offered him limited opportunity during peacetime, Lindbergh spent a year working for various commercial enterprises, including a flying circus that entertained crowds in more than twenty states. In

April of 1926, Robertson Aircraft Corporation inaugurated its contract air-mail service and named him chief pilot of its St. Louis–Chicago route.

After Lindbergh had contributed $2,000 of savings from his barn-storming days to the venture, he set out to raise an additional $13,000 needed to finance a flight to Paris. He sought the funds from a group of aviation-minded businessmen in St. Louis. Banker Harold M. Bixby, the treasurer of a local flying club, questioned the wisdom of flying with only one engine.

"A pilot can't fly at all without taking *some* risk," said Lindbergh. "I've weighed my chances pretty carefully."

"You've only got a life to lose, Slim," said Bixby. "But don't forget, I've got a reputation to lose." Then, a few seconds later: "If you're going to make the flight, we've got to get started right away."[3] The nine sponsors from St. Louis soon raised $8,500 in subscriptions against a $15,000 loan from a local bank.[4]

Lindbergh's initial discussions with airplane manufacturers went in circles. On February 3, 1927, he sent a telegram to Ryan Airlines, Inc. in San Diego: "CAN YOU CONSTRUCT WHIRLWIND ENGINE PLANE CAPABLE OF FLYING NONSTOP BETWEEN NEW YORK AND PARIS..." Ryan, a little-known company that operated out of a dilapidated factory by the city's harbor, replied that it could deliver a plane with enough fuel capacity to reach Paris—and within two months of receipt of a down payment. Three weeks later, Lindbergh toured the factory and sat down in the office of the company's chief engineer, Donald Hall, to discuss design strategy. Because he would "rather have extra gasoline than an extra man," Lindbergh insisted on only one cockpit.[5] "I preferred the independence of flying alone," he would write more than four decades later.[6] Despite the resulting elimination of the pilot's forward vision, Hall set back the cockpit in the fuselage. Lindbergh and Ryan agreed on a $10,850 price for a monoplane with a Wright Whirlwind J-5 engine.

Determined to oversee every aspect of design, Lindbergh hovered over the factory as Ryan worked twenty-four hours a day to build the *Spirit of St. Louis* to his precise specifications. With his obsessive eye for detail, he evaluated the trade-offs necessary to strip every ounce of excess weight to maximize the fuel his plane could carry; he even trimmed the edges of his maps. The French writer Antoine de Saint-Exupéry, himself an aviator destined to perish in flight, best defined the ideal: "A designer knows he has achieved perfection not when there is nothing left to add, but when there is nothing left to take away."[7]

At two o'clock in the morning of April 25, Lindbergh wired his investors: "FACTORY WORK COMPLETE TODAY." Though the news was reassuring, it was actually the prior accidents, delays, and legal entanglements of other contestants that would give the dark horse airmail pilot a chance to win the great Trans-Atlantic Air Race. On April 16, the polar explorer Richard Evelyn Byrd had crash-landed on his first test flight. Ten days later, two more airmen with dreams of glory died after their multi-engine Keystone biplane crashed on its final trial flight in Virginia.

Two weeks before Lindbergh's flight, two French flying aces, Captain Charles Nungesser and Captain François Coli, had gone missing en route to New York in their Levasseur PL-8 biplane. With the deaths of the two pilots of *L'Oiseau Blanc*, six men had lost their lives in pursuit of the Orteig Prize.

Seven days before Lindbergh's takeoff from Roosevelt Field, a telegram arrived at the Garden City Hotel.

| | |
|---|---|
| CAPT. CHARLES A. LINDBERGH | DETROIT, MICH. |
| CURTISS FIELD, LONG ISLAND | MAY 13, 1927 |
| ARRIVE NEW YORK TOMORROW MORNING | |
| MOTHER[8] | |

*It's the newspapers*, Lindbergh realized. A steady stream of phone calls from reporters and a flood of articles predicting his demise had so disturbed his mother that she decided to see him in person to reassure herself that "he really wanted to go and felt it was the right thing to do."[9] Upon her arrival, the press bombarded Evangeline Lindbergh with questions about her only child's chances of survival.

The aviator in his flying togs climbed into his cockpit at 7:40 a.m. on Friday, May 20, 1927. Carrying 450 gallons of gasoline in five tanks, the *Spirit of St. Louis* staggered nearly a mile down the narrow, rain-softened grass runway, sloshed through shallow pools, and bounced three times before lifting into the misty air.[10] A thousand feet ahead, a web of telephone wires loomed just beyond the runway. At this point, there was no turning back. Climb or crash. Nose down, the *Spirit* picked up speed

*Charles Lindbergh with his plane, the* Spirit of St. Louis, *just days before his flight to Paris*

and continued its slow ascent. As Lindbergh wrote in his Pulitzer Prize–winning book about the flight more than twenty years later, "wires flash by underneath—*twenty feet to spare!*"[11] With the little silver monoplane high in the sky, the world began its breathless wait for news.

By the evening of Saturday, May 21, France had gone Lindbergh-mad. Mobs formed in the streets of downtown Paris after the radio announced the sighting of the *Spirit of St. Louis* over southern England. A chorus of cheers erupted as *Le Matin* posted an illuminated bulletin: Lindbergh had flown over Cherbourg and the coast of Normandy. As the *Spirit* approached its destination, 150,000 people had flocked to Le Bourget, where a chill wind was blowing.

After the *Spirit* touched down, swung around, and rolled to a stop in the center of the airfield at 10:22 p.m.,[12] thousands broke through stout steel fences on the field's edge, swept past police and two companies of soldiers with bayonets, and swarmed up to the plane. Within seconds, Lindbergh could feel the *Spirit* shudder from the pressure of the mob. Above the mingled shouts of thousands of rejoicing French voices, he heard the ripping of the fine-knit cotton cloth fabric that covered his plane and the cracking of wood as vandals broke off fairing strips. "Fame— Opportunity—Wealth—and also tragedy & loneliness & frustration rushed at him in those running figures on the field at Le Bourget," his future wife, Anne, would write. "And he is so innocent and unaware."[13]

No sooner had Lindbergh opened the door and stuck his foot out of the cockpit than the crowd dragged him out of the *Spirit*, hoisted him into the air, and began parading him about the airfield. George "Toto" Delage, a pilot with Air Union, recognized that Lindbergh needed help and called out to his friend Sergeant Michel Détroyat, one of the French military's most skillful acrobatic and combat pilots. Delage ran to get his car.

Moments later, Détroyat, in full military uniform, whisked Lindbergh into his friend's "shabby" 6-horsepower Renault. After Delage zoomed into the Air Union hangar on the side of the airfield, the fliers ducked into a waiting room inside.

When he discovered that Détroyat could speak some English, Lindbergh asked: "Is there any news from Nungesser and Coli?"[14] Détroyat shook his head: there was no word regarding *The White Bird*, which had last been sighted over Ireland. The somber mood in the room instantly disappeared when Lindbergh, passport in hand, asked how to proceed with immigration and customs. After a few minutes, Détroyat, whose friendship with the man he would call "dear Charley"[15] would endure for decades, set off to search for an officer of higher rank. He returned with Major Pierre Weiss of the Bombardment Group of the 34th (Le Bourget) French Aviation regiment.[16]

Major Weiss escorted Lindbergh to his office on the military side of the aerodrome, about a mile away. The American pilot refused an offer of champagne and requested a glass of water. Meanwhile, a group of soldiers wheeled off the *Spirit* to the hangar Lindbergh had just left and placed the plane under a military guard. Souvenir hunters had punctured gaping holes in the sides of the fuselage and made off with the engine and navigation logs.

Myron T. Herrick, seventy-two, the U.S. ambassador to France, appeared forty minutes later and invited Lindbergh to stay at the embassy. Once there, Lindbergh fielded questions from reporters who had been shown up to his elegant blue-and-gold guest room. After a few minutes, Herrick asked the journalists to allow his guest to retire. Paris clocks marked four-fifteen in the morning. Not counting three hours of sleep he managed to snatch before takeoff, the flier had been awake for sixty-three hours. The *New York Times* hailed the triumph with a banner three-decked headline: LINDBERGH DOES IT! TO PARIS IN 33 1/2 HOURS; FLIES 1,000 MILES THROUGH SNOW AND SLEET; CHEERING FRENCH CARRY HIM OFF FIELD. Radio commentators talked round the clock about the twenty-five-year-old airmail pilot who had become the most famous person on earth.

Advances in technology had readied the public for its first media sensation. The radiograph, the Bartlane cable picture transmission system, the radio, and the telephone all brought the world news and images of Lindbergh's landing in Paris. Moreover, the arrival of synchronized sound in motion pictures allowed footage of his takeoff from Roosevelt Field and the mob scene at Le Bourget to be viewed around the globe.

Lindbergh awoke a little before noon and read a congratulatory telegram from President Calvin Coolidge. Afterwards, the ambassador's son coaxed him onto the front balcony to greet a throng gathered outside the embassy hoping to glimpse the new hero. As the aviator looked out on a sea of humanity, a thunderous chant erupted: "*Vive* Lindbergh! *Vive l'Amérique!*" Accustomed to crowds applauding such stunts as barrel rolls, loop-the-loops, and taking his dog for a walk on the wing of an airplane, the man once billed as "Aerial Daredevil Lindbergh" felt embarrassed by the thought of people cheering him while he was just standing around doing nothing.

Mid-afternoon, Lindbergh visited the mother of Charles Nungesser, one of the French fliers whose open cockpit biplane wsas presumed to have crashed in the ocean. Marveling at her guest's bravery, Madame Nungesser begged him tearfully to find her son who she remained convinced was somehow on his way back to civilization. Lindbegh encouraged her not to lose hope.

On Lindbergh's second day in Paris, the president of the French Republic, Gaston Doumergue, pinned the Cross of the Legion of Honor on the lapel of his ill-fitting borrowed suit. The flood of tributes during the first days following Lindbergh's arrival at Le Bourget—including a dinner at the U.S. Embassy, a luncheon hosted by the American Club in Paris, and a ride in an open car down the *Champs-Élysées* with half-a-million cheering admirers lining the route to the *Hôtel de Ville*—had already made him feel a prisoner of his celebrity, which he considered a meaningless burden.[17]

Only when Lindbergh was in the sky, where he could glory in his "love of wind and height and wings"[18] and behold the beauties of the earth below—could he obtain a sense of freedom. On May 28, he went flying at sunrise with his new friend Michel Détroyat, the French combat pilot. Their planes were only five meters apart when Lindbergh gave a wave that said "Let's do some acrobatics."

"I did not keep you waiting too long—Loops came upon spins and rolls in quick succession. You were enjoying the show to your heart's content," wrote Détroyat in a letter to Lindbergh some twenty-four years later. "Unfortunately, the officials on the ground were getting panicky. A red rocket was fired. I immediately obeyed it and landed without further argument. But you were enjoying yourself and you kept on for some time 'putting your feet to the ceiling.'"[19]

On Lindbergh's next stop after France, he flew the repaired *Spirit of St. Louis* to Belgium, where King Albert made him a Knight of the Order of Leopold. The following day, a welcoming delegation called the Old Volunteers of the Great War held a civic reception at the five-hundred-year-old Gothic town hall. Declaring that Lindbergh had earned "the right to claim the title of Citizen of the World," Burgomaster Max credited the aviator with having united "[his] young country with the old soil of Europe" in a way no diplomat could have achieved.[20]

As he left the country, Lindbergh flew low over a cemetery where white crosses marked the graves of American soldiers. He tossed a floral wreath out of the cockpit, circled the cemetery twice, and headed for Great Britain. It would not be the last time he would pay such a tribute from the air.

In England, a crowd of 150,000 swarmed the *Spirit* after it landed at Croydon Aerodrome. At a banquet and reception arranged jointly by the American Society in London, the American Chamber of Commerce, and the American Club, a comment by Lindbergh brought the attendees to their feet in a frenzy of applause: his generation should not allow the aerial transatlantic crossing to eclipse the contribution of fliers to the winning of the war, men who had received little recognition for their valor. In a ceremony at Buckingham Palace, King George V decorated Lindbergh with the Royal Air Force Cross—the British crown's highest peacetime honor for a foreign aviator.

Because the flight to Paris was his first trip abroad, Lindbergh had intended to spend a few weeks studying Europe's airports, aircraft factories, and aeronautical activities. Yet America clamored for her own celebrations. The U.S. ambassador to Great Britain informed the flier that President Coolidge was sending the flagship of the U.S. European fleet, the 7,500-ton cruiser USS *Memphis*, to Cherbourg to bring the hero home.

With the *Spirit of St. Louis* crated into what Lindbergh would describe as "a coffin," Admiral Guy Hamilton Burrage greeted the aviator at the dock in Cherbourg.[21] As the *Memphis* cast off, crowds shouted their good-byes, seaplanes soared overhead, and every whistle in the port blared praise to the man whose flight had thrilled the world as would no other spectacle until another man stepped foot onto the Moon two generations later. Still bigger crowds awaited him in America, and with them a level of adulation he had never sought. Other young men might envy such acclaim, but something about it left Charles Lindbergh uneasy and wary. He would remark years later, after the worst had come to pass, "As one gains fame one loses life."[22]

# 3

# Reconnaissance

On the morning of June 11, 1927, Lindbergh caught his first glimpse of the new life that lay ahead of him in America. As A. Scott Berg describes the scene in his Pulitzer Prize–winning biography, saluting guns fired from the president's yacht, the *Mayflower*, greeting the *Memphis* as it appeared around the bend of the Potomac. A crowd of 25,000 at the Washington Navy Yard shouted, Navy factory whistles screamed, and the Navy Department band struck up "Sailing, Sailing, Over the Bounding Main" as Lindbergh, hat in hand, stood erect on the bridge in a blue serge suit and waved, his sandy-colored, wavy hair ruffled by the breeze. Because he had made his flight as a civilian, he decided to wear a suit rather than his officer's uniform.[1]

A great roar of welcome went up from the crowd as the cruiser came alongside the brick pier and eased into her berthing place. Admiral Burrage escorted Lindbergh's mother aboard as ecstatic whoops and military music filled the air. She had spent the previous night as the guest of Calvin and Grace Coolidge at the temporary White House on Du Pont Circle. Also visiting was the President's Amherst College classmate Dwight W. Morrow, head of the recently established Aircraft Board and a senior partner at J. P. Morgan and Company—"probably the most formidable financial combine in history."[2] Recognizing the importance of "studying the application of airplanes to national defense," Coolidge had appointed Morrow to chair the newly commissioned Aircraft Inquiry Board two years earlier. A wonderful raconteur, Evangeline Lindbergh entertained the diminutive, bespectacled international financier for hours with stories and anecdotes about her son's adventures in the sky.[3]

A large gathering of army, navy, marine, commerce, and post office aviators stood at attention as the honorees alighted from the warship. Members of a reception committee hoisted top hats into the air. Amid chants of "Lindy, Lindy," the aviator shouldered his way through the crowd and climbed into the back seat of the president's convertible touring car for a one-mile ride to the Peace Monument at the base of Capitol Hill—the starting point for a 1,600-person military parade with brass bands, soldiers, sailors, and dignitaries.

Hundreds of children crowding the Capitol steps watched the touring car creep along Pennsylvania Avenue to the cheers of a flag-waving throng on the Capitol grounds. As the only son of a Republican congressman from Minnesota, Lindbergh was accustomed to Washington fanfare. One day, the young boy witnessed President Theodore Roosevelt riding in his open car. On another occasion, he saw President William Howard Taft taking his exercise behind a horse-drawn carriage in Rock Creek Park. In the White House, he watched President Woodrow Wilson sign a bill, one his own father, Representative Charles August Lindbergh, Sr., had sponsored.

As a host of dignitaries looked on, Calvin Coolidge paid tribute to the flier in a ceremony at the foot of the Washington Monument, the President's storied reticence suspended for the occasion: "The absence of self-acclaim, the refusal to become commercialized, which has marked the conduct of this sincere and genuine exemplar of fine and noble virtues, has endeared him to everyone . . . a conqueror of the air and strength for the ties which bind us to our sister nations."[4] The loudest hurrahs erupted when Coolidge gave Lindbergh his commission as a Colonel of the United States Reserve Corps and pinned the Distinguished Flying Cross on the lapel of the aviator's suit.

As Lindbergh approached the microphones to speak to the crowd of 250,000 packed solid on the Monument grounds and to a radio audience of thirty million, forty-eight homing pigeons, one from each state, fluttered up into the air upon their release from a box under the grandstand. With an innate sense of comedic timing, Lindbergh said, "I was informed that while it wasn't an order to come back home, that there would be a battleship waiting for me next week." Never mentioning his flight, the aviator shared his message of affection from the people of Europe and closed with: "I thank you."

Two days later, Lindbergh flew to New York for the greatest reception ever accorded a private citizen in the City's history—including a ticker-tape parade viewed by over four million witnesses. Minutes after landing at Mitchel Field on Long Island, he boarded the amphibian *San Francisco*, which took off for New York Harbor.

"How much happier I would be if I could spend the afternoon flying your plane, which is a new type to me, than having to go through the experience which awaits me," Lindbergh said to the pilot, Ira C. Eaker, who would be named commander of the Eighth Air Force during the Second World War.[5]

Pulled aboard the municipal reception boat *Macom* after the amphibian landed in the waters, Lindbergh observed his escort: a harbor full of yachts, excursion boats, tugs, and motorboats, all flying American flags. Making its slow passage forward, the flotilla sounded sirens, whistles, and tooters as, farther up the bay, the bass notes of liners caused the air to vibrate.

A crowd of 300,000 in Battery Park watched twenty-two planes in battle formation sweep over the reception boat and circle Manhattan. After the *Macom* docked at the pier at 12:40 p.m., Lindbergh stepped into the back seat of a convertible limousine, perched on the folded top, and rode up Broadway from Battery Park to City Hall. A full military parade of more than ten thousand soldiers and sailors led the march. With the stock market, banks, and businesses closed for "Lindbergh Day," a blizzard of ticker tape, torn-up phone books, and confetti streamed out of building windows as people jammed the sidewalks along the mile-long route and cheered.

After a ceremony at City Hall hosted by Mayor James J. Walker, Lindbergh climbed back into the parade limousine as marching troops led the way through streets packed with a roaring, hat-waving crowd. From the balcony of the three-story Lafayette Hotel, Raymond Orteig looked down on the celebration with joy. Lindbergh's feat had fulfilled the long-awaited dream of the hotel baron who had come to the States from France at the age of twelve: the first nonstop flight between New York and Paris had mended relations between the two great nations he loved.

The crowd extended along the avenue into Central Park and into the park to the Mall, where Governor Alfred E. Smith was awaiting the airman's arrival. In a ceremony attended by hundreds of thousands, the governor draped the blue ribbon of the Medal of Valor from the State of New York over Lindbergh's neck. Accorded the role of "chief spokesman for the new world of commercial aviation,"[6] Lindbergh flew to each of the forty-eight states, heralded and adored in one city after another. Within a month following his return from France, he had received offers totaling more than five million dollars to endorse products and star in motion pictures. On June 14, William Randolph Hearst invited the aviator to his Manhattan apartment on Riverside Drive. Dazzling in its opulence, the cavernous home imitated the grandeur of the Palace of Versailles. Everywhere Lindbergh looked, he saw priceless paintings: Gérômes, Vouets, Greuezes, and Fragonards jostling one another for the best-lit spots on the walls. The newspaper magnate presented a contract from his movie production company, Cosmopolitan Pictures. Lindbergh would receive $500,000 plus ten percent of gross receipts to portray himself in a film about his life story that would co-star Hearst's thirty-year-old blonde mistress Marion Davies, a silent film star. As Lindbergh contemplated the staggering sum, he explained his decision not to go into pictures. At Hearst's request, the flier tore up the contract and tossed it into the fireplace.[7]

As Lindbergh considered what mattered most to him, the development of aviation or the millions he could make, he realized that "money would always be minor to the other terms of the life [he] led."[8] In surveying routes and landing sites for Transcontinental Air Transport (TAT), the company that would become Trans World Airlines, Lindbergh helped create a passenger airline that would connect New York to California. The company gave him a $250,000 signing bonus, plus a yearly retainer of $10,000 a year to chair its Technical Committee. Lindbergh reached another agreement to serve as Technical Advisor with Pan American Airways for a $10,000 annual salary and the option to purchase ten percent of the company's stock at a steep discount.

Lindbergh handled his status as the most admired, celebrated man on earth with modesty, a virtue that enhanced his reputation and heightened public interest. There was an aura about the boyish-looking flier, something intangible beyond his heroism that drew people to him. Eager to cash in on Lindbergh's fame, musicians and lyricists composed over a hundred songs inspired by the flight to Paris. At gala dinners across the country, Lindbergh endured one rendition after another of "Lucky Lindy."

"Apart from the sleep problem over the Atlantic, there was no element of chance," he would comment years later. ". . . There was no luck, one of the reasons I hate the 'Lucky Lindy' nickname."[9] Yet Lindbergh was quick to acknowledge the contributions of the men who had embraced his vision. "Aside from taking over the burden of finances, it was the attitude of my partners in St. Louis which made success possible," he would write to Harold Bixby twenty-five years later, "and that was due largely to your wisdom and guidance . . . The more I study the other transatlantic flights, . . . the more clearly I appreciate the tremendous asset I had in the character of the men who were behind me."[10]

As would become his standard practice, the flier ignored inquiries into his personal matters. In a press interview after a parade in Hartford, a young reporter asked, "Is it true, Colonel, that girls don't interest you at all?"

"If you can show me what that has to do with aviation," said Lindbergh, "I'll be glad to answer you."

She persisted. "Then aviation is your only interest?"

"That is the purpose of this tour, to promote aviation."

"Are you always so evasive?"

"I shall be glad to tell you anything I know—on aviation."[11]

In the fall of 1927, President Coolidge persuaded Dwight Morrow to close the door on his investment banking career and named him U.S. Ambassador to Mexico. At the request of one of Lindbergh's sponsors from St. Louis, Morrow had raised $10,500 from the Morgan partners to complete the financing of the flight to Paris, permitting the aviator's own contribution to be returned to his personal account. The net effect, notes historian Ron Chernow, was that Morrow and his partners had paid for the flight.[12] Upon Morrow's appointment, Lindbergh sent a congratulatory note, ending with: "And if, by any chance, an opportunity should arise where I might be of any aid to you, please call on me."[13] Recognizing the diplomatic value of a flight by Lindbergh to help disentangle Mexico's "subtle and complicated puzzles"[14] and following up on a comment the aviator had made about "doing a little flying in Latin America,[15] Morrow proposed an idea for a goodwill mission and followed up with a letter: "As one interested in Mexico, in aviation, and in you personally, I am exceedingly anxious that you should fly down here."[16] Lindbergh accepted President Plutarco Elías Calles's invitation to be a guest of the Mexican government and took off from Washington, D.C., on December 13, 1927. The following afternoon, the *Spirit of St. Louis* landed to a euphoric welcome at Valbuena Field outside Mexico City as 150,000 thronged to watch his plane arrive. The arrangement of the aviator's flight connecting the capital cities would be attributed to Morrow as a stroke of diplomatic genius.

Shortly after his appointment, Morrow ordered construction to begin on a mansion in Englewood. Reminiscent of the Long Island estates built during the heyday of the Gilded Age and designed in the Georgian Revival style, it was Betty Morrow's dream home, a colossal affair with elaborate formal gardens on fifty-two acres of rolling meadows and woodlands. The Morrows would call the home Next Day Hill, a play on the family name.

Dwight and Betty Morrow had already hosted Lindbergh at the U.S. Embassy in Mexico for a week when their second daughter arrived by sleeper train for Christmas break from her senior year at Smith College. While Anne Spencer Morrow was shy, self-conscious, and bookish, her older sister, Elisabeth, was sophisticated and graceful—at ease in every social situation. Engulfed in self-doubt, Anne felt an "odious" envy of her sister's self-confidence, charm, and wit.[17]

Dressed in formal attire, Lindbergh was standing at the top of the embassy stairs when Anne's eyes fell on him. "He was so much slimmer, so much taller, so much more poised than I expected," she wrote in her diary.[18] "Tremendous hands, he has, too, and wrists—strong but not clumsy—steady and firm."[19]

Betty Morrow had issued a warning: "Don't try to make conversation with him!" Although Anne—"in awe and tongue-tied shyness"[20]— was the one who made Lindbergh feel comfortable around a girl for the first time in his life, she assumed that he would prefer Elisabeth. Anne had bloomed into a lovely, petite, brown-haired woman with radiant blue eyes, but she fretted about her attractiveness and regarded herself as "the youngest, shiest, most self-conscious adolescent that ever lived."[21]

"I fell in love with Anne almost as soon as I saw her," Lindbergh would write privately more than forty years later. "Elisabeth was a lovely girl, but she was not more beautiful."[22]

In the autumn of 1928, Lindbergh telephoned the Morrow residence in Englewood. It was his first time to call someone for a date. When he asked to speak to "Miss Morrow," the servant who answered the phone assumed that he meant Elisabeth.

"No, no," said Lindbergh. "Anne Morrow."

Anne was out of town, but she arrived home on the midnight train. At nine-thirty the next morning, the servant, Jo, asked her, "Guess who called up last night?"

Anne shrugged.

"Charles Augustus Lindbergh," said Jo. "He is going to call up at ten today."

And so when the telephone rang, Anne said, "Jo, I *can't*—I simply *can't*—I *can't* speak to him."

"You've *got* to, Anne," said Jo. "Go ahead—it won't be long."

At this point, Anne would recall, she looked at the telephone "paralyzed, gulping, like standing in front of a glass of castor oil." Finally, she picked up the receiver and answered very sheepishly, "Hello?"

"Hello. This is . . . Lindbergh himself."

As if reading from a preflight checklist, he reminded Anne of a promise he had made in Mexico to take her flying. Her anxiety during the brief conversation matched the awkwardness of his clipped sentences.

"But—you—you're very busy, aren't you?" she asked.

"Not particularly."[23]

After only one day alone together, the vestige of nervousness each had felt disappeared. Still under a romantic spell after her afternoon up in the clouds, Anne wrote to her younger sister, Constance, of the "glorious" flight over Long Island in an open-cockpit biplane.[24] "It was an inexplicable connection," the Lindberghs' daughter Reeve would say of her shy parents' attraction to each other.[25]

Lindbergh soon came calling again and took Anne for a drive. They sat in his black Franklin sedan and talked on for hours. Charles

*Charles and Anne Morrow Lindbergh*

described his vision of aviation's role in bringing the countries of the world together in harmony, while Anne revealed her goals as a writer. *Scribner's* had already published her poem "Height," and she had received two prestigious prizes awarded by Smith College for literary work.[26] Her yearning for the life of adventure he led and his admiration for her literary skills helped draw them together.[27] For Anne, who had written poems and stories about voyages to countries undiscovered, the time had come to fulfill her dreams and leave the "walled garden" of her privileged upbringing.[28] Moreover, she admired Charles's idealism, and although her vision of her own contribution to society was still vague, she wanted to "make [her] world count." "What do I want to do—what *can* I do?" she had written in her diary.[29]

Following but a week or two of flights, Anne accepted Charles's proposal of marriage. She had told her classmates at her high school graduation dinner that she wanted to marry a hero.[30] "The press did not learn about my interest in Anne until our engagement was announced," Lindbergh would write decades later.[31] With reporters prowling about Next Day Hill to pry out the undisclosed wedding date, with suspicions swirling that the phone line had been tapped, with a reporter offering servants a $2,000 bribe "to betray the secrets of the household," the couple determined to keep their wedding plans private.[32] Lindbergh, knowing that reporters were tracking the movement of his plane, ordered it flown to the airport at Rochester, New York.[33] Perhaps he was taking a cue from his late father, a congressman who had confounded the media by making preposterous comments with a straight face; on one occasion, he suggested the abolishment of the Senate and the vice presidency. A group of publishers agreed it might be an excellent idea.

On Sunday, May 26, the Morrows hosted a reception in honor of Lindbergh's mother. The next morning, they called up several relatives and close friends and invited them over for lunch and a game of bridge. At 3:15 p.m., Betty Morrow collected the group in the living room. Wearing a cream-white chiffon wedding gown and carrying a bouquet of light blue larkspur and other handpicked flowers Elisabeth had arranged, Anne walked in on her father's arm. After she said her vows, Charles slipped a gold band onto her finger. There were no photographs.[34]

When Lindbergh drove through the gates of the mansion, the reporters and photographers milling about the entrance were unaware that his bride was lying on the floor of his car. He drove to Long Island Sound and rowed out in a dinghy to his dual-cabin "motor-launch," the *Mouette*, which he had anchored near shore. The newlyweds made their way into the Sound by nightfall and headed up the coast.

Four days later, reporters and news photographers swarmed the couple after they were spotted refueling in Maine. A reward had been posted for information regarding their whereabouts. After Charles dropped anchor in an island bay, a "motion-picture photographer" stopped alongside in a speedboat and shouted at the Lindberghs to come aboard for pictures. Though they made it clear that they had no intention to do so, the boat circled them for hours, making a wake that rocked the *Mouette*.[35]

On April 20, 1930, Easter Sunday, Lindbergh and his copilot wife, seven months pregnant, broke the transcontinental speed record on a flight from Los Angeles to New York. The Lindberghs retreated to Next Day Hill, where Anne, whose doctors had advised against the trip, recuperated from nausea and exhaustion. For nearly fifteen hours at high altitude, she had breathed in gas fumes. Anne was airsick and in pain for the last four hours of the flight.

Journalists and photographers camped out in front of the gated mansion and waited for news of the birth. The refusal of five of the New York newspapers to observe rules of press ethics regarding private rights of citizens and unwritten rules of common courtesy and respect disgusted Lindbergh.[36] Ever since the flight to Paris, reporters had exhausted themselves stalking him and scrambling to uncover stories. Many had little or no interest in aviation. The biggest news about Lindbergh, observed social historian Daniel Boorstin, was that he was such big news.[37]

On Sunday, June 22, Anne gave birth to Charles Augustus Lindbergh, Jr. It was her twenty-fourth birthday. The press called the infant "Baby Lindy" and "Eaglet," a play on the aviator's moniker the "Lone Eagle." Well-wishers from all parts of the world flooded Next Day Hill with 300,000 letters, flowers, and piles of gifts for the baby.

By the time of his son's birth, Lindbergh had become as obsessed with privacy as the public was with him. One day, a carload of "sightseers" zoomed through the gates of Next Day Hill, hit Anne's and her sister Constance's West Highland white terrier, Daffin, and sped away. The dog let out a pained cry and began panting furiously. As Daffin yipped and thrashed about in a death agony, the family's other white terrier, Peter, stood watch and growled whenever anyone approached the bloodstained driveway. A veterinarian rushed over, but Daffin had already lost consciousness. An injection of morphine and it was over. "Charles really wanted to shoot them," Anne wrote to Constance. "The house has been so lonely—I think of him all the time . . . I see the print his little body made in the chair he has jumped down from."[38]

Lindbergh began search for a homesite that would provide seclusion and protection from intruders and also supply reasonable access to Manhattan. During the summer of 1930, he flew over the Sourland Mountains in central New Jersey and spotted 425 acres of meadows and leafy woods three miles from the borough of Hopewell. A brook meandered through the rural property, which was reachable only by little-used roads that wound through sparse woods. Lindbergh, envisioning Highfields as a haven where he could escape the eye of the public, fell in love with the land. He hired the architect of Next Day Hill to draw up a set of blueprints and cleared an area for a landing field. At five hundred feet above sea level, the home would sit on a hill in the center of the estate at one of the highest points in New Jersey.

The architect designed a plan for a two-and-a-half story native fieldstone house with whitewashed cement. Lindbergh added his own design specification: a thick slate roof whose rippled pattern, when viewed from the sky, would give the impression of ocean waves. Although the Lindberghs rented a farmhouse near Princeton while their new home was under construction, they spent most of their time at Next Day Hill, where Anne felt safer. In September of 1930, her father, whose great passion was politics, returned to New Jersey and ran as a Republican for a seat in the U.S. Senate.[39] He won in a landslide.

In the spring of 1929, Constance Morrow, a student at Milton Academy, had received a letter demanding $50,000 from her father; if he did not pay up, she would be kidnapped. "Don't open your trap to a living soul or it will be your last talk," the letter warned. "Your going away will not help as you are MARKED."[40]

Anne worried because the newspapers provided constantly updated information about her family's whereabouts. The Lindberghs spent their weekends at the farmhouse. "The house is rather unprotected," Anne wrote to her mother-in-law. "The baby sleeps outside. Unless he is watched every second, anyone could walk in and photograph him, etc. Perhaps this is all very silly."[41]

The Morrows had staffed their 40,000-square-foot, irregular C-shaped mansion with twenty-nine servants. Because his family was a prime target for kidnappers, Dwight Morrow had erected a tall iron fence around Next Day Hill and hired a team of full-time security guards. Shortly before he died of a cerebral hemorrhage in October 1931, not even a full year into his Senate term, he had cautioned his son-in-law about failing to maintain adequate security. Assuming that his family would be safe in the countryside, Lindbergh ignored the advice.

*An aerial view of Next Day Hill in Englewood, NJ*
(Courtesy of Amherst College Archives and Special Collections)

Anyone on a reconnaissance mission who peered through the bars of the iron fence would have conceded Next Day Hill's impregnability. Had an intruder somehow managed to penetrate the security perimeter and break into the mansion, threading its labyrinth of wings and rooms to find the nursery and escaping with the baby would have been even more daunting. The Lindberghs' new estate outside Hopewell would be far easier for a kidnapper to infiltrate. The design of the two-story home and the location of the baby's room, however, would require the participation of accomplices.

It was understandable that an aviator might mistake distance and remoteness for relative safety, but in reality the Lindberghs' new home, without so much as a single private security guard, invited danger. In the parlance of today's security experts, the estate was a soft target whose seclusion increased its vulnerability.

Most potential kidnappers would have been deterred by the remoteness of the Hopewell area and by the fame of the target. Why take unnecessary risks when easier and wealthier targets lived closer to the City? But Dwight Morrow, in his advice to Lindbergh about protection, had perhaps understood that his son-in-law was a unique figure, likelier than much richer men to come to grief unless he was careful. To a certain kind of criminal, the theft of the most famous baby in America would confer something he coveted far more than a ransom. It would present the opportunity to pull off a feat even bigger, even more daring, than Lindbergh himself had accomplished.

Common criminals don't conceive such grandiose ideas. The criminals who do so fall into the specialty of Ed Sulzbach, who spent seventeen years tracking down, capturing, interviewing, and studying serial killers, rapists, pedophiles, and murderers of children. "Lindbergh was beyond famous," he said, "which made him a tremendous lure for a psychopath. The anonymous fame such a person stood to gain from the kidnapping would have been as alluring to him as public acclaim.

"The investigation would have been handled much differently had it taken place today," said the retired FBI special agent. "If I were on the case, I'd be looking for an antisocial personality type in his twenties or early thirties. The leader of the kidnapping gang would likely possess a boundless ego, a gift of high intelligence and articulateness, an impulsive nature, and little or no regard for others or capacity for relationships. And no conscience whatsoever."

The man eventually convicted of the murder—as Sulzbach puts it, "a common criminal"—does not fit this description.[42] To profilers today, Bruno Hauptmann still has the look of a follower who went along with someone else's big idea, convinced and manipulated by a stronger, more aggressive, and more malevolent personality. But who was that someone, where could Hauptmann have met him, and how did it all begin?

# 4

# Johannes

In December of 1926, three months after Charles Lindbergh conceived the ambition to fly a plane nonstop from New York to Paris, a short, stocky German immigrant with a high forehead and pointed chin was settling into the Melrose neighborhood in the South Bronx.[1] Melrose and two neighborhoods in its immediate vicinity, Morrisania and Mott Haven, were home to the densest German populations in the borough.[2]

The eighth of nine children, Johannes Knoll—John, as he would call himself in America—was born on June 24, 1904, in Herxheimweyher, a tobacco farming village of five hundred in Rheinland Pfalz. The predominantly Catholic village recently celebrated its 950th anniversary. At the time of Johannes's birth, his father was forty-three, his mother thirty-nine.

My journey took me to Herxheimweyher in 2010, in search of people who still remembered him or knew of him, and also to Kempten im Allgäu, where the niece of John's second wife lives today. As on my visits to Michigan and other states to meet other Knoll relatives, everyone I spoke to about John was friendly and gracious—to the point of inviting me to a family reunion in Richmond, Michigan, and even putting me up for a couple of nights. To judge from my experience, John Knoll came from a family of first-rate people.

In the 1960s, when Gene Zorn first suspected Knoll's involvement in the Lindbergh kidnapping, he recalled the strong interest his former neighbor had shown in him. As he began to study the case, the thought never occurred to him that anyone in the gang might have had any motive other than quick riches. "Good people are rarely suspicious," wrote William March in *The Bad Seed*. They cannot image others doing the things they themselves are incapable of doing."[3] Indeed, as I began my own investigation, I assumed that if the uneducated immigrant John Knoll was guilty, he had likely viewed a kidnapping-for-ransom scheme solely as a means of escaping the struggles of the Depression.

Stories that have survived about Knoll, however, portray a person whose behavior and personality were unlike anything I'd ever observed. Indeed, only the veteran FBI criminal profilers, forensic psychiatrists, and psychology researchers whose counsel I've sought seem ever to have encountered many people like him. To them, as I reported what I had learned from others who knew John Knoll, the stories had a familiar ring, even the little incidents in his early life that all by themselves wouldn't seem very troubling.

Gene Zorn, an economist trained to appreciate the implications of financial decisions, considered Knoll's circumstances at the time of the kidnapping. In 1932, the worst year of the Depression, advancement opportunities for uneducated German immigrants were practically nonexistent. How else, then, might this deli clerk have had a chance to get rich while the economy was in ruins other than through criminal activity?

In story after story, we always seem to find John Knoll demeaning others or somehow trying to draw attention to himself. He comes across as reckless, impulsive, unpredictable, lacking in empathy, and at times imperious enough to have earned the boyhood nickname of "Schah"— German for "shah," or Persian king. My father remembered Knoll ringing the doorbell aggressively, stomping about the Zorns' apartment, and sniffing under the lids of his mother's pots on her coal stove. My grandmother called him the "crazy Dutchman," and she always got an uneasy feeling when Knoll was around, like something about him was a little off. It turns out she wasn't the first.

It's difficult to piece together a clear picture of his youth, yet his parents must have concluded early on that Johannes was unlikely to follow his two older brothers into the priesthood or into academia. Johannes's childhood was undoubtedly influenced by larger events that his older brothers never had to endure growing up in the Pfalz. He was ten and his brother Walter five at the beginning of the Great War.

"The Pfalz was one of the first regions of Europe to know what the outbreak of war between modern nations would entail," writes historian Dr. Celia Applegate. ". . . Although the Pfalz never became the scene of actual fighting, as many of its inhabitants initially feared, its proximity to the front for four years brought it not only the sounds of this loudest of wars, but also a constant stream of prisoners and wounded and dying soldiers from one direction, and supplies and ever more troops from the other."[4] Indeed, a Russian prisoner of war lived with the Knolls during the war, and a family member, Julius Knoll, died in battle just as hostilities were about to cease. "The war itself or some particular incident related to it could have shaped John Knoll's emotional responsivity," said Dr. Craig S. Neumann, a renowned psychology researcher. "It could have had a callousing effect on him."[5]

As a ten-year-old boy, Johannes had preferred to stand away from his nearest schoolmates in a class picture. In the photo, taken near the beginning of the war, all the kids look a little glum. But everyone else is shoulder to shoulder, and only one boy in the scene, by a full step, has set himself apart from the rest. He's turned slightly away from the group, too, with an oddly superior expression, as if he were the sole subject and the others weren't even there. It's much the same with pictures of Knoll well into adulthood that capture an emotional range from surliness to indifference.

During his teenage years, his sister Agnes discovered a pistol beneath his pillow while making up his bed one day. The explanation for that incident is long forgotten; it's just one of those stories that got traction in family lore as an example of the guy he was, like the one about Johannes and the French soldiers who occupied the Rheinland after the armistice and commandeered the Knolls' home and tobacco barn. Behind the family's home was their barn, where tobacco leaves hung from crossbeams to dry. The visitors made a habit of pulling snails off the family's grapevines and frying them in vats of lard; just one sniff of the odor was enough to disgust Johannes. One day, as the soldiers were practicing their marching in the barn, he crept inside, climbed a ladder to the rafters, and spat on them. Then he unbuttoned his trousers and urinated on the soldiers, who immediately seized him and threw him in jail. Knoll was about fourteen at the time, and this was a pretty daring thing for a kid that age to do. Johannes's father was the Bürgermeister of Herxheimweyher, how-ever, and he quickly secured his son's release.[6]

The third of four sons born to Philipp Jakob and Elisabeth Keller Knoll, Johannes was set to become laird of the paternal home and tobacco farm. A photograph taken in 1863 of the chalet-style home shows his distinguished-looking grandfather, also named Philipp Jakob Knoll, dining with four other gentlemen dressed to the nines and drinking wine from elegant crystal goblets. Yet the charming home and the life of a to-bacco farmer seemed to have been of no interest to any of the four Knoll boys. Overcoming the misgivings of his father, Johannes's brother Leo, the eldest and his senior by sixteen years, joined the Order of Salesian priests and spent his life in Peru ministering to the poor. Born two years after Leo in 1890, Emil earned a degree in philology in Sweden but died in his early twenties when Johannes was still a boy.

Philipp Jakob Knoll and his wife sought to teach their children the values of faith, education, industriousness, and selflessness. By all accounts, however, Johannes found little excitement in the serious pur-suits of his ambitious and devout older siblings. Both a few years older than Johannes, Maria and Elisabetha became sisters of the Dominican Order. During the Holocaust, Elisabetha would receive Jewish children from their parents, teach them how to pass for Catholics, and harbor them from the Nazis. Such willingness to risk execution stood as the most powerful evidence of the strength of her faith, yet for the rest of his life, Elisabetha's younger brother would disparage her and her good works. He took to calling her *"Mutter Gottes,"* or Mother of God, and it wasn't said in pious admiration.

At age twenty, Knoll boarded the steamship *Republic* and cast off for America in January 1925.[7] It was the year F. Scott Fitzgerald published his novel about young Jay Gatsby's obsessive dream of success. The sur-viving memories of Knoll's family members portray a man with a few illusions of his own about the new life that lay ahead. In any case, that life began with an apparent lie to immigration authorities. On the ship's man-ifest he put down the Bronx as his destination, but upon arrival promptly moved into the more exciting precincts of Manhattan. Whether it was a case of deliberate misrepresentation can best be judged by considering that, as we'll see, nearly fifty years later Knoll would misrepresent the year of his arrival in the Bronx, claiming to have come not in 1926 but in 1932. He was given to misstatements of the kind, and in the latter case, of course, a 1932 arrival date takes him out of the picture at the very time when the Lindbergh kidnapping was planned.

In 1925—the year records clearly place him in the United States—the Bronx was in his future anyway. Maybe it was the loss of a job, or the signs throughout New York City reading HELP WANTED—GERMANS NEED NOT APPLY when he tried to find another. In any case, Knoll ended up in the South Bronx in December of 1926 in a neighborhood more congenial to immigrants. Like many spots in the melting pot of the City, Jackson Avenue reflected the wave of immigration into New York in the preceding half-century. Knoll found work as a clerk of a delicatessen on Westchester Avenue owned by a German immigrant named Henry Woltmann, who had come to New York at the turn of the century. The deli store was around the corner from the furnished room on Jackson Avenue where Knoll lived, just three doors away from my grandparents' place.

My grandparents rented their third floor apartment at 732 Jackson Avenue from a caterer named Oscar Rietschel, a drinking companion of John Knoll. A German immigrant in his fifties from Kamenz, a town of 13,000 in eastern Saxony, Rietschel was a fixture in the neighborhood. With his thick accent, walrus moustache, beer belly, and ever-present cigar, he would have looked right in place in the square of a German village. According to his Petition for Naturalization, his previous petition had been denied "for the following reasons and causes, to wit, Lack of Intelligence, and the cause of such denial has been since cured or removed."[8]

Six feet tall with a dark complexion and oval face, Rietschel made "gallon upon gallon" of homebrewed beer at least once a month.[9] During Prohibition, the neighborhood kept silent about such activities. The beverage satisfied the cravings of hard-drinking John Knoll, a frequent visitor in the Rietschels' house. It seems likely that conversation between the two men might now and then have turned to life back in Germany, or to fellow immigrants from the Fatherland now living in the Bronx. If so, perhaps Oscar Rietschel mentioned the name of another man from Kamenz—Bruno Richard Hauptmann.

The Rietschels lived at *Rosengaesschen* 6, the Hauptmanns at *Bautzner Straße* 64, a distance of 125 yards apart. Would the families have been acquainted? I asked Odette Küntsler of the Kamenz City Archives. "Because the Rietschels and the Hauptmanns lived so close by," she said, "the families certainly would have known each other."[10] Adding even more to the likelihood of an acquaintance, Hauptmann had come to America in 1923 as a friendless stowaway and fugitive, and was known to look up people from his hometown. A sociable person who enjoyed sing-a-longs, camping trips, and outings at amusement parks, he went as far as Elizabeth, New Jersey, to visit a man from Kamenz named Otto Heyne.[11]

The Kamenz connection offers a simple explanation as to how John Knoll and Bruno Hauptmann came to know each other—through a mutual association with Oscar Rietschel. When they met is unknown. All we know is that it was sometime between December 1926, when Knoll moved to Jackson Avenue, and the summer of 1931, when my father's eyewitness account places Knoll and "Bruno" outside Palisades Park, nine months before a crime the ransom notes said was "pland for a year allredy," speaking in German about a place called Englewood.

# 5

# The Stamp Collector

More typical than Oscar Rietschel among the Jackson Avenue land-lords was Emma Schaefer, one of several widows on the Zorns' block who rented out apartments or rooms either to subsist or supplement their incomes. Emma lived on the second floor of the home at 738 Jackson Avenue. Facing the street in her "railroad" flat were two adjoining rooms—the living room, called a parlor in those days, and a little bedroom. John Knoll rented the room for ten dollars a month and entered from the outside hallway. He could lock the door to the parlor to ensure complete privacy and come and go with no one noticing. His younger brother also leased a room in the apartment.

In February 1926, Walter Knoll had made his crossing to America at age sixteen and moved in with his sister Agnes Breiling and her husband, Ludwig, in a suburb of Detroit. Five-foot-eleven and slim, Walter had a full head of dark, wavy hair, blue eyes, and a long, angular face. Finding little to keep him in Michigan, the younger and quieter Knoll—"Lazy Walter" as he was called in Herxheimweyher—came to the Bronx a couple of years later and got a job at Woltmann's.[1]

Emma Schaefer's daughter Alice, a dressmaker in Manhattan in her mid-thirties, occupied a back bedroom. Alice's older brother, Bill, also lived in the apartment from time to time.[2] The Schaefers treated the Knoll brothers as members of the family and allowed them to use their kitchen and their telephone, which Alice listed in her name. John fancied himself an adroit coiner of nicknames—to him she was "Alice Chiffonier." He also called my father's long-legged teenage sister Glady *Honigplatz* ("honey seat") as he leered at her rear end.

A row of seven three-story attached wooden houses stood on the east side of the 700 block of Jackson Avenue. Down the street were an elevated subway stop, Jackson Avenue Station, and a tall, high-ceilinged building that had once housed a motion picture studio. Devoid of lawns or landscaping in the front, the homes on the block had no pretensions to architectural elegance. Wrought-iron gates provided direct access to the cellar from the street. The neighborhood bore no resemblance to Herxheimweyher's picturesque *Hauptstraße*, or Main Street, on which John Knoll had lived in his family's storybook home.

In each house on Jackson Avenue lived at least one—and usually two—middle-class German families. On the block lived the Boydstons, the Bendels, the Gerhardts, the Koehlers, the Snyders, the Hillebrands, the Huths, the Kuhns, the Gerckens, the Hennickes, the Schattgens, the Schalks, and a Chinese launderer named Lee Sing. The breadwinners in the neighborhood included a policeman, a fireman, a paper cutter, a stenographer, a barber, a garment presser, a machinist, a horseman, a cement finisher, a riveter, a steamfitter, a butcher, and a baker.[3] Another man scratched a living as the proprietor of a tiny store that sold nothing but French fries. Each of the houses had three flats, with six rooms in those on the second floor.

Life for Knoll in the Bronx was not easy, and the grind of his job as a deli clerk wasn't exactly how he had pictured life in America. Whatever the reasons, he is remembered as quick to take offense at the slightest perceived insult. He once used a broom to chase my father and his friend out of Woltmann's delicatessen after the boys had played a harmless practical joke on him.[4]

He was a secretive man, too, managing to conceal from his landlady and most everyone else even the fact that he had been married. For all the years the Zorns knew him, he had represented himself as a bachelor. Yet on October 13, 1927, as his marriage record shows, he exchanged vows with a showgirl named Paula Trauth at St. Thomas the Apostle Church in Manhattan.[5] Three years older than her groom, Paula was petite with dark hair and a gap between her front teeth. A native of a neighboring village of Herxheimweyher called Hayna, she had set forth on her new life in America aboard the express liner *Bremen*, arriving in New York on October 31, 1926.[6] Knoll's sister Agnes, who had immigrated to the States three years earlier, accompanied her on the voyage. Agnes and Knoll's friend Karl Dickgiesser from Herxheimweyher both signed as witnesses to the marriage. Knoll and Dickgiesser had sailed to America together twenty-two months earlier.

Knoll lived in the room he rented from Emma Schaefer from 1926 to 1934. What had drawn the showgirl to her odd-looking husband and where she lived after the ceremony are mysteries.[7]

"John was very good at flattering women and they were really attracted to him," recalled his niece Sharon Breiling. "His marriage to Paula lasted only a few months, however."[8] We don't know whether or not John and Paul ever officially divorced. At the time, one had to prove adultery to obtain a divorce in New York. U.S. Census records reveal that Paula was using her maiden name in 1930 and was employed at that time as a live-in servant for the family of a Herman Wolfheim in St. Louis. The Wolfheims' son Richie was ten at the time. "We had a lot of maids live with us, but I don't remember Paula," ninety-two-year old Richie Wolfheim said. "Just my luck: a showgirl moves into our place, and I'm too young to take advantage of it."[9]

On Knoll's October 31, 1931, Petition for Citizenship, he listed Paula as his wife but described her whereabouts as "Unknown." The record indicates that he had lived in the Bronx since December 16, 1926. Knoll's employer, Henry Woltmann, signed the petition as a witness.[10] Her marriage to Knoll having been ill-fated from the start, Paula would eventually return to Hayna and remarry, leaving Knoll without further need of stealth and secrecy about Mrs. Knoll.

Even after her marriage to Knoll, Paula remains a mystery. In ship records, we find her again bound for America from Germany in August 1935, but for some reason her name is crossed out, suggesting that she had changed her plans at the last minute. When she finally does make the return trip in February 1936, two months before Hauptmann's execution, she designates Hamburg as her last permanent address. Beyond this, we know only that Paula would meet in Germany with John Knoll's second wife on one occasion sometime in the mid-1930s.

What does seem striking is that Knoll's second wife, Lilly, was an aviator. Karoline Lillian Karg was an accomplished flier, and trained by the best. In 1921, she took lessons from Lothar von Richthofen, one of Germany's most victorious combat aces of the Great War and the younger brother of the Red Baron. Born in 1902 in Niederingelheim, Germany, Lilly had come to America from Bucharest, Romania, docking in New York on the SS *Columbus* on June 8, 1929, less than five months before the Great Crash.

Though we don't know their wedding date, Lilly Karg and John Knoll were married when they departed America in December 1934, three and a half weeks before Bruno Hauptmann went on trial for the murder. At that time John and Lilly could not have been married very long. In September of 1933, Lilly, traveling under her maiden name, had sailed from Hamburg to New York on the SS *President Harding*; the ship's manifest listed her last permanent residence as Brightwaters, a village on Long Island in western Suffolk County.[11]

When John Knoll sailed back to America in February 1935, just days after the conviction of Hauptmann, Lilly did not accompany him. She stayed in Germany an additional four months.[12] In August 1935, she gave birth to their son, John Robert "Bobby" Knoll, in Mt. Clemens, Michigan. The Knolls had moved there from the Bronx, living with John's sister and brother-in-law, sometime shortly before or after the arrest of Bruno Hauptmann. When Bobby was eight months old, she returned to Germany, leaving her husband and taking the baby with her. This was right about at the time of Hauptmann's execution in April 1936. Lilly would not move back to the States for a decade—preferring, as surviving family members attest, a life in Hitler's Germany to life with John Knoll.

Lilly's niece Brigitte Geiger, now in her early seventies, lives in Kempten im Allgäu in southwest Bavaria. Her face twists in revulsion at the mention of John Knoll. In the stories she heard growing up, her family had described him as harsh, controlling, and unfaithful. "John was an alcoholic and was very unpredictable," she said. "Lilly worried that he was on the edge of the law."[13] Knoll's father-in-law, Robert Karg, seems to have had a similar impression. "Please, Lilly," he begged, "get rid of that bum!"

She acted on the advice, but we don't know what had drawn Lilly into that miserable situation in the first place. Although John displayed no capacity for maintaining relationships, he clearly had an instinct for how to initiate them. One wife vanished and the other fled, but both apparently saw something attractive at the outset, and it couldn't have been the prospect of a bright future at Henry Woltmann's delicatessen. The criminal profilers view him as a skillful manipulator, typical of many abusive husbands.[14] He could appear considerate, friendly, and perhaps even charming. But his behavior would soon be revealed as a put-on, much as Knoll could take an eager fifteen-year-old on an outing in New Jersey only to abandon the boy and instruct him to go back to the Bronx by himself. Whatever his first two wives saw on first impression, what followed was bad enough to send both out of his life in a hurry. Even Knoll's son, in his own adulthood, would remain on the opposite coast from his father.

All of this fits with my father's recollections of Knoll, especially in regards to stamp collecting. The shared hobby brought out John's more amicable side, and, in fact, it was Knoll who had first interested my father in stamps. Collectible stamps issued in the 1920s had risen dramatically in value, and many who were investing in stamps issued in the 1930s assumed the trend woud continue. It seemed a good way to make money, and in those days, it was also a form of entertainment.

My father took to stamps immediately. An eye injury had prevented him from playing stickball with the kids on the block, but one day, John Knoll invited him to his room in Emma Schaefer's apartment. Knoll took out his collection of stamps and First Day Covers and let my father look at them. A new world suddenly opened up, and soon Gene Zorn had his own albums filled with stamps of all shapes, sizes, and colors. "There is no frigate like a book," wrote Emily Dickinson, "to take us lands away."[15] For the boy whose little room in that cramped apartment on Jackson Avenue overlooked the street, books were fine, but there was no frigate like a stamp. Stamps transported him to India, Egypt, Portuguese East Africa, France, Italy, and other faraway lands from which each had traveled all the way to the Bronx. There were commemorative stamps, too, to mark such highlights in history as the rule of Caesar Augustus, the British surrender at Yorktown, the VIII *Olympiade* in France, and the solo flight of Charles Lindbergh to Paris.

The "Lindbergh Airmail" stamp, issued on June 18, 1927, was a gift from John Knoll to my father. In 1928, Knoll had mailed a letter bearing the stamp to his brother-in-law Ernst Schlachter in Queichheim, Germany.[16] In the lower left-hand corner of the envelope is the artwork on First Day Covers and commemorative covers known as a cachet, featuring the dirigible *Graf Zeppelin*, a symbol of German engineering triumph. The airship had carried this same letter across the Atlantic. The artwork includes two globes and the words "First Flight Air Mail," "Via *Graf Zeppelin*," and "United States–Germany." Next to the cachet is the 10-cent Lindbergh stamp, depicting the *Spirit of St. Louis* and its route from New York to Paris. Looking slightly out of place along with these images of the two most acclaimed aircraft in the world is a one-dollar stamp honoring the Lincoln Memorial. In the upper left-hand corner of the envelope, Knoll had written "German Airship *L.Z.* 127 from Lakehurst, N.J."

*This envelope bearing the "Lindbergh Airmail" stamp was a gift from John Knoll to my father. The artwork in the lower left-hand corner is known as a cachet.*

This envelope, with its $1.15 worth of stamps (the equivalent of $17.26 today), seemed an extravagant gift to my father.[17] To this day, it remains the centerpiece of his stamp collection. At the time, he counted the envelope as his most prized possession, surpassing even the baseball he had caught at Yankee Stadium.[18] More gifts from his German neighbor would come, too, including a commemorative cover with a cachet celebrating the five-year anniversary of Lindbergh's flight to Paris. The envelope bears a postmark of May 20, 1932. Altogether, Knoll made eighteen contributions to my father's boyhood stamp collection, including four First Day Covers and a commemorative cover all postmarked April 22, 1932. Even at the time, Gene Zorn, a future economist who possessed a keen understanding of money, wondered about this curious sudden generosity. How was a man with the slender wages of a deli clerk able to afford to purchase an entire stamp collection from another philatelist in the City and to give a boy down the block one fabulous collectible after another?

# 6

## The *Singnature*

On the night of the kidnapping, the one who discovered the ransom note left in the nursery was Lindbergh himself. As he looked about the room, his eyes fell on an envelope on top of the windowsill. Recognizing that the envelope contained a letter from the kidnappers, he told Anne and Betty Gow to leave it alone. Lindbergh observed small traces of yellowish clay on the windowsill and on a suitcase that sat on top of a cedar chest against the wall and directly below the window. A Tinkertoy rabbit on top of the suitcase and a beer stein on the windowsill remained undisturbed. Lindbergh saw another smudge on the floor by the window but none between the window and the crib on the opposite wall.

Olly Whateley, acting on Lindbergh's order, called the Hopewell Police Department. The kidnappers had not cut the wires. At 10:30 p.m., Lindbergh telephoned the New Jersey State Police Headquarters in Trenton, and then made a second call to his close friend Colonel Henry Breckinridge in Manhattan. Breckinridge, forty-five, a tall, dashing lawyer educated at Princeton and Harvard, served as Lindbergh's primary sounding board. Breckinridge and his wife, the pioneering aviator Aida de Acosta, had visited the Lindberghs at Highfields the previous weekend.

Lindbergh, a crack shot who could put a hole through a quarter from a distance of fifty feet, stepped out into the darkness with his rifle and searched the grounds with Whateley. The Hopewell police chief and his constable arrived at 10:35 p.m.

Anne stood in the foyer holding back tears as her husband motioned the men to follow him upstairs. The officers examined the baby's room then made a circuit of the house with Lindbergh. The police chief, using his flashlight, spotted the two lower sections of a homemade ladder sixty feet from the house. An unused top section lay another ten feet beyond. The builder of the device had designed the sections to nest together so that it could fit into an automobile.[1] The two connected sections were attached by a dowel rod pushed through matching holes, the narrower upper section fitting into and overlapped by the lower. Both side rails of the upper section, however, had split near the bottom. As he took a look for himself, Lindbergh assumed that the cracking noise he had heard earlier was the sound of the ladder breaking. Spaced at nineteen-inch intervals, the rungs were seven inches farther apart than those of a standard ladder. A wood-handled, three-quarter-inch Buck Brothers chisel lay on the ground a little way off from the ladder.

At 10:46 p.m., the police Teletype system transmitted an alarm: COLONEL LINDBERGS [SIC] BABY WAS KIDNAPPED FROM LINDBERGHS HOME IN HOPEWELL SOMETIME BETWEEN 7-30 PM AND 10-PM.[2] Police had set up roadblocks on New Jersey streets by eleven o'clock. Aroused from sleep, Police Commissioner Edward P. Mulrooney took charge of the New York City search and ordered patrolmen and motorcycle men to inspect every vehicle that came into Manhattan by way of the New Jersey ferries, the George Washington Bridge, and the Holland Tunnel.

The officers from Hopewell had been at the crime scene for twenty minutes when Corporal Joseph A. Wolf of the New Jersey State Police appeared and began his own investigation. About three feet from the east side of the house where the kidnappers had leaned the ladder up against the wall, the two shafts of its bottom section had left depressions an inch and a half deep in the muddy ground.[3] The ladder had been positioned to the side of the window rather than directly below it.

The strength and gymnastic ability demanded of a single kidnapper all but eliminated the possibility that the crime was the work of a lone wolf. The intruder would have to open the window, pull himself into the nursery without disturbing any of the items on or near the windowsill, squeeze back through the thirty-inch-wide window with a baby weighing about thirty pounds, maneuver to land on the appropriate rung of the ladder in total darkness and descend safely. Doubtless the intruder would have kicked over the ladder as he tried to land on it; the device would have tended to slide against the house rather than remain in a fixed position. The plan required the participation of three people: one to steady the ladder, another to climb it and receive the baby, and a third to steal into the home, grab Charlie from the crib, and make the hand-off out the window.

Retired FBI criminal profiler Dr. Mary Ellen O'Toole, a leading expert on child abduction, psychopathy, and targeted violence, stresses the amount of planning required for a kidnapping-for-ransom plot.[4] One imagines the difficulty of capturing the victim and escaping unnoticed, negotiating a ransom, identifying a safe spot to receive the money, taking delivery of the cash without the benefit of having an accomplice on the lookout for police, then spending bills likely to be marked. If the kidnapper's plan calls for him to take care of the victim and return him unharmed, how challenging would it be for one person to accomplish this? And if the victim is dead, what are the chances of collecting the money without returning him?

In our day, no profiler is better known or more admired for his expertise than John Douglas himself, a pioneer of modern criminal investigative analysis during his twenty-five-year FBI career.[5] Douglas has written about the Lindbergh case and examined the former crime scene. He contends that it is "virtually inconceivable" that it was the work of one man working alone. "The only efficient way to get the child from the nursery window to the ladder is through a handoff," Douglas writes.[6] He also concludes that the UNSUB—as the unknown subject would be referred to in today's jargon—was "someone who took great personal risks."[7] But in the 1930s, investigators gave little thought to the inner workings of the criminal mind.

Corporal Wolf's crime report would state that the kidnappers consisted "apparently of a party of at least two persons."[8] He observed that the thirty-eight-pound ladder had been moved seventy-five feet[9] from the southeast corner of the house—an improbable action for a lone kidnapper to take while fleeing the crime scene with a child in his arms. The report also noted the discovery of "two sets of fresh footprints leading off in a southeast direction" from the home.

*The ladder used by the kidnappers propped against the wall of the Lindbergh home. Although it is shown directly below the window at the nursery, it was actually positioned to the right of the window from the climber's perspective.*

"Everything pointed to the fact that there must have been three people engaged in the act of kidnapping," said Betty Gow. "It would not have been possible for anyone to have taken the child in their arms, stepped through the window and descend without outside aid."[10] Several hours before the crime occurred, Anne had tossed a pebble at one of the windows in the nursery to attract her attention.[11] Betty opened the window and held up the baby to wave to his mother. The nursemaid recognized the near impossibility of escaping the nursery in pitch darkness and descending a flimsy ladder positioned well below the window ledge—and to the side of the window as well.

After Wolf examined the clues by the southeast corner window, he used a penknife to transfer the envelope to the fireplace mantle, where the evidence would remain untouched until the arrival of a fingerprint specialist. Soon scores of investigators and reporters would arrive at the crime scene.

Colonel H. Norman Schwarzkopf, thirty-seven, the tall, athletic, and mustachioed superintendent of the New Jersey State Police, showed up just before midnight with Major Charles Schoeffel, Captain John J. Lamb, head of the State Police detective branch, and Lieutenant Arthur T. "Buster" Keaten, the local investigative bureau chief. In 1921, the New Jersey State Police had awarded Badge #1 to Schwarzkopf, a West Point graduate who had served on the front in France during the war, and would serve again in the Second World War. West Point "had shaped his entire life," and its motto, "Duty, Honor, Country," was his creed, as Schwarzkopf's famous son would write sixty years later.[12]

Making no pretense of possessing experience in detective work, Schwarzkopf turned over the investigation to Lamb, who had received recognition for his work in a high profile double-murder case.[13] Another trooper arrived after midnight and powdered the nursery and the envelope. After the process failed to yield a single fingerprint, one of the men slit open the envelope. Inside was a letter that read:

> Dear Sir!
> Have 50.000 $ redy 25000 $ in
> 20$ bills 15000 $ in 10$ bills and
> 10000$ in 5$ bills. After 2-4 days
> we will inform you were to deliver
> the mony.
> We warn you for making
> anyding public or for notify the Polise
> the child is in gut care.
> Indication for all letters are
> Singnature
> and three hohls.[14]

The amount demanded was the equivalent of $750,000 today. The "*singnature*" referred to a pair of interlocking blue circles appearing in the lower right-hand corner of a sheet of cheap bond paper. The symbol itself, with its three evenly spaced holes, pointed to the likelihood of a three-man operation.

At the time, the police viewed the signature-symbol as nothing more

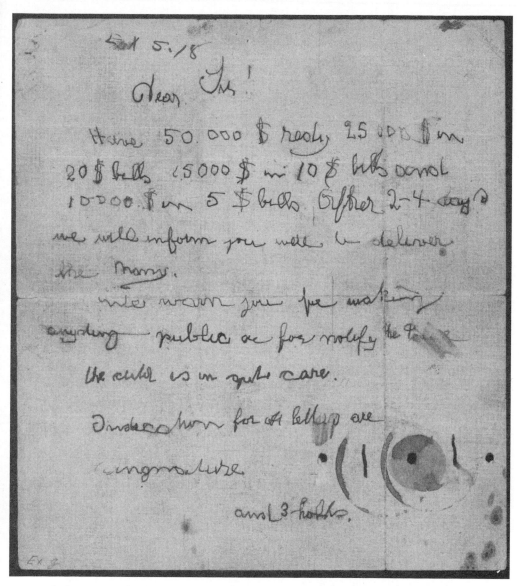

*The first ransom letter, found in the baby's nursery. Note the kidnappers' signature symbol—two interlocking circles and three punched holes—in the lower right hand corner.*

than a way for the kidnappers to ensure that the Lindberghs would know they were dealing with the right people. But it was a case of the criminal having more imagination than the investigators, for, of course, the kidnappers could have accomplished the same purpose by much less elaborate means. Why such intricate symbolism, drawn and repeated on each ransom letter? Why not a simple code word? In profiler Dr. Mary Ellen O'Toole's opinion, the symbol was unnecessary to the accomplishment of the crime, and it was the mark of a game player.[15] And it likely brought great emotional satisfaction to its creator.

The stated mission of the National Security Agency is "to protect U.S. national security systems and to produce foreign signals intelligence information,"[16] and for that purpose hires the country's top cryptanalysts "to code and decode information."[17] Former NSA analyst Ken Scarborough has devised a theory about the meaning underlying the kidnappers' signature-symbol. "The three circles represent the participation of three kidnappers," said Scarborough. "The interlocking circles—a symbol whose origin dates back to ancient Rome—signify solidarity among the gang members. If any of the three is caught, he will refuse to name his accomplices."[18]

In the 1930s, ordinary criminals rarely exercised much creativity in their extortion notes. It's a different type altogether that adds the artistic touch, seeking to communicate something beyond threats, instructions, and the demand for money. Much like the separate sets of footprints leading away from the Lindbergh house, the interlocking circles and three holes signify the mark of more than one man. And whoever devised the signature-symbol was almost certainly the mastermind, not just an accomplice.

# 7
# Butterflies

With operating margins in bootlegging in decline, kidnapping for ransom had evolved into a booming business for the mob. The legal system had seemed powerless against the industry from the mid-1920s to the early 1930s, when kidnapping posed a threat in major metropolitan areas throughout the country. Newspaper publicity surrounding a series of abductions and plots against the rich and famous, including one never carried out to steal the children of Edsel Ford, had the public on alert. In almost every kidnapping case, the primary motive was the same—money.

In 1983, forensic psychiatrist Dr. Emanuel Tanay presented an academic paper on the Lindbergh case at the annual meeting of the American Academy of Forensic Sciences. Dr. Tanay remarked that kidnapping a child "secures a great deal of emotional impact with relatively modest means" and that when small children are targeted, "reasons other than criminal expediency" would likely factor into the equation. "Kidnapping a child of a national hero would be a particularly unsuitable method for achieving financial success through extortion," he wrote. "It seems reasonable to assume that the kidnapping of the Lindbergh child was motivated by factors other than mere desire to procure money by criminal means."[1]

Because of the kidnappers' superior position in negotiations, Lindbergh informed the investigators of his intention to pay the ransom. Henry Breckinridge concurred. Not given to self-doubt, Lindbergh let

Colonel Schwarzkopf have his say, then did exactly as his own judgment dictated. He believed that through cooperation with those who had stolen his boy, he ought to be able to negotiate for his safe return.

Sympathetic to Lindbergh's concern about impeding negotiations with the kidnappers, Schwarzkopf agreed not to interfere. The discussion of strategy over, Lindbergh and three state troopers tramped the woodlands about the property in search of additional clues. About the time they reached the main road, a figure emerged from the darkness near the entrance to the estate. Sam Blackman, twenty-seven, had arrived thirty-two minutes ahead of his competition. Having recently lost his job with *The Home News* in New Brunswick because of cutbacks, he was on his first assignment with the Associated Press.[2] Blackman introduced himself to Lindbergh, who replied that he had nothing to say.

The search continued until long past midnight. The efforts were futile—a mere chasing after the wind. A reporter overheard a conversation in a local restaurant about an area game trapper named Oscar Bush and urged him to put his skills to work. Arriving at 4 a.m., Bush observed two sets of footprints and followed them from the spot where the kidnappers had discarded the ladder through a field to an abandoned road that ran parallel to the Lindberghs' driveway. The getaway car had made marks in the bushes and the grass. Bush rejected the notion that anyone would have possessed the acrobatic ability to enter the nursery through the window.

Reporters who had arrived at the crime scene rushed back off to phone their bosses: "Gimme the desk!"[3] Newspaper editors across the country stopped the presses and remade page one to run the story under banner headlines. The *New York Times* announced:

LINDBERGH BABY KIDNAPPED FROM HOME OF PARENTS ON FARM
NEAR PRINCETON; TAKEN FROM HIS CRIB; WIDE SEARCH ON.

The newspaper reported that the case involved "the greatest police effort in the history of the city" and "the most intensive manhunt in the history of this continent."[4]

The *New York Evening Post* ran an editorial: "[The kidnappers] must know that if they [harm the baby] that they face the possibility of being torn limb from limb by the people of the U.S."[5] The crime made page one news in France, where the aviator remained a hero, and across the globe.

"The news of the tragedy struck the nation a blow unmatched in our history," recalled Hearst reporter Adela Rogers St. John. "Remember, little Lindy was everybody's other baby. Or if they had none, their only child. We were shot down from heights that up until then had been serene no matter what else went on below. . . . Kidnapped? The Lindbergh baby? Who would *dare*?"[6]

Will Rogers, who often remarked "I never met a man I didn't like," seemed to have second thoughts when he wrote in his syndicated column "Why don't lynching parties expand their scope and take in kidnappings?"[7]

Herbert Hoover sent a letter of sympathy to the Lindberghs. The morning after the kidnapping, he met with U.S. Attorney General William D. Mitchell to discuss how the federal government might assist the New Jersey authorities. The President also summoned J. Edgar Hoover to the White House. The thirty-seven-year-old chief of the Bureau of Investigation set up a special twenty-man Lindbergh squad in New York. Hoover sought the enormous publicity his organization would receive if his men could rescue the baby.

The Bureau chief was at home when a night dispatcher had called at 11 p.m. to alert him of the news. Hoover rushed to headquarters a little after one o'clock in the morning after a second call had informed him of the ransom demand. He met later in the day with Attorney General Mitchell, then directed the Los Angeles office of the Bureau of Investigation to assign a special agent to provide extra protection for the family of Herbert Hoover, Jr., in Pasadena.

New York Governor Franklin D. Roosevelt offered the full assistance of the state police system. Meanwhile, Congress hastened to enact legislation that would make transporting a kidnap victim across state lines a federal crime. Subsequently passed in June, the Federal Kidnapping Act became known as the Lindbergh Law.

Governor A. Harry Moore came to the Lindbergh estate the day after the baby's disappearance to announce that the State of New Jersey would pay a $25,000 reward—the equivalent of $375,000 today—for information leading to the arrest of those responsible. Lindbergh feared that such an aggressive stance might anger the kidnappers and demanded that the governor rescind the offer. Moore quickly complied.

Convinced that he needed the cooperation of the press, Lindbergh asked the police not to close off his property.[8] As a result, swarms of reporters, press photographers, and amateur detectives descended on the crime scene. Letters and telegrams poured in "by the thousands" and telephone calls became "so numerous as to virtually paralyze the telephone system."[9] The head of the New Jersey Motor Vehicle Commission, Harold G. Hoffman, made a public appeal over the airwaves not to drive by the home. On the national scene, the song "Who Stole the Lindbergh Baby?" hit a high note of tastelessness. Worse, gossipmongers started a rumor that the baby's parents had resorted to euthanasia because he was deaf and dumb.

Lindbergh referred all questions from the media to the State Police and requested that an auxiliary police station with a twenty-line switchboard be set up in his three-car garage, which became the command center for the investigation. Mattresses and makeshift beds for the forty men assigned to the case lined the floors of the dining room and other rooms. Anne assimilated some of the police lingo: "wheel," meaning a mental case—"see the pretty wheels go round"—and "butterfly," referring to a clue that leads nowhere.[10]

A partner at J. P. Morgan and Company informed Lindbergh that the Department of Labor was investigating the kidnapping and that he had received a call from Special Assistant Secretary Murray Garsson. The official had claimed the ability to solve the case within forty-eight hours. One night, Lindbergh, who was planning to be in conference with Breckinridge until dawn, telephoned his wife at 1 a.m. and told her that a team of investigators was en route to Highfields. Unbeknownst to Lindbergh and the men at the House of Morgan, Garsson was a shady operator with ties to mob kingpins—a man capable of immense fraud.

Anne, her houseguest Aida de Acosta Breckinridge, and Betty Morrow, who had moved in to give her daughter emotional support, all got dressed. At three o'clock in the morning, Garsson arrived accompanied by another labor official and hauled a large black bag into the foyer. Nearly shattered by the macabre sight, Anne feared that the bag contained her baby.

With his slicked back hair, big ears, and long, oval face, Garsson was repulsive both in manners and appearance. He insisted that the crime was an inside job and that an intruder in the nursery could be heard downstairs. To prove his point, he told Anne, three months pregnant with her second child, to run upstairs and walk about the room. She carried out the instructions, then asked Garsson whether he had been able to hear her. "Oh, I was busy talking, I forgot to listen," he said. "Run up and do it again."[11]

Betty Morrow put an end to this rubbish, but she could not stop Garsson from playing out the rest of his game. Garsson ordered the women to rouse the servants for an interview. Betty Gow recalled how Colonel Lindbergh had once hidden the baby in a closet as a practical joke. Lindbergh, Garsson told the group, had been rehearsing the kidnap of his own son. Then he demanded to be taken to the cellar. Down in the boiler room, he began staring at the furnace. As Anne looked on in horror, he poked around in the ashes for evidence of the baby's bones. The implication was that the Lindberghs had murdered their son. Garsson smiled in her face—then poked around some more.[12]

Anne's encounters with such "madness, cruelty, and indifference" went on and on.[13] One day, a well-dressed man claiming to possess "a secret he would tell no one else but Anne Morrow Lindbergh" showed up at Highfields.[14] The police escorted him upstairs to her room. As Anne sat up in bed to listen, the man stretched out his arms and delivered a few lines from a Hamlet soliloquy. In a letter to her mother-in-law, Anne wrote, "It is so terrifically unreal that I do not feel anything."[15]

# 8
# Underworld

With her husband focused on his mission of securing the baby's return, Anne kept her distance for the first couple of days following the abduction. "Calm, clear, alert, and observing," as she described him during the crisis,[1] he had no tolerance for displays of weakness or hopelessness. Anne came to believe that her self-control was absolutely necessary—and that she was "willing to barter *anything*" to maintain it.[2] She sought refuge by writing to her mother-in-law, a chemistry teacher in Michigan. Evangeline Lindbergh returned to her laboratory and Bunsen burners the day after the kidnapping. "I cannot see interviewers," she said to her principal. "I have no news for them but I do have classes to teach. Chem II must go on."[3]

Anne wandered about alone through the grounds and gazed up through the branches of the winter-stripped trees. "It is dreadful not to be able to do *anything* to help," she wrote. "I want *so* to help."[4] The thought occurred to her to write an appeal to the kidnappers and submit it to the media. She composed a note that would appear in the March third editions of newspapers all across the country.

Mrs. Anne Morrow Lindbergh asks that the baby's diet be adhered to, as follows:

A half cup of orange juice on waking.

One quart of milk during the day.

Three tablespoons of cooked cereal morning and night.

Two tablespoons of cooked vegetables once a day.

The yolk of one egg daily.

One baked potato or rice once a day.

Two tablespoons of stewed fruit daily.

A half cup of prune juice after the afternoon nap.

Fourteen drops of viosterol, a vitamin preparation, during the day.

Because Anne's idea seemed to provide the most effective means of communicating with the gang, the Lindberghs wrote a second letter and submitted it to Breckinridge for approval. The attorney modified the language to stress the couple's commitment to the kidnappers' safety.

Mrs. Lindbergh and I desire to make a personal contact with the kidnappers of our child.

Our only interest is in his immediate and safe return and we feel certain that the kidnappers will realize that this interest is strong enough to justify them in having complete confidence and trust in any promises that we may make in connection with his return.

We urge those who have the child to select any representatives of ours who will be suitable to them at any time and at any place that they may designate.

If this is accepted, we promise that we will keep whatever arrangements that may be made by their representative and ours strictly confidential and we further pledge ourselves that we will not try to injure in any way those connected with the return of the child.

Charles A. Lindbergh

Anne Lindbergh[5]

"In crowded theatres, restaurants, street cars, everywhere, people talked of only one thing—the Lindbergh baby," reported the *Detroit Free Press*. "Hysteria swept along, leaving a trail of rumor and conjecture, wild, impossible, even ludicrous, in its wake."[6]

The crime sent an electric shock of terror in homes throughout the country. Born five years after the kidnapping, author Barbara Goldsmith recalls that the crime "put fear into the hearts of a generation of children." If this could happen to the Lindbergh baby, "then who was safe"?[7]

"At night, after I'd been tucked into bed, I would lie awake waiting—knowing that this was the night the ladder would go thwack against my bedroom window and I'd be *taken away*," writes Goldsmith, who as a young girl had lived in Central Park West. Her family's apartment was on the eleventh floor.[8]

Three days after the abduction, the police arrested Betty Gow's boyfriend, Henry "Red" Johnson, at the home of his brother in West Hartford, Connecticut. Johnson's relationship with the baby's nursemaid had given him a clear knowledge of the Lindbergh estate. The family's butler, Olly Whateley, had toured him through the home and walked him about the grounds. Whateley had also given unauthorized tours to curiosity seekers who had shown up on the doorstep. "Quite often people came prowling around the Lindbergh house," he said.[9]

At 8:47 p.m. on the night of the kidnapping, Johnson had telephoned Betty from Englewood to express his disappointment that he would not see her that evening. The timing of his call raised suspicions that he had been delivering a coded message. When the authorities discovered an empty milk carton in his car, they concluded he was the kidnapper. Though Johnson's alibi for the night of the baby's disappearance exonerated him, he was taken to Ellis Island and deported. Johnson would never see Betty Gow again.

Letters from crackpots, amateur detectives, astrologers, occultists, scam artists and people sharing their dreams arrived by the sackful. The inventor of a window protection device wrote to Lindbergh seeking an endorsement. Particularly shocking and upsetting to Anne were demands for money.[10] "Three to four thousand letters come here a day," she wrote in a letter to her mother-in-law.[11] According to a Bureau of Investigation report, the crank letters were written by "insane persons, nitwits, persons with a degraded sense of humor, and others with a fraudulent intent."[12] Frustrating investigators, the letters undermined the case by obstructing the mail and compelling them to waste time on worthless clues.

Because kidnapping was not a federal offense at the time, the Bureau of Investigation had no jurisdiction in the case. Nonetheless, on the day of Johnson's arrest, J. Edgar Hoover came to Hopewell to offer his assistance to the Lindberghs. Knowing that Dwight Morrow had been one of Hoover's harshest critics, Lindbergh referred him to Colonel Schwarzkopf.

Because of the colliding ambitions between their two organizations, Schwarzkopf, who loomed over the five-foot-seven, bulldog-like Hoover, responded that the New Jersey State Police needed no outside help. Hoover viewed the brush-off as the beginnings of "the manifested hostility of the New Jersey State Police" toward the Bureau" and the result of the "jealous and narrow attitude" of the New Jersey police officials.[13] Over the course of the investigation Schwarzkopf would send one dismissive, overly polite letter after another to "My dear Director Hoover," spurning pleas to share information and files.[14] "When Lindbergh case is finished," Schwarzkopf wrote in one letter, "I will be very glad to give you copies of everything you wish." The animosity between the New Jersey State Police and the FBI would last for decades.[15]

On Saturday, March 5, a ransom letter postmarked in Brooklyn at nine o'clock the previous evening arrived at the Lindbergh estate. This was the first in a series of ransom notes that the kidnappers would mail from locations near subway stops along the Lexington Avenue line. Easily accessible from the Bronx, the line runs to the southern tip of Manhattan and tunnels underneath the East River. A member of the kidnapping gang likely got off at Borough Hall Station, the first stop in Brooklyn. Right across the street in a municipal building was the Post Office where the letter was postmarked. A familiarity with postmarking practices would have assured the kidnappers that the letter would be untraceable to the borough of their residence. In any case, the police made no connection between the letter's having been mailed across the street from Borough Hall Station and the possibility that whoever had deposited it into the mail might have ridden the subway to get there. Nor did they consider that the person might not own a car.

The kidnappers' *singnature*—the identifying symbol of three holes and two interlocking circles—distinguished the note from the many crank letters the Lindberghs had received. In the lower left-hand corner of page one are the words "*Singnature* on all letters"—along with an arrow pointing to the symbol. In the ransom note left in the nursery, the kidnappers had already made the point clearly: "Indication for all letters are *singnature* and three holes." Why the need, then, for emphasis and repetition? Written on two sides of the same sheet, the note read:

Dear Sir. We have warned you note to make anyding public also notify the Police now you have to take the consequence. It means we will hold the baby until everyding is quiet. We can note make any appointment just now. We know very well what it means to us. It is realy necessary to make a world affair out off this, or to get your baby back as soon as possible to settle those affair in a quick way will be better for both seids. Don't by afraid about the baby two ladys keeping care of us day and night. We also will feed him according to the diet

We are interested to send him back in gut health. Ouer ransom was made aus for 50000$ but now we have to take another person to it and probable have to keep the baby for a longer time as we expected So the amount will be 70000$ 20.000$ in 50$ bills 25.000 in 20$ bills 15000 in 10$ bills and 10.000 in 5$ bills. dont mark any bills or take them from one serial nomer. We will inform you latter were to deliver the mony. But we will note to so until the Police is out of this case and the pappers are quiet.
the kidnapping we preparet in years. so we are preparet for everyding.

Dr. Wilmer Souder, the leading handwriting expert of the Bureau of Standards in the 1930s, examined the ransom letters and concluded that the writer was German. "One thing puzzles me," he said. "[The writer's] choice of words and his phrasing indicate a superior mentality. His spelling and his penmanship do not."[16] Eighty years after the crime took place, internationally renowned forensic linguist Dr. Robert A. Leonard studied the text of the ransom notes. "It's possible that the notes were intentionally dumbed down and that whoever was writing them was laying it on thick," said Dr. Leonard. "Or perhaps the person might have been under a lot of stress."[17]

Engaged by Colonel Schwarzkopf, handwriting analyst Albert S. Osborn examined the ransom note alongside the first one discovered on the windowsill in the nursery. Osborn observed that the kidnappers had torn a sheet of paper in half and written the first ransom note on one half and the second on the other.[18] He also noted that both letters had been inserted into envelopes with the same "Fifth Avenue Linen" script watermark. "The watermark is the property of the F. W. Woolworth

Company 5¢ and 10¢ Stores and the paper is sold in their stores," Osborn wrote in his report.[19]

Postmarked on March 7, the third ransom note arrived at Colonel Breckinridge's law offices at 25 Broadway. There was no "l" in "Col." on the envelope. A member of Breckinridge's staff rushed the letter to the Lindbergh estate. Marked with the signature-symbol of interlocking circles and three holes, the letter read:

Dear Sir:

Did you receive ouer letter from March 4 we sent the mail on one off the letter—near Boro Hall Brooklyn. We know Police interfer with your privatmail how can we come to any arrangements this way. In the future we will send our letters to Mr. Breckinbridge at 25 Broadway. We believe Polise capturet two letter and let not forwarded to you We will not accept any go-between from your sent. We will arrangh theas latter. There is no worry about the Boy. he is very well and will be feed according to the diet. Best dank for information about it We are inter-ested to send your Boy back in gut health.

It is necessary to make a world-affair out off it, or to get your Boy back as soon as possible. Why did you ignore ouer letter which we left in the room. the baby would be back long ago. You would not get any result from Police becauce our kidnaping was pland for a year allredy. but we were afraid the boy would not be strong enough.

Ouer ransam was made out for 50.000$ but now we have to put another lady to it and propperly have to hold the baby longer as we expected so it will be 70000$. 20000 in 50$ bills 25000 in 25$ bills 15000 in 10$ bills and 10000 in 5$ bill. We warn you again not to mark any bills or take them from one serial No. We will inform you latter how to deliver the mony. but not befor the Police is out of this cace and the pappers are quite.

Please get a short notise about this letter in the New-York American.

In the lower left-hand corner of page one was an isolated word: "Singnature." The leader of the kidnapping gang—the creator of the "singnature"—seemed to be enjoying the negotiations by dictating to

Lindbergh how they would be handled. Just as with the omitted "l" in "Col." on the envelope addressed to Breckinridge, the letter also displays an overlooked detail of the crime: the author appears not to have bothered with proofreading. A 25$ bill? Just like the inability to foresee that Lindbergh might not open the first ransom note ordering him not to notify the police, this mistake is evidence of the mix of disorganized and organized aspects of the crime.[20]

This third ransom note bears a postmark from Station "D"—132 Fourth Avenue in Manhattan.[21] Clearly, the kidnappers were sending ransom notes from different locations to complicate the investigation. Another aspect of their modus operandi remained unchanged: they had mailed the letter from a location close to a subway stop, this one near the 14th Street (Union Square) stop off the Lexington Avenue line. The stop was about a block away from Station "D." The line also had stops at 8th Street and at 23rd Street.

Lindbergh's status as the most famous man in the world allowed him to dictate what he would and would not allow the police to do. Just as he had overseen every detail of the design of the *Spirit of St. Louis*, he wanted to maintain control of the investigation. Skeptical of Lindbergh's strategy, Colonel Schwarzkopf did not know what to expect after he had acceded to the young father's wishes.

Robert Helyer Thayer, age thirty, was a Harvard lawyer and a friend of the Lindberghs.[22] The managing partner of his law firm, Colonel William Joseph "Wild Bill" Donovan, was an arch-nemesis of J. Edgar Hoover and the future head of the country's first national spy agency, the Office of Strategic Services. A hero of the First World War and former prosecutor who had earned a fortune in corporate law, Donovan had a close friendship with Henry Breckinridge. On Wednesday, March 2, after he read about the kidnapping in the newspapers, Thayer contacted Morris "Mickey" Rosner, a Romanian-born bootlegger and confidence man. Thayer's idea was to determine if Rosner "could render any assistance to the family in recovering the child."[23] The son-in-law of a millionaire Republican congresswoman, Thayer was somewhat of a playboy. Rosner had toured him through underworld haunts and introduced him to notorious bootlegger Jack "Legs" Diamond.

Rosner warned that "the child was in serious danger of his life as the result of the tremendous pressure of international publicity unless immediate contact is established with the underworld pointing to direct negotiations for the payment of the ransom."[24] He claimed to possess the contacts who could determine who was responsible for the kidnapping and agreed to help. Within hours, he called Donovan's law offices in Manhattan with a lead on an underworld figure who had suddenly disappeared. Suspicious of the mobster's motives, Donovan relayed the information to Breckinridge but cautioned him to meet with Rosner before agreeing to any deals. Despite the kidnappers' statement that they would not accept any go-between chosen by the Lindberghs, Breckinridge insisted that the couple appoint an intermediary with ties to organized crime. He did not understand that the kidnappers were saying in their ransom notes that the game would be played their way, not Lindbergh's.

On the third of March, Breckinridge, Thayer, and Rosner drove to Hopewell for a 6:30 a.m. meeting with Lindbergh and Colonel Schwarzkopf.[25] Rosner offered the services of two of his associates to act as intermediaries. Schwarzkopf balked at accepting assistance from such worthless characters and bristled at the gangster's request for twenty-five hundred dollars; as Thayer noted, the reason Rosner gave for needing the money—at a time when gas was twenty cents a gallon—was "to defray expenses for traveling etc."[26] Lindbergh had already made up his mind, however, and bootlegger Salvatore "Salvy" Spitale and his right-hand man, Irving G. Bitz, came over to discuss strategy that evening.

The dapper and high-rolling Spitale, an Italian-born racketeer, was a regular in midtown speakeasies and Harlem nightclubs. He lived in an apartment overlooking Central Park, maintained a collection of rare books, and sent his children to private school. Years earlier, a jury had acquitted him of a homicide committed during a fur robbery. "Bitzy" had served a one-year sentence in the Atlanta Federal Penitentiary on a narcotics charge for Spitale. After Bitz got out, Spitale made him a partner in his drug smuggling operation. "As a man of my word," said Spitale, "my promise that I'll play ball with the kidnappers assures them of a square deal."[27] For the gambit to succeed, however, the kidnappers would have to have underworld connections. "If this is a professional job, I am absolutely confident I will be able to obtain the release of the Lindbergh child," Spitale went on. "If some amateur did it, I don't know if he will be willing to trust me or not."[28]

SEEK KIDNAPPER IN UNDERWORLD announced the March seventh edition of the *New York Daily News.* Below the headline was a letter that appeared on the front page of newspapers across the country.[29]

> If the kidnappers of our child are unwilling to deal direct we fully authorize "Salvy" Spitale and Irving Bitz to act as our go-between. We will also follow any other method suggested by the kidnappers that we can be sure will bring the return of our child.
>
> Charles A. Lindbergh
> Anne Lindbergh

Anne wrote in her diary that those brought in to help—"two of the biggest men of the underworld"—showed "more sincerity in their sympathy" than many of the politicians who had descended on the crime scene to pose for pictures with the kidnap ladder.[30] The underworld knew Spitale and Bitz as men "who [had] never double-crossed a friend."[31] They went right to work, ordering their henchmen to circulate through speakeasies and other hangouts of organized crime. The thugs looked for anyone who might have information about the kidnapping, but the search yielded not a single clue. "If it was someone I knew, I'll be damned if I wouldn't name him," said Spitale. "I been in touch all around, and I come to the conclusion that this one was pulled by an independent."[32]

A lawyer representing Owney Madden, the boss of the largest gang in New York, said that the most powerful mob leaders in the City were as outraged by the kidnapping as the rest of the population. Frustrated that policemen looking for the Lindbergh baby were stopping bootleggers on New Jersey's roadways and confiscating their inventories, the mob itself offered a $10,000 reward for information leading to the kidnappers' arrest.

Rosner reported to Robert Thayer, the attorney who had facilitated his introduction to Lindbergh, that the underworld was not responsible for the kidnapping. The mobster said that Madden knew the child's whereabouts and who had him. Having caught Rosner in "multiple mis-statements," however, Thayer had himself grown skeptical.[33]

Although Lindbergh applied the same focus and rigorous logic he had used to conquer the Atlantic to the mission of securing the return of his son, his efforts degenerated into micromanagement. Engineering design was easy for him to understand, human nature much less so. Anne confided to her diary that he looked "like a desperate man."[34] "And the security we felt we were living in!" he said.[35]

Lindbergh possessed an uncommon clarity of thought: many years later, as he drafted *The Spirit of St. Louis* in longhand, he often wrote paragraph after paragraph without a single cross-out or correction.[36] His ability to anticipate potential dangers in flight—and guard against them—had proved invaluable. He had viewed the move to the Sourland Mountains as a strategic decision that would enhance his family's safety, but he miscalculated. The leader of the kidnapping gang had recognized the vulnerability of an unguarded country estate. And now, it galled him to read newspaper accounts of mobsters making deals with the baby's father. As a later ransom note would ask, "How can Mr. Lindbergh follow so many false clues?"

# 9

## The Go-Between

In Chicago, Al Capone awaited a transfer from the Cook County Jail to the Atlanta Federal Penitentiary. The week after the kidnapping, Hearst columnist Arthur Brisbane visited him in his cell. Capone claimed that a former member of his gang had stolen the baby and issued a public statement: he would use his influence to rescue the child in return for his freedom and a full pardon. Brisbane relayed the offer to millions of readers.

Lindbergh called his friend Ogden L. Mills, President Hoover's newly appointed Secretary of the Treasury. After the St. Valentine's Day Massacre and a string of other violent crimes for which Capone was responsible had gone unpunished, the Treasury's investigative unit—the "T-men"—had succeeded in putting the country's most notorious criminal behind bars for income-tax evasion. Elmer Irey, the Chief of the Special Intelligence Section of the United States Treasury, was a fierce rival of J. Edgar Hoover, whom Capone had eluded. Mills ordered Irey to Hopewell to meet with Lindbergh, who had snubbed Hoover. Irey offered the full services of his unit and agreed that the situation called for a minimum of police interference. He assured Lindbergh, however, of the T-men's commitment to helping recover the baby.

As the search for the child continued, a hoax was getting underway in Norfolk, Virginia, where John Hughes Curtis, the president of a shipbuilding business, was facing financial collapse. Curtis approached the Very Reverend Harold Dobson-Peacock with a phony tale about a rumrunner who had hired him to repair his boat. As the story went, the gangster, who was holding the Lindbergh baby, had asked him to act as a go-between. Curtis knew that Dobson-Peacock had met the Morrows when he served as rector of the Episcopalian cathedral in Mexico City. The priest telephoned the Lindbergh residence but could not get past the man who fielded the call—Morris Rosner. The mobsters were answering the phone, bossing around servants, and tapping cigar ashes onto the carpets.

Another Norfolk resident was retired Admiral Guy Hamilton Burrage, the commander of the warship that had carried Lindbergh home from France. Curtis persuaded Burrage to call Lindbergh. When the admiral put Curtis on the line, however, the flier reacted with surprising indifference. An unlikely new player in the case had just appeared—Dr. John F. Condon.

*Dr. John F. Condon, better known as "Jafsie."*

The son of an Irish immigrant, Condon, seventy-one, had taught and served as a principal in city schools for forty-six years. Broad-shouldered, athletic, and six feet tall, arrogant and opinionated, he was an imposing presence. In all the Bronx it would have been difficult to find a man more eager to trade the twilight of his life for the spotlight. Over the years, the neighborhood paper that employed my father as a delivery boy, the *Bronx Home News*, had published letters and poems penned by the old man under such pseudonyms as P. A. Triot, L. O. Nestar, and J. U. Stice.

Condon belonged to the Bronx Old Timers Association, a social organization of men bound to one another by devotion to the borough and its traditions. Early members had met for dinners to reminisce about marching off to fight in the Union Army. The predominant colors of the club's emblem appealed to Condon's sense of patriotism: red standing for being red-blooded Americans, white symbolizing the protection of innocence and living a life of purity, and blue representing being true blue and forever remembering boyhood friendships.[1] My grandfather knew Condon as a fellow member of the Bronx Old Timers and referred to him as "an old coot."

Viewing the kidnapping of the Lindbergh baby as an attack on America, Condon was disturbed that "the greatest hero of this age"[2] had decided to seek the aid of gangsters. An editorial regarding "a baffled Uncle Sam futilely admitting that he could not solve the Lindbergh case"[3] irked Condon, who saw such acceptance of defeat as a disgrace. Despite his family's protests, he stayed up until three o'clock in the morning writing a letter to the *Bronx Home News*. The letter, penned in elegant script with homemade purple ink, read:

> I offer all I can scrape together so a loving mother may again have her child and Col. Lindbergh may know that the American people are grateful for the honor bestowed upon them by his pluck and daring. Let the kidnapers know that no testimony of mine, or information coming from me, will be used against them. I offer $1000 which I have saved from my salary as additional to the suggested $50,000 which is said to have been demanded of Col. Lindbergh. I stand ready at my own expense to go anywhere, alone, to give the kidnaper the extra money and promise never to utter his name to any person. If this is not agreeable, then I ask the kidnapers to go to any Catholic priest and return the child unharmed, with the knowledge that any priest must hold inviolate any statement which may be made by the kidnapers.[4]

On March 8, the *Bronx Home News* outlined the appeal in the front-page article "Dr. John F. Condon Offers to Add $1,000 of His Savings to Ransom Lindbergh Child."[5] The paper hit the newsstands at 3:45 p.m.[6] Condon sifted through his mail the following evening and found a long white envelope.

> Mr. Dr. John F. Condon
> 2974 Decatur Avenue
> New York

The peculiar form of the address—the use of multiple indentations—caught his eye. The kidnappers would use multiple indentations on the envelopes of every ransom note they would send through the mail. Only the word "Mr." was in cursive.

The first two ransom letters sent through the mail bore postmarks from Brooklyn and from Station "D"—132 Fourth Avenue in Manhattan. The one received by Condon was postmarked on March ninth at Station "T," located at 165th Street and Third Avenue in the South Bronx.[7] Station "T" was right in my father's neighborhood, only several blocks away from the apartment where John Knoll lived.

Condon examined the crude printed scrawl on the envelope and noted the typical German salutation "Mr. Dr." Tearing open the envelope was, he would later recall, the most "thrilling moment" of his life.[8] Inside were a sealed envelope addressed to Lindbergh and a letter that read:

Dear Sir: If you are willing to act as go-between in Lindbergh cace please follow stricly instruction. Handel incloced letter personaly to Mr. Lindbergh. It will explain everyding. don't tell anyone about it as soon we find out the Press or Police is notified everyding are cansell and it will be a further delay.

After you gett the mony from Mr. Lindbergh put these 3 words in the New-York American

mony is redy.

affter that we will give you further instruction. Don't be affrait we are not out fore your 1000$ keep it. Only act stricly. Be at house every night between 6-12 by this time you will hear from us

The phrase "act stricly," despite having no meaning in English, reflects the kidnappers' sense of urgency. The opportunity Condon presented was the one the leader of the kidnapping gang had been waiting for.[9] The letter had likely been mailed within hours after the *Bronx Home News* had published the squib describing Condon's offer.

The immature handwriting and odd-looking symbol made Condon suspicious that the letter might have been a prank. Because of his wife's anxiety about his potential involvement with mobsters, he decided against his first impulse to consult her about the note. Condon rode the trolley to a restaurant on the Grand Concourse where his friend Al Reich often stopped by at night. Not spotting Reich's car out front, Condon went inside and, after showing the letter to the proprietor, Max Rosenhain, excused himself to place a call to the Lindbergh residence —which, incredibly enough, anyone could still reach by telephone. Robert Thayer, the attorney who had introduced Lindbergh to gangster Morris Rosner, answered the phone and listened as Condon read the "*incloced* letter."

> Dear Sir:
> Mr Condon may act as go-between You may give him the 70000$. make one packet the size will be about—
>
> [drawing of a box with dimensions of seven by six by fourteen inches]
>
> We have notifyt you already in what kind of bills. We warn you not to set any trapp in any way. If you or someone els will notify the Police ther will be a further delay Affter we have the mony in hand we will tell you where to find your boy You may have a airplain redy it is about 150 mil awy. But befor telling you the adr. a delay of 8 houers will be between.

As Jim Fisher, author of two books the case, describes what happened next, as soon as Condon began to describe the intersecting circles that formed the kidnappers' signature-symbol, Thayer broke in and asked him to come to Hopewell at once. It was a few minutes past midnight. Rosenhain suggested that his friend Milton Gaglio had a car and asked to come along. The men set off for New Jersey and arrived at the Lindbergh estate at three o'clock in the morning.[10]

Condon followed Breckinridge upstairs and handed the letter to Lindbergh, who compared it with the previous ransom notes. The writing appeared a match, and the holes in the signature-symbol coincided. Lindbergh and Breckinridge agreed they were dealing with the bona fide kidnappers and decided right on the spot to appoint Condon go-between.

Because Breckinridge and Anne's mother occupied the two guest beds, Lindbergh hauled a handful of army blankets into the nursery and set up a "camp fashion" bed for Condon on the floor. With nowhere for them to stay, Rosenhain and Gaglio left. Condon asked to meet Mrs. Lindbergh before he retired. A "gleam of tears" in her eyes, Anne was sitting on the edge of her bed.

"If one of those tears drops," said Condon, "I shall go off the case immediately."

Anne wiped her eyes and smiled. "You see, Doctor, I am not crying."

"That is better. That is much, much better."[11]

The next morning, the breakfast table was laden with a platter of bacon and eggs, stacks of toast, a pitcher of orange juice, and a pot of coffee. Lindbergh left half his food on the plate and excused himself. Interested in the football team at Princeton, Breckinridge's alma mater, Condon carried on a lively conversation as he went on eating. A few minutes later, Lindbergh called the men upstairs and handed Condon a sheet of paper. The Lindberghs had signed the note, which read:

> March 10, 1932
>
> We hereby authorize Dr. John F. Condon to act as go-between for us.
>
> Charles A. Lindbergh
>
> Anne Lindbergh

Breckinridge planned to forward the "Money is ready" message to the *New York American* that afternoon, but he needed an alias for Condon to use that the kidnappers would recognize and that anyone else would find meaningless. It would be a disaster, he pointed out, if the newspapers figured out that Condon was in touch with the kidnappers. Condon came up with an idea: If his initials—JFC—were pronounced quickly, the result was "Jafsie." Lindbergh approved the suggestion, and Breckinridge edited the message to read:

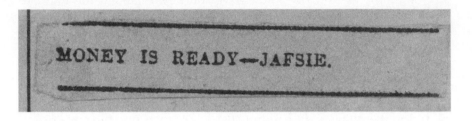

After Condon had spent an hour studying photographs of the baby, Breckinridge drove him back to the Bronx and asked to stay at Condon's home during the course of negotiations. Elated by the opportunity to latch onto one of Lindbergh's close associates, Condon extended an open invitation and bought a special ashtray for Breckinridge. Meanwhile, Anne, her anxieties temporarily assuaged by the new intermediary's involvement in the case, wrote to her mother-in-law, "Yesterday things began to move again and it was a great relief to everyone."[12]

# 10
## The Cemetery

To the dismay of Myra Condon, her home in the Bedford Park section of the Bronx had become command central for the operation. A little after noon on Friday, March 11, the family's telephone rang, just hours after the morning edition of the *New York American* went on sale. The "MONEY IS READY—JAFSIE." ad appeared in the classifieds. Myra answered the phone, and a man with a German accent asked to speak to "Dr. Condon." Her husband was not at home, she replied. Tell him to wait for another call about seven o'clock, the caller said. Then he hung up.[1] Because Lindbergh had refused to allow the police to tap the line, the call could not be traced.

Colonel Breckinridge arrived in the Bronx a little after 6 p.m. Myra Hacker, Condon's daughter, and his friend Al Reich also dropped by. The group congregated in the living room and sat waiting.

The Tiffany clock on the mantle began to chime seven times. "Something's wrong," said Breckinridge, looking up at the clock. "Why doesn't he call?" At this point he began pacing about the room. It was a few minutes past seven when the telephone in the hallway finally rang. Condon sprang from his chair and picked up the receiver.

A guttural voice came on the line. "Is this Dr. John F. Condon?"

"Yes. Who is calling?"

"Did you *gotted* the letter with the *singnature*?"

"Of course. How else would I have known about the message to put in the *American*?"

"I saw your ad."

"Where are you calling from?"

"Westchester." Then, after a pause: "Doctor Condon, do you write sometimes pieces for the papers?"

"Yes, I sometimes write articles for the papers."

It was then that Condon heard the caller speak to someone else: "He say sometimes he writes pieces for the papers."

*The man has an accomplice*, Condon thought. His opinion would never change.

The voice instructed Condon to stay at home every evening that week between six o'clock and midnight; he would receive another note, and the gang would contact him again very soon. He heard a sharp click and the line went dead.

"We are to receive further word soon," Condon said to the group. "Probably tomorrow night." He then sat down and described the conversation. The man on the phone had sounded German, he noted.

Breckinridge lit a cigarette. "His opening statement to you, then, Doctor, was: 'Did you get my letter with the signature?'"

"Yes, except that he said it this way: 'Did you *gotted* the letter with the *sing-nature?*'"

Breckinridge was exultant. "Doctor, that man was the kidnapper as sure as you're born."[2]

The following night of Saturday, March 12, Bronx taxi driver Joseph Perrone was looking for customers. At 8:15 p.m., a man wearing a heavy brown, double-breasted overcoat and a brown fedora flagged him down at the corner of Knox Place and Gun Hill Road. The man handed him a dollar and instructed him to deliver an envelope to Condon's home, a mile and a half away. Perrone described the man who had hired him to Condon and left. The letter, which bore the kidnappers' signature-symbol, read:

Mr Condon

We trust you but we will note come in your Haus it is to danger. even you can not know if Police or secret servise is watching you follow this instruction. take a car and drive to the last supway station from Jerome Ave here 100 feet from the last station on the left seide is a empty frank-further stand with a big open Porch around, you will find a notise in senter of the porch underneath a stone this notise will tell you were to find us.

Act accordingly.

After ¾ of a houer be on the place. bring the mony with you

Forensic linguist Dr. Robert A. Leonard observes that the word "subway" appears prominently on signs at every stop in the boroughs of New York. It's hard to believe, therefore, that the writer of the ransom letters would not have known how to spell the word.[3] It's possible that the spelling of *supway* is a case of the dumbing down of the ransom letters— as well as an instance of game-playing on the part of the author.

My father was familiar with the Jerome Avenue line, the Woodlawn Station subway stop, and the abandoned hot dog stand. He and his family often passed the shack on the way to St. Mark's Lutheran Church in Yonkers, and his Sunday school class held May Day celebrations at the park right down the street. He recalled the layout of the area vividly as he began researching the case, and he was fairly certain that the subway would have been quite empty at this late hour, particularly on such a bitter-cold, windy night. Woodlawn Station, an elevated stop and the last on the Jerome Avenue line, was a stone's throw from the vacant frankfurter stand.

The leader of the kidnapping gang had likely reconnoitered the area surrounding Woodlawn Cemetery to find a place to hide the *notise* where it would not blow away. Because earlier ransom notes had been mailed near subway stops along the Lexington Avenue line and because the hot dog stand was less than a hundred feet away from Woodlawn Station, it's probable that he rode the subway there. If this was the case, he would have noticed the little wooden structure after he got off the el and reached the street level.

Breckinridge, understanding that the gang expected the money that night, fretted that he had not assembled the bills. Yet Condon convinced him of the importance of meeting with the kidnappers. Al Reich offered to act as chauffeur. Condon put on an overcoat and went out of the front door with his friend. Breckinridge shook their hands and wished them luck.

Traffic was light on Jerome Avenue as Reich wheeled his Ford coupe to a stop in front of the frankfurter stand. Condon found an envelope beneath a rock on the porch. Back in the car, he opened the letter and read aloud:

cross the street and follow
the fence from the cemetery.
direction to 233rd Street
I will meet you.

On the west side of Jerome Avenue lay one section of Van Cortlandt Park. Across the street was Woodlawn Cemetery, enclosed by a seven-foot iron fence with ornate spires. A product of the Romantic Era, Woodlawn with its four hundred acres of rolling hills and lakes had been laid out as a rural cemetery during the Civil War.[4]

Reich drove for another half-mile and parked near the entrance to the cemetery at the southeast corner of Jerome Avenue and 233rd Street. A rush of adrenaline surged through him as he scanned the deserted streets. A six-foot-three former heavyweight boxer, he had once knocked Jack Dempsey out of the ring in the Polo Grounds. Reich imagined himself felling the kidnapper with a flurry of jabs and punches. "When they shoot you tonight, they won't have to carry you far to bury you," Reich said to his friend.[5]

The cold wind penetrated Condon's overcoat as he stood near the entrance gate and looked around. It was a few minutes later when a man holding a handkerchief to his face walked by on the sidewalk. From the car Reich watched them. The man was a lookout, his brain registered automatically—someone assigned to watch for police and signal an accomplice after he had spotted Condon. Then a second man who had hidden himself inside the locked cemetery waved a handkerchief between the iron bars of the gate.

"Did you *gotted* my note?" the man called out in a German accent. He held the lapels of his coat well up over his face. The coat was lightweight and black. The man who had hired the cab driver to deliver the envelope, however, had worn a heavy brown overcoat and a fedora with the brim pulled down over his eyes.

"Yes, I received it," Condon said.

"Have you *gotted* the money?"

"No, I can't bring the money until I see the package."

"No. The gang would not stand for it."

"Well, then, I will go and get the money if you will take me to the child as a hostage."

Suddenly, from one of the tree-lined paths that twisted among the headstones came a crunching sound of dead leaves being trampled. A uniformed security guard making his rounds appeared about twenty-five feet away. With what Condon would describe as "the agility of an athlete," the man seized the top of the iron fence, clambered up on it, swung his legs over, and landed next to him on the sidewalk like a cat. In the light of a streetlamp, Condon observed that his face "looked like an inverted, doughy triangle, its point lopped off."[6]

"It is too dangerous," the man said and sprinted north across 233rd Street.

"Don't run away!" shouted Condon. "Do you want to run away and leave me here to get drilled?"

At this point he chased after the man, who had dashed into the huge, wooded expanse of Van Cortlandt Park. Condon spotted the man standing in a clump of trees. "You should be ashamed of yourself," he said. "Here you are, my guest. No one will hurt you." Condon cajoled the man out of hiding and guided him to a park bench next to a tool shed. The bench was far out of sight from 233rd Street. Condon invited the man to sit down at his right.

"Tell me how I am to know that I am talking to the right person," Condon said.

"You *gottit* my letter with the *singnature*."[7]

Recognizing the potential value of the information, Condon had come to the meeting prepared to make close observations of the kidnapper's features. The descriptions Condon would give the police of his "guest" varied somewhat, but not by much: a "middle weight" between 158 and 165 pounds and between five-foot-eight and five-foot-ten. "Dr. Condon, during that dramatic interview, felt the arm muscles of the kidnapper, in order to be able, when the time came, to guess accurately at his weight," the *New York Times* would report.[8] The educator commented on the light fabric of his coat.

Condon would describe the man as having a stocky build, a light complexion, a prominent forehead, large ears, a pointed chin, and an "unusually large muscular or fleshy development"[9] at the base of his left thumb. Because Condon had put him at his right on the park bench, the man's left hand was in plain sight. There was a street intersection lamp close enough to provide enough light for Condon to see the man's features distinctly.

"Do you know Colonel Lindbergh personally?" the man asked.

"Yes," said Condon. After a brief pause, he asked, "What is your name?"

"John."[10]

John identified himself as an intermediary who worked for "Number One." Four men and two "womens"—both nurses—were involved in the kidnapping plot. The baby was in the nurses' care on a boat six hours away. The $70,000 ransom would result in a $20,000 payoff for "Number One" and $10,000 for each of the other five.[11] A nice even split.

Because of the delays caused by Lindbergh's decision to contact the police, John said, the gang had decided to increase the ransom to $70,000. In other words, Lindbergh had no one else but himself to blame that the ransom had been raised. In response to Condon's offer reported in the *Bronx Home News* to add a thousand dollars of his own money to the ransom amount, the kidnappers had replied: "We are not out fore your 1000$ keep it."

What clues about the mindset of the leader of the kidnapping were they communicating here? Would the profilers in today's FBI's Behavioral Science Unit conclude that he was concerned that a hard-working teacher might be giving up his life savings? No—the mastermind cared about no one but himself. In essence, he was saying that this isn't about you and me, Dr. Condon. It's about Lindbergh and me.[12]

Condon admonished John for not abiding by the original bargain of $50,000. But no one would ever question that the numbers in the supposed split wouldn't have been in easily divisible multiples of $10,000 had the amount remained fixed at $50,000—and that his story about a six-person gang didn't add up.[13]

"What if the baby is dead?" asked John at a lull in the conversation. "Would I burn if the baby is dead?"

"What is the use of this?" asked Condon. ". . . Why should we be here, carrying on negotiations, if the baby is dead?"

"The baby is not dead," said John. "The baby is better as it was… The baby is all right."[14]

Condon wanted to know whether or not Betty Gow's boyfriend had any connection to the kidnapping. "John, what about Henry Johnson?"

"Red Johnson?"

"Yes."

It was then that John raised his voice and showed strong emotion for the first time: "Red Johnson is innocent! Betty Gow she is innocent too!"[15]

Because any false leads could only divert police attention from the real kidnappers, it was an odd comment for a hunted man to make. Perhaps, as John Douglas surmises, Cemetery John resented the untrue stories reported in the newspapers that were diminishing his own role in the biggest news story of the day. In effect, Cemetery John was saying, "Hey! *I'm* the guy!"[16]

Douglas notes that the media often plays a major role in such highly publicized cases. "The UNSUB," he says, "always reacts to the press coverage."[17]

Condon probed for John's nationality. "I am Scandinavian," he replied. Then the go-between demanded assurance that John was in direct contact with those holding the child. "You *gottit* my letter with the *singnature*," said John. "It is the same like the letter with the *singnature* which was left in the baby's crib."[18]

*In the crib?* Condon knew that Lindbergh had found the original ransom letter on the windowsill. Whoever had left it there was not the same person now sitting beside him. Condon was now certain that the kidnapping had not been a one-man job. Then, for a second time, he offered to give himself up as a hostage: "I shall stay with the baby until the money is in your hands."

"No," said John. "They would *schmack* me out."

"Leave them. Don't you see? Sooner or later, you will be caught."

"Oh, no. We have planned this case for a year already."

"But you must take me to the baby, let me see him."

John shook his head. "I will give you the evidence."

"How?"

"I will send the sleeping suit from the baby."

John explained that he had to prove to his boss he had performed his job and asked Condon to insert another ad in the *Bronx Home News*:

BABY IS ALIVE AND WELL. MONEY IS READY.

In the meantime, he would send the sleeping suit. As their conversation on the park bench trickled to a stop after an hour and fifteen minutes, the two men shook hands. John slipped away and disappeared deep into the woods of the park. Condon returned to the car. The man who had walked along the sidewalk holding a handkerchief to his face, Reich told him, was surely an envoy of the kidnappers. He started the engine and drove off.

Condon turned the conversation on the drive back to his house to the man calling himself John. "You'll never know how close I came to following after you tonight. I wanted to hit that fellow. I'd give a lot to hit him—just once!" said Reich. "You'll *never* see the baby. I don't think that that – – – intends to give you the baby. I don't think he *can* give you the baby. I think the baby is dead."[19]

# 11
## The Little Package

Arriving home from Woodlawn Cemetery at 11:45 p.m., Condon briefed Breckinridge on the meeting. One particular comment John had made—that the crime had been "planned for a year"—convinced Breckinridge that John was a member of the gang that had stolen the baby. The go-between did not know that the kidnappers had made the same claim in a ransom note.

Condon received no reply from his ad in the Sunday, March thirteenth edition of the *Bronx Home News:*

BABY ALIVE AND WELL. MONEY IS READY. CALL AND SEE US. JAFSIE.

He submitted another:

MONEY IS READY. NO COPS. NO SECRET SERVICE. NO PRESS. I COME ALONE LIKE THE LAST TIME. PLEASE CALL. JAFSIE.

It ran for two days. Still eliciting no response, he prodded the kidnappers again:

I ACCEPT. MONEY IS READY. YOU KNOW THEY WON'T LET ME DELIVER WITHOUT GETTING THE PACKAGE. PLEASE MAKE IT SOME SORT OF C.O.D. TRANSACTION . . . YOU KNOW YOU CAN TRUST JAFSIE.

On Wednesday, March 16, Condon's mailman delivered a package wrapped in brown paper—the kind used by butcher shop and delicatessen employees to wrap meat. The package had been dropped into a mailbox rather than taken to a Post Office window. On the package was a canceled 10-cent stamp bearing an image of President Monroe.

To serious students of the case, the stamp is one of the more baffling aspects of the Lindbergh kidnapping. Investigators at the time, however, attached little importance to it, never considering why the kidnappers would use—or even have—a 10-cent stamp. The attention of the State of New Jersey did turn briefly to the stamps on the ransom envelopes during the trial of Bruno Hauptmann when a curious feature was noted. As syndicated radio program host Walter Winchell would explain to his listeners:

> To the *Daily Mirror* and all Hearst newspapers the other day I wired a new clue that the State has. It is a certain type of penny postage stamps, which the post office department recalled in early 1932. They intended to testify—that the ransom notes contained these stamps— and that only two in the vicinity of Hauptmann's home were late in returning those stamps to Washington. I am now informed, however, that the State will not risk using that as evidence—as it did to temporarily keep the kidnap ladder out of the record.[1]

Even without any defects that might have interested stamp collectors, ten cents' worth of postage in 1932 was enough to mail a package weighing up to four pounds, far in excess of the weight of the sleeping suit.[2] Because the Post Office charged only two cents to mail a letter in those days, stamps of five times that value were uncommon in day-to-day use. In itself, of course, the presence of a 10-cent stamp on the package does not prove that a stamp collector sent it. But along with the kidnappers' knowledge of postmarking practices and the resemblance of the signature-symbol to a cachet, it is one more piece of evidence pointing in that direction.

Inside the package was a folded, spotlessly clean gray woolen sleeping suit. Back at Highfields, an army of reporters was following Lindbergh's every move. Disguised in amber glasses and wearing a cap pulled down low over his forehead, he left around 11 p.m. and made it to the Bronx by one o'clock in the morning. Breckinridge was waiting for him with Condon when he arrived.

Lindbergh spread out the sleeping suit on top of the grand piano and approached his examination as if it were a preflight inspection. He felt the material. He noted the pocket. He counted the buttons. He held up the sleeping suit and looked at the flap. He studied the sleeves. He observed the manufacturer's trademark in the neckband.

The sleeping suit, Lindbergh told the others, was precisely like his son's. But why, he wondered aloud, had the kidnappers taken the trouble to have it cleaned? Also inside the package was a note, which read:

Dear Sir: ouer man faill to collect the mony. There are no more confidential conference after the meeting from March 12. those arrangements to hazardous for us.

We will note allow ouer man to confer in a way like befor. Circumstance will note allow us to make a transfare like you wish. it is impossibly for us Wy should we move the baby and face danger to take another person to the place is entirely out of question. It seems you are afraid if we are the right party and if the boy is allright. Well you have ouer singnature. It is always the same as the first one specialy them 3 holes
[design drawn in here]
Now we will send you the sleepingsuit from the baby besides it means 3$ extra exspenses becauce we have to pay another one. Pleace tell Mrs. Lindbergh note to worry the baby is well. we only have to give him more food as the diet says

You are willing to pay the 70000 note 50000$ without seeing the baby first or note. let us know about that in the New York-American. We can't do it other ways becauce we don't like to give up ouer safty plase or to move the baby If you are willing to accept this deal put these in the paper.

I accept mony is redy

ouer program is:

after 8 houers we have the mony received we will notify you where to find the baby. If there is any trap, you will be responsible what will follows.

"Don't you think, Colonel, that one of us should see and identify the baby before any money is paid over?" Condon asked.

"Yes, of course, if it can possibly be arranged that way," said Lindbergh. "But we must not let negotiations go on too long. If he despairs of getting the money, if word leaks out to the newspapers, if any one of a dozen things happens, it might endanger my son's life. This man, after all, is in a position to dictate his own terms."[3]

An ad appeared in the *New York American*:

I ACCEPT. MONEY IS READY. JOHN, YOUR PACKAGE IS DELIVERED AND IS O.K. DIRECT ME. JAFSIE.

This time, the money *was* ready. On Thursday, March 17, armed guards hired by J. P. Morgan and Company delivered fifty thousand dollars to the Fordham branch of the Corn Exchange Bank. Lindbergh informed Breckinridge that he would obtain the balance of the ransom money demanded by the kidnappers.

On Monday, March 21, a letter bearing the familiar symbol of interlocking circles and three holes arrived in Condon's mail. The letter was postmarked in Manhattan at Station "N" (203 E. 69th Street), which was near another subway stop off the Lexington Avenue line. The note read:

Dear Sir: You and Mr. Lindbergh know ouer Program. If you don't accept den we will wait untill you agree with ouer deal. we know you have to come to us any way But why should Mrs. and Mr. Lindbergh suffer longer as necessary We will note communicate with you or Mr. Lindbergh until you write so in the paper.

We will tell you again; this kidnapping cace whas prepared for a year already so the Police won't have any luck to find us or the child You only puch everyding farther out did you sent that little package to Mr. Lindbergh? it contains the sleepingsuit from the baby

the baby is well.

On the reverse side was a final comment: "Mr. Linbergh only wasting time with his search." Upon receipt of the letter, Lindbergh, Breckinridge, and Condon composed another ad and ran it the following day in the *Bronx Home News* and in the *New York American*:

THANKS. THAT LITTLE PACKAGE YOU SENT ME WAS IMMEDI-
ATELY DELIVERED AND ACCEPTED AS REAL ARTICLE. SEE MY
POSITION. OVER FIFTY YEARS IN BUSINESS AND CAN I PAY WITH-
OUT SEEING THE GOODS? COMMON SENSE MAKES ME TRUST
YOU. PLEASE UNDERSTAND MY POSITION. JAFSIE.

On Tuesday, March 29, Condon received another letter postmarked
at Station "N" in Manhattan:

Dear Sir: It is note necessary to furnish any code. you and Mr.
Lindbergh know ouer Program very well. We will keep the child in
ouer save plase until we have the money in hand, but if the deal is
note closed until the 8 of April we will ask for 30000 more. also note
70000 – 100000.
how can Mr. Lindbergh follow so many false clues he knows we are the
right party ouer singnature is still the same as in the ransom note. But
if Mr. Lindbergh likes to fool around for another month we can help it.
Once he has to come to us anyway but if he keeps on waiting we will
double ouer amount there is absolute no fear aboud the child
it is well.

The "false clues" refer to the hoax of Norfolk shipbuilder John
Hughes Curtis. The story of his efforts to rescue the baby was making
headlines, and no one other than Curtis and the kidnappers themselves
knew for certain it was nonsense. Though Lindbergh believed that Condon was dealing with the right people, he decided to explore every lead
he thought serious. On Friday, April 1, another ransom letter
instructed him to have the money ready by Saturday evening. The kidnappers warned again not to set a *"trapp."* A subsequent communica-
tion would instruct him where and how to deliver it.

Elmer Irey, head of the Treasury Department's investigative unit,
met with Lindbergh and spelled out his concerns about the package of
ransom money. The package, he pointed out, had contained no gold certificates, which would soon become illegal to possess and thus far easier
to spot and trace. Each bill should be listed and a record kept of its

serial number. Lindbergh, believing that such an action would violate his sense of fair play, rejected the idea.

"Colonel Lindbergh," said Irey, "unless you comply with our suggestion to record the serial numbers, we shall have to withdraw from the case. We cannot compound a felony."[4]

Lindbergh did not reply; in an uncharacteristic moment of acquiescence, however, he acceded to the ultimatum the following day. A team of clerks at J. P. Morgan and Company created two new packages of bills according to the T-man's specifications. The 5,150 bills were bound with identifiable paper and string, and no two serial numbers were in sequence. The first package of $50,000 contained $35,000 in gold certificates, and 400 fifty-dollar gold notes comprised the second.

On Friday, the first of April, Betty Gow and Elsie Whateley took a walk down the Lindberghs' gravel driveway, which was six-tenths of a mile long. As they neared Wertsville Road, Betty picked up a shiny metal object—one of the thumb guards she had put on the baby the night he disappeared. Both women had seen the thumb guard at the same time.[5] It was like new and lay in the middle of the driveway. Teams of investigators had combed the grounds for clues in the weeks since the crime; reporters and others had tramped up and down the driveway many times over. As historian Lloyd Gardner notes, a photographer with the *Philadelphia Inquirer* would comment that he "had walked over that entire area the morning after the crime, taking pictures and looking for 'clues' and saw nothing in the road where the thumb guard was found."[6] What were the odds that the thumb guard, in mint condition and with a long string attached to it, would lie in the driveway unnoticed for a month? More likely, observes John Douglas, it was left there sometime afterward as evidence that the kidnappers were in possession of the baby. If anything had gone wrong with the collection of the ransom money, the kidnappers would have included a reference in their next communiqué to the thumb guard lying in the driveway just inside the Lindberghs' property line.[7]

# 12

# Payment

O n Saturday, April 2, Condon tried to cram the 5,150 bills into the custom-made box. The box, however, split on one side. With the ransom money ready, Lindbergh, Breckinridge, and Condon's friend Al Reich sat down with the go-between and his family to wait. The Condons' doorbell rang a little before 8 p.m. A taxi driver handed an envelope to Condon's daughter and left. No one thought to ask who had sent him. Lindbergh opened the letter, which read:

> Dear Sir: take a car and follow tremont Ave to the east until you reach the number 3225 east tremont Ave.
>
> It is a nursery.
>
> Bergen
>
> Greenhauses florist
>
> there is a table standing outside right on the door, you find a letter undernead the table covert with a stone, read and follow intstruction.
>
> don't speak to anyone on the way. If there is a ratio alarm for policecar, we warn you. we have the same equipment. have the money in one bundle.
>
> We give you ¾ of a houer to reach the place.

Al Reich persuaded Lindbergh to take his Ford coupe rather than his own automobile. Breckinridge agreed with the suggestion: John and his lookout had seen Reich's car at Woodlawn Cemetery.

Armed with a handgun, Lindbergh drove to the East Bronx with Condon. Surrounded by residences and other stores, the flower shop was a one-story building with a stone façade and a table beneath an awning with thick stripes. The shop, catty-corner to St. Raymond's Cemetery, was closed. Condon found an envelope covered by a stone beneath the table and returned to the car. Lindbergh switched on his flashlight and read the note inside.

> cross the street and
> walk to the next corner
> and follow Whittemore Ave
> to the soud
> take the money with
> you. Come alone
> and walk
> I will meet you.

Condon convinced Lindbergh to stay in the automobile. Ignoring the note's instructions to take the money with him, Condon started off toward Whittemore Avenue, a dirt road that bordered the cemetery and sloped down a hill. Lindbergh's eyes followed a man walking along a sidewalk across the street. The man's hat was pulled down over his eyes, and the lower part of his face was covered with a handkerchief. From his nervous movements Lindbergh concluded that the man was a lookout.

Further disregarding the instructions, Condon crossed Whittemore Avenue and continued east on Tremont Avenue. After a hundred yards, he reached the cemetery gate and paused. He turned around and walked back toward the car. "I guess there's no one here!" he shouted. "We'd better go back!"

Just then, a loud German voice boomed from within the cemetery: "Hey, Doctor!" A dim figure emerged from behind a monument and loomed in the darkness. The man waved his arms. Then: "Hey, Doctor, over here!"

Lindbergh heard the shout from the car. Condon watched a silhouette dart among the headstones and angle toward Whittemore Avenue. The old man walked down the unlighted dirt road and continued to a narrow connecting road on his left that entered the cemetery. A five-foot wall formed its northern boundary. The man mounted the wall, jumped down, crossed the road, and hopped over a low fence. He stopped and stooped low behind a thick hedge that was four feet high.

"Have you *gottit* the money?"

Condon recognized him as the man he had met twenty-one days earlier. It was Cemetery John. "No," said Condon. "It is up in the car."

"Who is up there?"

"Colonel Lindbergh."

"Is he armed?"

"No. No, he is not. Where is the baby?"

"You could not get the baby for about six, eight hours."

Condon requested directions to the location of the child. Once again, however, John demanded the money.

"Listen, these are times of Depression," said Condon. "It is difficult today for any man to raise seventy thousand dollars. Colonel Lindbergh is not so rich. He has had a hard time raising fifty thousand and that is what you bargained with him for. Why don't you be decent to him? He can't raise the extra money, but I can go up to the auto right now and get the fifty thousand."

"Since it is so hard it will be all right, I guess. I suppose if we can't get seventy, we take fifty."

"That will be paid. But tell me, where is the note?"

"In ten minutes I come back again and give you the note."

Condon retraced his steps up the slope of the dirt road. As he neared the car, a pang of suspicion shot through him. During the conversation on the park bench, John had expressed fear that "Number One" might *schmack* him up, but now it seemed clear that John was the man in charge. How else could he have quickly agreed to reduce the ransom payment to fifty thousand dollars when "Number One" had wanted twenty thousand more?

Lindbergh, following Condon's instructions, withdrew the package of fifty-dollar bills and handed him the box of money. Moments after Condon started back down Whittemore Avenue, Lindbergh saw the suspicious-looking man with the handkerchief again. The man paused near the cemetery fence, searched all around, and suddenly backtracked.

Lindbergh heard him blow his nose loudly. With that, the man dropped his handkerchief and ran off.

John reappeared behind the hedge thirteen minutes after Condon had left to retrieve the ransom money. It was 9:29 p.m. Condon rested the box on his left forearm and reached out with his right hand to receive the note of directions. As John grabbed the box, Condon grasped the piece of paper John had pulled out of his coat pocket. John placed the box at his feet and knelt down to inspect it. "Wait until I see if it is all right, if these bills are marked."

"It is all right, as far as I know," said Condon. "I am only an intermediary. There is fifty thousand dollars in fives, tens, and twenties as you instructed in your note."

"I guess it is all right. Don't open that note for six hours."

"I will not open it. You can trust me."

"Thank you, Doctor. We trust you. Everybody says your work has been perfect."

The two men shook hands across the hedge.

"If you double-cross me—," began Condon.

"The baby is all right," broke in John quickly. "You find him on the *Boad Nelly* like the note says. Good-bye, Doctor."[1] John zigzagged among the tombstones and was instantly lost in darkness, never to be seen again.

Back in the car, Lindbergh hesitated to ignore John's order to wait before opening the note. Condon shook his head: although John had warned *him* not to open it for six hours, someone else could do so right away. Lindbergh pulled over under a streetlamp near Westchester Square, about a mile from the cemetery, and read the note.

> The boy is on Boad Nelly
> It is a small boad 28 feet
> long two persons are on the Boad. the are innosent.
> you will find the Boad between
> Horseneck Beach and gay Head
>                 near Elizabeth Island.[2]

It was almost midnight when the two men returned to Condon's home, where Breckinridge and Reich had been waiting. After a few minutes, Lindbergh and Breckinridge announced that they were going into the City for a meeting and invited Condon and Reich to join them.

The men drove to Betty Morrow's townhouse on East 72nd Street, where Elmer Irey and two other investigators from the Special Intelligence Unit, Frank J. Wilson and Arthur P. Madden, were sitting in the library. Considered "a genius for detail" by Irey,[3] Wilson had helped design the strategy to capture Al Capone. As the T-men listened in disbelief, Condon regaled the group with his story of having saved Lindbergh twenty thousand dollars by outsmarting John. Disgusted, Irey explained that the second package of money had contained nothing but fifty-dollar gold certificates—bills that would have drawn maximum attention when the kidnappers tried to pass them. Condon, trying to wash his hands of the matter, explained that he didn't know anything about the bills. His meddling, however, had ruined the T-men's plan.

It was three o'clock in the morning when Lindbergh and Breckinridge set off with Irey, Condon, and Reich for Bridgeport, Connecticut. They reached the airport there two hours later and waited another hour for daylight and the arrival of a chartered two-engine Sikorsky amphibian. Soon after the plane touched down in the water, Lindbergh, Breckinridge, and Irey in flying togs boarded the aircraft with Condon. Breckinridge sat beside the pilot, Irey and Condon in the rear of the cabin with a bottle of milk and a set of the baby's clothes. After the plane took off, Reich drove Lindbergh's car to the Aviation Country Club in Hicksville, Long Island, where the group planned to return with the baby.

When the Sikorsky had gained altitude, Lindbergh allowed Breckinridge to take over the controls. Whenever Breckinridge attempted to turn in one direction, however, Lindbergh would cross the controls by pressing the opposite rudder pedal, causing the plane to veer left when the pilot wanted to go right, and vice versa. "It was quite a scene," Irey would recall, "Lindbergh playing practical jokes, Breckinridge wondering if he was crazy, and Jafsie yowling excerpts from Song of Solomon."[4]

The morning sky was bright and clear as the amphibian flew over a triangular section of Vineyard Sound near Martha's Vineyard. Lindbergh's honeymoon cruise had familiarized him with the waters. Coast Guard cutters from nearby Cuttyhunk Island arrived at Irey's request, and word spread that the pilot of the Sikorsky was looking for the Lindbergh baby.

Reporters rushed to the scene as the plane crisscrossed low over the sea and buzzed the coastline in search of the *Nelly*. Lindbergh dove at every boat he saw and swept alongside to read the name. He landed in Buzzards Bay at noon and taxied to Cuttyhunk Island, where a horde of journalists had gathered on the dock. Lindbergh brushed them off.

"There is no news," Breckinridge said.

The men stopped for a hasty lunch at a hotel. Lindbergh hardly touched his food, but Condon gobbled his with a hearty appetite. After the break, it was straight back into the airplane. The hunt continued throughout the afternoon, but the search team saw no boat even vaguely resembling the *Nelly*. Condon tried to defuse the tension in the cabin with a few words of inspiration.

In his memoirs, Irey would write, "Nobody could speak because Jafsie was roaring in rolling accents:

> To be or not to be: that is the question:
> Whether 'tis nobler in the mind, etc., etc.

When he wasn't reciting from *Hamlet*, he was reeling off Biblical quotations by the hour. That was Jafsie, the only man the kidnapper would deal with."[5]

The plane turned southward at the end of the afternoon, and Lindbergh headed for Long Island. "We've been double-crossed," he said.[6]

After he landed in Hicksville, Lindbergh phoned home. He had given Anne two code words to indicate whether or not the search was a success. As she had awaited the call, the nursery bloomed with light in expectation of the baby's imminent return; the Lindberghs had kept the room dark since the night of the kidnapping. But the tone of Charles's voice was enough to dissolve away her hope as once again, anticipation yielded to angst. She trudged upstairs and kept to her bedroom. *My baby*, she thought, *is surely dead*.

Lindbergh and Breckinridge repeated the exercise the following day, flying over the Sound in another futile hunt for the *Nelly* as Coast Guard cutters patrolled the waters. Hours later, Lindbergh climbed out of the plane with a baby blanket tucked under his arm and made another long, lonely drive home.

Back in the Bronx, Condon suggested to Breckinridge that John would soon be back in touch. Yes, Breckinridge agreed, they should remain patient and not lose optimism. In the meantime, perhaps they could reestablish contact with the gang and nudge John along to resume communications. Condon placed another ad in the newspapers:

WHAT IS WRONG? HAVE YOU CROSSED ME? PLEASE, BETTER DIRECTIONS JAFSIE.

While Condon waited in vain for a reply to the "What is wrong?" ad, Lindbergh sought additional assistance from the government. The treasurer of the United States sent a fifty-seven-page circular with the recorded serial numbers of the ransom bills to banks across the country. The Treasury issued a plea not to divulge its contents, but a clerk at a bank in Newark sold a copy to a local newspaper for five dollars. On April 10, 1932, the list appeared in the newspapers despite Lindbergh's pleas to the AP and the United Press to withhold publication. The media also reported that the Treasury had charged all banking institutions with keeping a lookout for the ransom bills.

On April 9, Colonel Schwarzkopf announced in a national radio broadcast that although a ransom of $50,000 was paid to an emissary of the gang, the baby was not returned. Because the kidnappers had ceased their communications, he said, the cooperation of the federal government had been enlisted to trace the ransom bills.

Two days later, after a page one article in the *Bronx Home News* had revealed Condon's secret role as an intermediary in the Lindbergh case, journalists and autograph-seekers flocked to his doorstep. Some police officials speculated that members of the gang, including Cemetery John, might have gotten themselves thrown in jail for a petty crime to lie low for a while. Condon went to police headquarters downtown to observe lineups of new prisoners and inspect rogues-gallery photographs. No one resembled Cemetery John.

On April 18, John Hughes Curtis, the shipbuilder from Norfolk, came to call on the Lindberghs and spun a tale about having met with a gang of five Scandinavians holding the baby on a boat. The leader was John—the same man who had collected the ransom money from Condon at St. Raymond's Cemetery. Curtis's story when Anne listened to it struck her as "a lot of hooey."[7] Clutching at some faint hope, however, her husband decided to follow it through.

As the story went, John had invited Curtis to his home in Cape May at the southern tip of New Jersey. The kidnapping was an inside job, John said. He and another man had climbed the ladder, chloroformed the baby, and walked out the front door. The gang had hired a German nurse to write the ransom notes. When Curtis had demanded proof he was dealing with the right people, John spread out a few ransom bills on a table and pointed out how their serial numbers matched ones on the published list.

Curtis told Lindbergh that he had scheduled a follow-up meeting with the kidnappers near Cape May, where they had taken the baby. Because an underworld operation was offering a huge sum for the package, the gang was about to move the child again. Lindbergh said that he would rent a hotel room in Cape May and call upon his arrival. When he did so the following evening, Curtis said that the gang had contacted him and would take him aboard its schooner and resume negotiations.

Curtis appeared at daybreak and said that he had been on the schooner, a two-masted Gloucester fisherman. The baby had not been aboard, but the kidnappers had promised to have the vessel, with the child, near Block Island the following morning, the twenty-first of April. For the next three weeks, Curtis inflated Lindbergh's hopes with one invention after another, only to dash them each time with news that the gang had again altered its plans.

# 13

# Hand of the Kidnapper

I t was around this time, after the ransom money had been paid, that Gene Zorn made a curious observation about his neighbor's behavior: The money John Knoll was investing in stamps seemed excessive considering the modest paychecks of a deli clerk living in a ten-dollar-a-month rented room. Knoll boasted about his many new stamps, including an entire collection he had acquired from a man in Yorkville. He also bragged about his ability to dicker. "It was a pretty substantial amount of money," recounted my father.[1]

He was the type to make such observations; my father had an eye for patterns and breaks in pattern that served him well later on in his career as an economist. And these offerings from Knoll, a man so frugal he saved scraps of cardboard to stuff into the envelopes of his First Day Covers, were certainly a break in the pattern. Something about his neighbor's burgeoning stamp collection seemed askew. It was strange how generous Knoll had suddenly become with gifts of First Day Covers and other commemoratives; the Depression, after all, was growing worse.

"It was not until late in the month of April 1932 that John began donating items to my collection," my father recalled. "He even gave me four identical copies of a First Day Cover commemorating Arbor Day. Each bears a postmark of April 22, 1932. Starting at this point his gift-giving became very frequent and abundantly generous."

One day, Knoll handed my father an astonishing gift. As usual, because he had not been offered a chair, he sat on the bed in Knoll's room. The envelope—the one that bears a "Lindbergh Airmail" stamp and a *Graf Zeppelin* cachet—contained a whopping dollar and fifteen cents worth of stamps. Gene Zorn had never seen a more amazing collectible, nor one of such value.

Toward the end of April 1932, Knoll began making one addition after another to my father's collection. In addition to the envelope with the "Lindbergh Airmail" stamp and the *Graf Zeppelin* cachet, Knoll also gave my father a commemorative cover celebrating the five-year anniversary of Lindbergh's flight to Paris. Including the envelopes bearing stamps and cachets pertaining to the *Graf Zeppelin*, the *Spirit of St. Louis*, and Lindbergh, Knoll gave my father eight collectibles related to flying. There were also commemorative covers celebrating the Wright Brothers and Kitty Hawk, the Omaha Air Races, the tactical training flight of the U.S.S. *Akron*, the First Flight Air Mail Route, and the All American Aircraft Show in Detroit. Another cachet paid tribute in the first voyage of the SS *Manhattan*, the "largest ship ever built in America." The timing of Knoll's gifts to my father and the Lindbergh theme of the two most notable keepsakes could be dismissed as mildly unusual except for two features. First, there was artwork of the First Day Covers and something about these cachets that brings to mind the notes from the kidnappers. In the lower right-hand corner of the ransom note left in the nursery, and on subsequent ransom letters, was a pair of interlocking blue circles. Three small, evenly spaced holes were punched through the symbol in a straight horizontal line. A solid red area covered the middle hole and filled in the ellipse formed by the circles' intersection. Investigators never attached much significance to this symbol beyond its clear intention as a calling card, a means at identifying authentic communications from the kidnappers.

The image of the interlocking circles with three holes remains one of the most overlooked clues in the case. The symbol is also among the most significant because it was a deliberate clue by its designer to tell the world something about himself and the historic nature of the letters. The kidnappers repeatedly referred to the image as their *"singnature,"* but perhaps it was something even more revealing. Once it is known that the prime suspect is a stamp collector, this cryptic symbol begins to look very much like a cachet.

There was something else peculiar about the First Day Covers that Knoll gave to my father: the appearance of the handwriting on these

*Three different commemorative covers given to my father by John Knoll. The first shows his normal handwriting. In the second, Knoll attempted to disguise his handwriting. The third was clearly written by someone else.*

envelopes varied markedly. Each was addressed to 706 Westchester Avenue, the location of Knoll's employment in the Bronx. On some of the envelopes, Knoll wrote in his normal manner; his signature matches those on his Declaration of Intention and on his marriage license.[2] On others, however, Knoll tried to disguise his writing by changing the way he wrote the *J* and *K* in *John Knoll* and the *W* and *A* in *Westchester Avenue*.[3] The *ohn* in *John* and the *noll* in *Knoll* resemble his normal handwriting. On a few of the envelopes, Knoll had someone else write his name and address; the handwriting on these looks nothing like his own. This caught my father's attention even at the time, if only in passing and without making any sinister associations. Why was John trying to disguise his handwriting?

It was a matter of chance that the intermediary in the Lindbergh case, Dr. John F. Condon, happened to share his first name. On the ransom envelopes addressed to Condon, the *J* in *John* was written in different ways. And the last three letters—*ohn*—were printed at times, written in cursive at others. The cursive *ohn* on the ransom envelope delivered by taxi driver Joseph Perrone is nearly identical to the *ohn* on John Knoll's self-addressed Armistice Day/Harry Coppendyke Post 171 commemorative covers—almost as if one *ohn* had been traced over another. A gap at the top of the *o* slants upward to a looped *h* and continues with a nearly identical *n*.

*One of the ransom envelopes addressed to John Condon. Note the similarity of the "-ohn" to that in Knoll's disguised handwriting on the middle envelope on the previous page.*

In search of expert opinion on these handwriting samples, I submitted them for analysis by Dr. Sargur N. Srihari, a leading authority on the application of computer technology to document analysis. Ever since the late nineteenth century, when courts first allowed testimony from handwriting experts to help resolve questions of "writership," the entire discipline rested on a premise that had never been proved to the satisfaction of the scientific and legal communities—that each person's handwriting is unique and, under expert scrutiny, distinguishable from that of all others. The problem was that different experts often arrived at different conclusions, causing courts with increasing frequency to dismiss handwriting-related evidence and testimony and casting doubt on the entire field. To address this issue, in the early 1990s the National Institute of Justice turned to the University of Buffalo's Center of Excellence for Document Analysis and Recognition (CEDAR), headed by Dr. Srihari. The principal focus of CEDAR is optical handwriting recognition (OHR), analogous to optical character recognition (OCR).

Dr. Srihari set out to establish a scientific basis and computational method for handwriting examination. Building on work CEDAR had conducted for the U.S. Postal Service, he developed algorithms, statistical models, and software to determine whether "two writing samples compared side-by-side originate from the same person."[4] The CEDAR-FOX system ("FOX" is short for "forensic examination") can make such a determination with a 96 percent rate of accuracy. Even when just one or two words are compared, the proven accuracy rate is 80 percent. The software recognizes and measures such facets of handwriting as the spacing and slant of letters and the manner in which loops in letters are opened and closed. In all, the program analyzes 512 features of individual letters and numbers as well as eleven structural features such as line spacing and the size of margins.[5]

The CEDAR-FOX software produces a positive or negative Logarithmic Likelihood Ratio (LLR) as the result of comparing two handwritten items. It is the logarithm of the ratio of two probabilities: the probability of the known and questioned items under the hypothesis that they were written by the same person, and under the hypothesis that they were written by different individuals. The LLR can be readily converted into probability, or odds, of same writership using this formula: probability of same writer = exp(LLR)/1+ exp(LLR). Finally, the program issues an opinion: identified as same, high probability same, probably did, indicates did, no conclusion, indicates did not, probably did not, high probability did not, or identified as different.

So what conclusions did the CEDAR-FOX system yield in the case of John Knoll's handwriting? The writing on his First Day Covers and commemorative covers he gave my father were used for comparison. No letters he might have written to relatives are known to be in existence. Four samples of "John" in Knoll's handwriting were compared by the program to nine samples of "John" found on ransom envelopes addressed to John Condon, for a total of thirty-six comparisons. "This resulted in an average positive LLR of 1.5, which indicates an 81% probability that they were written by the same individual," said Dr. Srihari. "Since some of the 'Johns' in the questioned writing were hand-printed, while the known 'Johns' were cursively written, if the unlike types are discounted, the average LLR increases to 3, which indicates a 95% probability of same writership." In other words, Dr. Srihari's analysis demonstrates a 95% probability that John Knoll's handwriting appears on the ransom envelopes.[6]

The handwriting evidence against John Knoll is strong; even more compelling is evidence centering on the hand itself. As a former boxer and longtime boxing coach, Condon was a proficient estimator of weight, and he paid particular attention to Cemetery John's hands. Moreover, unlike an eyewitness who had not been expecting to see a crime suddenly take place, Condon came prepared to carefully observe the physical characteristics of the man he was about to meet. He gauged Cemetery John's height as between five-foot-eight and five-foot-ten and his weight at between 158 to 165 pounds—similar to that of a "middle weight boxer."[7]

Condon also described Cemetery John's distinguishing physical characteristics, which included a high forehead, large ears, a pointed chin, and an "unusually large muscular or fleshy development" or lump on the thumb of his left hand.[8] This is not a description of just another average-looking face in the crowd. Condon's description narrows the focus considerably to a face one would likely remember and could readily pick out

*John Knoll holding his son Bobby in 1936. Note the fleshy lump at the base of his left thumb.*

of a police lineup—as Condon himself would later demonstrate when he saw Bruno Hauptmann in a lineup. Pressed by investigators to identify Hauptmann as the man with whom he had spent over an hour conversing, side-by-side on a park bench, Condon said that he could not do so.

How might Condon have reacted to the sight of John Knoll standing before him in a police lineup? That chance slipped away when Cemetery John darted between the tombstones with a boxful of money and vanished into the darkness. In pictures, we can see exactly what John Knoll looked like. His Declaration of Intention form, filed on September 20, 1926, puts his height at five-foot-seven, his weight at 164 pounds.[9] His Army enlistment record dated September 22, 1942, shows little variation: five-foot-seven and 167 pounds.[10] Knoll had a high forehead, large ears, and a pointed chin. All of these are the very characteristics that Condon remembered most clearly. To this extent, at least, it seems safe to say that Condon's reaction would have been one of instant recognition.

But what about the left thumb? Was there the "large fleshy mass" that Condon had noticed at the cemetery, described to police, and looked for on the left hand of Hauptmann? Had Condon been able to inspect Knoll's hand in a police lineup, he would have seen exactly what he was looking for. John Knoll had a large fleshy mass on his left thumb. "I remember noticing something wrong with his hand," Knoll's niece Sharon Breiling recalled to me."[11] There is photogaphic evidence as well. In most surviving pictures from the time, his left hand is out of view, but it's clearly visible in this 1936 photo of Knoll holding up his infant son.

Dr. J. Daniel Labs, a Florida hand surgeon trained at Harvard and Johns Hopkins, enlarged the photograph and examined it. "John Knoll's left thumb is not normal," said Dr. Labs. "His other fingers do appear to be normal. He may have had a congenital defect of the left thumb."[12]

Whether or not the lump at the base of John Knoll's thumb was a congenital defect, the relevant point is this: Condon saw a strange growth on the left thumb of Cemetery John. Bruno Hauptmann had no such growth on his thumb. In addition to every other physical feature reported by Condon, John Knoll did possess that highly unusual identifying characteristic. Although some of Condon's description might apply to Hauptmann, it fits Knoll precisely.

# 14

# The Victim

I t was drizzly and overcast in the Sourland Mountains on the twelfth
of May—the seventy-second day of the search for the Lindbergh baby
and the manhunt for the kidnappers. At 3:15 p.m., William Allen and
Orville Wilson were hauling a truckload of timber down Hopewell–Mt.
Rose Highway in Mercer County. The deliverymen stopped on the side
of the road. Wilson waited in the truck as his partner walked about fifty
feet into the woods to relieve himself. A few feet ahead of him, a strange
sight caught Allen's attention. At first it appeared to be an animal skele-
ton. He inched closer. What he saw froze him in place. It was the corpse
of a baby.

The decomposed cadaver was facedown in a small hollow. Animals
prowling the woods—most likely foxes, raccoons, skunks, rodents, and
dogs—had scavenged the body, which was crawling with insects.[1] The
left leg had been gnawed off at the knee, the left arm at the elbow. The
right forearm was also missing. Allen shouted for his partner, who came
running. "Don't know about anybody losing a child except Colonel Lindbergh," said Allen. "Let's get out of here and see Charlie Williamson."[2]

The men drove to Hopewell and found Charles Williamson, one of
the first officials to arrive at the scene of the crime, in a barbershop. Allen
described his discovery, and Williamson, recognizing its importance,
bolted for the door. The deliverymen followed him to the township
police station and repeated the story to the police chief, who telephoned
Colonel Schwarzkopf at the New Jersey State Police Headquarters. Allen
led an array of officers, state troopers, and detectives to the shallow grave.

A state trooper and a detective discovered a burlap sack a few feet away from the corpse. The sack was stained with blood.

The details reveal what probably had happened in the woods. Forensic anthropologist Dr. Kathy Reichs, the model for Temperance "Bones" Brennan on the television series *Bones,* explains that animals will sometimes pull a body out of a sack and drag it to a place for scavenging.[3] One of her contemporaries is Dr. William M. Bass, founder of the University of Tennessee Anthropological Research Facility, also known as the "Body Farm." A longtime student of the Lindbergh case, Dr. Bass believes that an animal had scented gases emanating from the corpse and then ripped a grapefruit-sized hole in the sack and fished the corpse out.[4]

Dr. Arpad Vass, Senior Research Scientist at the Oak Ridge National Laboratory in Oak Ridge, Tennessee, explains that as a body decomposes, ammonia and elevated levels of carbon dioxide are dissipated quickly through the tissue and are among the first gases emitted. Animals are particularly attracted to sulfur compounds, insects to hydrogen compounds and ammonia. The dehydrogenization process begins upon the occurrence of a "decompositional event." The larvae of iridescent blowflies are often present on dead bodies found in wooded areas, but normally only when the temperature exceeds 50 degrees Fahrenheit.

Dr. Vass observes that the Post Mortem Interval (PMI) could have been gauged today within an accuracy of twelve hours. He is the co-inventor of the Lightweight Analyzer for Buried Remains and Decomposition Odor Recognition (LABRADOR), a device with twelve sensors that operates like a metal detector and hovers over the ground just like a dog's nose. Based on a pattern of recognition of sulfur, halogen, and various other compounds, LABRADOR can determine whether a decompositional event has occurred.

With today's technology, Dr. Vass explains, a scientist can determine how long a body has been in a particular spot. In one of his cases, he recalled, advanced technology revealed that a murderer had moved the corpse of his victim five times. If the Lindbergh kidnapping had taken place today, Dr. Vass could have taken a soil extract from beneath the corpse, a simple process. He would have looked for the presence of Volatile Fatty Acids, which are organic and are released from the breakdown of soft tissue, and for calcium, chloride, potassium, and other inorganic compounds. The extract would be compared to the decomposition fluid that had stained the burlap sack. The process would have enabled Dr. Vass to determine how long the body had been decomposing in the sack before it was removed.[5]

Although workers had strung up emergency telephone wires near the shallow grave, the police had not combed the woods this far from the crime scene. A body disposed of in such a casual fashion, explains John Douglas, reflects not only a complete lack of remorse—but also contempt for the victim.[6] Over the years, the FBI's Behavioral Science Unit has accumulated extensive data on the disposal of murder victims' bodies through long interviews of the most violent criminals in incarceration. Profilers have learned that how a corpse is treated provides clues about the murderer's mindset. If a body is shown a degree of respect—for example, if it is covered by a sheet—the murderer may be revealing some feelings of attachment to or caring for the victim. Charlie Lindbergh's body, however, was dumped in a random spot off the side of a highway, likely tossed away in the burlap sack and left to be scavenged like a dead rabbit. Whoever had ditched the body had about as much emotional attachment to the little boy as he had for the sack.[7]

One of the troopers used a stick to turn over the corpse. The face was well preserved. The decay, Dr. Bass would note fifty years later, had been much less rapid than it would have been had the crime occurred during the summer.[8] The trooper reached into his jacket pocket for a photograph of the Lindbergh baby and held it close to the face of the corpse. The dimpled chin and golden, curly locks were a match. Because the baby's grandmother Betty Morrow had saved a few snippets of his hair, a microscopic analysis performed on samples taken from the corpse proved that the hair belonged to Charlie Lindbergh.

Before he considered approaching the Lindberghs, Inspector Harry Walsh of the Jersey City Police met with Betty Gow to find out what the baby had worn the night of his abduction. Cautious not to alarm her, Walsh requested a sample of the material she had used to make the baby's nightshirt. She also retrieved the spool of blue thread needed for the stitches. Walsh returned to the gravesite, where investigators were continuing to search the area. The men filled ten wooden barrels with leaves and items raked up near the spot where the body was found. The investigators recovered twelve bones from the debris and put them into five glass vials with cork stoppers. In 1982, Dr. Bass would conduct an examination of the bones, which were still greasy and appeared almost new even after fifty years.[9] As far as Dr. Bass knows, he and Dr. Krogman are the only forensic anthropologists who have ever been allowed to examine the remaining material. The study would indicate that ten of the bones were human—four from the right hand, two from the left hand, and four from the left foot. They had all belonged to a child who had died between the ages of eighteen and twenty-four months. Both of the animal bones—a vertebral arch from the spinal column and a rib fragment—bore canine tooth marks.[10]

The clothing on the corpse matched Betty Gow's description down to the homemade flannel undershirt stitched with blue thread. Walsh removed what little remained of the baby's clothes to preserve as evidence.

The duty of breaking the news to the family fell to Colonel Schwarzkopf. Anne and her mother were at home when he arrived. The baby was dead, he said, and there could be no doubt about the identification. Charlie had died, it appeared, on the night of the kidnapping. Betty Morrow went to her daughter's bedroom and sat down next to her on the bed.

For Anne, "the hardest thing" to bear was a comment uttered by her mother: "The baby is with Daddy."[11] It had been seven months since Dwight Morrow's sudden death at fifty-eight. Anne expressed relief that her baby had not lived beyond that first night and that the information concerning him was, at last, definite. She had believed from the start that Charlie had died on the night of the kidnapping.[12]

"Everything is telescoped now into one moment, one of those eternal moments—the moment when I realized the baby had been taken and I saw the baby dead, killed violently, in the first flash of horror," she recorded in her diary. ". . . If you can say 'then he was living,' 'then he was dead,' it is final and finalities can be accepted." For Anne, the experience was like "sleeping in a grave."[13]

Coroner Walter H. Swayze's funeral home in Trenton received the baby's corpse at six o'clock in the evening. Two detectives arrived soon afterward with Betty Gow and led her into the embalming room. She could only bear to look at the blackened remains for a moment. Yet there was no uncertainty in her mind: this was the child she had taken care of for a year.

The New Jersey State Police reported that an announcement from Colonel Lindbergh's garage would be forthcoming. Two dozen journalists fought their way through rain to assemble for the news, which came at 6:45 p.m. Choking out the words, Schwarzkopf began, "We have to announce that apparently the body of the Lindbergh baby was found." As reporters sprang from their seats, he insisted that no one leave until he had finished reading his statement. Minutes later, four words came over the wires: "Lindbergh baby found dead."

In Times Square, the electric bulletin sign of the *New York Times* flashed the news. A stunned crowd stood in the rain and waited for more information. In the nation's capital, a meeting of the Democratic steering committee of the Senate broke up on receipt of the announcement. The fifteen senators in attendance tabled an important issue to seek further details surrounding the child's death. "I have never heard more shocking news," Senator Robert F. Wagner of New York said.[14]

Dr. Philip Van Ingen had examined the child ten days before the kidnapping and recorded a number of measurements in connection with a treatment for rickets. The pediatrician determined that the measurements of the corpse matched "almost exactly" with those he had taken of Charlie. Dr. Van Ingen observed that the skull, teeth, and toes of the corpse were identical to those of his patient.

New Jersey law required an autopsy to determine the cause, manner, and time of any violent death. Because of arthritic hands, the Mercer County physician, Dr. Charles H. Mitchell, could no longer perform surgeries. He directed the coroner where and how to make incisions. One of today's most renowned forensic pathologists, Dr. Michael M. Baden, called this highly unusual practice "improper."[15]

The stated cause of death in Dr. Mitchell's autopsy report was "a fractured skull caused by external violence."[16] Because of the hair color, the size of the head, and other observations, Dr. Mitchell concluded that the body belonged to Charlie Lindbergh. The autopsy confirmed that the baby had been dead for at least two months. Investigators assigned to the case presumed that the ladder had broken on the climber's descent, and that the baby had fallen to his death.

One of the leading forensic experts today on crimes involving children and in pediatric head trauma, forensic and neuropathologist Dr. Mary Case, has examined the autopsy report. It is certainly possible that the fall might have caused Charlie Lindbergh to die if he had gone untreated, she observes, but there is some possibility that it might not have. Although the injuries described in the report could have resulted either from such a fall or from one or more blows to the head, it is impossible to determine which scenario was more likely. In Dr. Case's opinion, the head injury would not necessarily have caused the child to die instantaneously although the death might have occurred in a short period.[17]

John Douglas believes that if Charlie Lindbergh had survived his skull fracture, the leader of the kidnapping gang might not have wanted an injured baby on his hands. Thus it's possible, Douglas says, that the child was killed intentionally—perhaps strangled to death while he was in the burlap sack. Not having to look at the baby would have dehumanized him to the killer.[18] Moreover, having the power to decide whether a victim lives or dies, or how he dies, "temporarily counteracts, for some, their feelings of inadequacy . . . and makes them feel grandiose and superior."[19] From a forensic standpoint, Dr. Case observes, there would be no way to determine if Charlie Lindbergh had been strangled; a child of twenty months could suffer such a fate without any external or internal injury present to indicate the cause of death.[20]

On the day his son's body was found, Lindbergh had telephoned his wife at seven o'clock in the morning. "Oh, Charles felt *so* encouraged and hopeful," she wrote in a letter to her mother.[21] Led to believe by John Hughes Curtis that the baby was aboard a black-hulled Gloucester fisherman far out at sea, he had been sailing in circles on an auxiliary ketch, the *Cachalot*, when the corpse was discovered. Soon after the *Cachalot* docked at Cape May Harbor, two men sent by Colonel Schwarzkopf, Edwin Bruce and George Richard, boarded the ketch. Lindbergh greeted them and reported another day of failure.

"Colonel, I have a message for you," said Bruce. "They have found the baby."

Lindbergh began, "Found—?"

"He is dead."

During the whole ordeal, and even after the couple had learned of their son's death, not once did Anne see Charles cry. On occasion he had reproached her for failing to control her emotions, and for his sake she had tried to maintain a surface composure.[22] From notes written by Lindbergh nearly fifty years later, it is clear how proud he was of his wife for the way she responded to their baby's kidnapping: "Anne bore up wonderfully. . . She was extraordinary."[23] Yet even toward the end of his life, he appeared not to understand her need to have shared her emotions with him about the tragedy: "There was not reason to discuss the case further with my wife. She went through all of it in detail."[24]

Without the freedom to discuss her feelings with her husband, Anne had to find her own way on her journey to learn how to move on from the most traumatic event she would ever endure—the type of tragedy human beings are simply not meant to get over.[25] "I think it was very difficult for her to be married to someone who couldn't express his emotions," the couple's daughter Reeve said nearly seventy years later.[26] It was clear to Reeve, however, that although her father had guarded his own emotions, he had felt the grief of his loss "very strongly and very deeply."[27] Indeed, Dr. Mary Ellen O'Toole believes, Charlie remained the love of Charles Lindbergh's life forever.[28]

As he dealt with the tragedy, Lindbergh may have considered how his late father would have coped under the circumstances. "He enjoyed life, and had a keen sense of its beauty and quality. No hardship could take this sense away from him," Lindbergh would write decades after the kidnapping. "My father had great depth of feeling, but did not believe in showing his feeling to others, and had extraordinary ability in hiding it . . . I have inherited from him much of the same tendency and ability. I remember my father saying to me, 'You and I are able to take hard knocks.'"[29]

Charles spent the rest of the night sitting by Anne's bedside, watching her and listening to her gasping sobs. "He has already been dead a hundred years," she wrote in her diary the next day.[30]

That afternoon, after Lindbergh had demanded to see the body, Breckinridge and a reluctant Schwarzkopf accompanied him to the Swayze & Margerum Funeral Home in Trenton. As several hundred mourners gathered outside in the rain, Lindbergh entered through the back door. A photographer had already stolen into the morgue to snap a picture of Charlie's corpse, copies of which were hawked on the streets for five dollars.

Writing in his journal nearly seventeen years later, Lindbergh would express the anger this act had stirred in him. The emotions he had submerged bobbed to the surface when a group of photographers vowed to give their "word of honor" to leave him alone in the future if he would consent to pose for just one picture. "Imagine a press photographer talking about his word of honor!" he wrote. "The type of men who broke through the window of the Trenton morgue to open my baby's casket and photograph its body—they talk to me of honor."[31]

The child's body covered by a sheet lay on the autopsy table. To Anne, the thought that Charles would have to endure the sight of their son's decomposed corpse was "unbearable."[32] A group of twenty hushed onlookers, many with tears streaming down their cheeks, including Special Agent Leon Turrou of the Bureau of Investigation, stood motionless as Lindbergh stepped forward in the cold light of the chamber. "Take that off," he said.

A member of the coroner's staff slipped off the sheet and edged away. Only the ticking of a clock on the wall broke the silence in the room. Lindbergh, expressionless, bent over the table and stared at the remains. He had always beamed at the sight of his cherished "Buster," who had called him "Hi." Charlie's squeals of laughter had bubbled out of him during rambunctious chases after his fox terrier Wahgoosh and aboard "ceiling flights" piloted by "Hi" in the living room. "Den!" ("Again!"), he had shouted as his father tossed him up into the air.[33] Playing with his son had brought Lindbergh utter joy—and perhaps the happiest moments of his life.[34]

His focus intact, Lindbergh observed that parts of the arms and left leg were missing. The bright blue eyes had turned charcoal-black and the corneas were clouded. The task before him triggering his habitual following of checklists, Lindbergh ran his fingertips along the upper and lower gumlines and counted sixteen teeth. Check. Toes that turned in slightly—another of the baby's features. Check.[35] The examination complete, Lindbergh walked out of the room. He had performed his self-appointed task with the clinical detachment of a forensic scientist. "There was not the slightest doubt about identification of the baby's body," he would write privately thirty-six years later.[36]

Lindbergh requested that his son's remains be cremated. On Friday, the thirteenth of May at 4:25 p.m., as policemen fanned out to restrain a crowd lingering outside the funeral home, the coffin was loaded onto a gray hearse. Colonel Schwarzkopf followed in his automobile with Lindbergh and Breckinridge in the back seat as the hearse headed for the Rosehill Cemetery and Crematory in Linden. After a forty-mile drive the procession of two cars reached the cemetery.

Schwarzkopf and Breckinridge stayed behind as Lindbergh descended a flight of stairs and entered the witnessing room. A clock on the wall marked a quarter past six o'clock. Four men in uniform—black suits, white shirts, and black hats of the type worn by train conductors—rolled the tiny oak coffin off a wheeled cart into the cremation chamber and closed the hinged cast-iron door. Because there had been no other cremations that day, the chamber was cold. Soon, however, its temperature would rise to 1500 degrees Fahrenheit. The father of the murdered child, standing alone, bent down and looked through a sighting port mounted to a brick wall. Flames erupted as the oil-fired burner was ignited. Lindbergh could see little more than an intense bright light as the blaze engulfed his baby's coffin. After an hour, the chamber was dark.

# PART II

# 15

# A New Life

After suffering seventy-two days of agonizing uncertainty whether her baby was alive, Anne Morrow Lindbergh tried to force herself to think of his death as a murder case.[1] She struggled every day, however, with severe depression and periods of numbness—a "terrible, terrible apathy of mind, spirit, and body."[2] She wanted to know the details regarding what had happened to Charlie—what he had suffered, even to feel it herself. As her eyes roved about the "horrible horrible-looking people" on the subway, she wanted to ask, "And which one of you killed my boy?"[3]

During her first pregnancy, Anne, the first woman to receive a first-class glider-pilot's license in the United States, had broken the transcontinental speed record.[4] Now, she was reduced to a person "terrified of a smashup" in the subway. She could not accept what had happened to her son. "It isn't death at all but something else," Anne wrote in her diary, "terrible and shaking and personal, something no one else ever suffered."[5] Her mind played tricks on her: if she thought about Charlie's death long or hard enough, or if she agonized about it enough, perhaps she could make it *un*-happen.[6] Or maybe the whole thing had happened to someone else. Then, once again, the realization would hit her: it did happen, it had happened to her, and there would be no recapturing the past. Charles's admonition—to try to "find some way of making Time go backwards"—forced Anne to bring back memories of the happiest days of her life.[7] It seemed incomprehensible that although those days were just a few weeks in the past, her baby was already very far away. "There is no greater sorrow," said Dante, "than to recall happiness in times of misery."[8]

On May 16, Schwarzkopf summoned John Condon, John Hughes Curtis, and Lindbergh's racketeer go-between, Morris Rosner, to Highfields. With the three men separated from one another, investigators circulated from room to room, then compared their stories. Each shifted blame onto the shoulders of the others. Inspector Harry Walsh of the Jersey City Police arrived as midnight approached. Plagued by insomnia, Curtis challenged him to a game of checkers. Because his opponent's mind was not on the game, Walsh suggested stepping outside into the courtyard to breathe in some fresh air.

After his business had failed, Curtis said, he had a nervous breakdown. You'd feel better, Walsh said, by clearing your conscience and telling the real story of your involvement in the Lindbergh case. But he *had* told the real story, Curtis insisted. Walsh repeated his rebuke as though the first one had not registered. There was no reply. As Walsh turned to leave, Curtis said that he had never seen the ransom money. It was the one comment that had convinced Lindbergh that Curtis was really in touch with the kidnappers.

Brought into the dining room a few minutes later, Curtis told Lindbergh that he had lied about having seen some of the ransom bills. He had believed it necessary to do so to convince him to act with haste in their dealings with the gang. Lindbergh made a gesture of disgust and without a word walked out of the room. With that, Curtis composed a voluntary statement of confession: "I exceedingly regret that I caused Colonel Linbergh [sic] and others any inconvenience."

Confronted about his actions, the ruined shipbuilder portrayed himself as a harmless prankster whose financial woes had driven him to perpetrate the hoax. Walsh dated the signed document: 4:35 a.m., May 17, 1932. Paramount Sound News sent a telegram to "Col. Schwartkopf [sic]" that afternoon: "IN VIEW OF THE FACT THAT A SIGNED CONFESSION HAS BEEN GIVEN TO THE PRESS BY CURTIS, NEWS REELS DESIRE SAME IN SOUND PICTURES, YOUR ASSISTANCE IN THIS MATTER WILL BE APPRECIATED."[9] Six weeks later, Curtis would be convicted of obstruction of justice in the Hunterdon County Courthouse. Lindbergh testified at the trial and attended every day of the proceedings. The judge imposed a $1,000 fine and gave Curtis a one-year jail sentence that was later suspended. Curtis smirked as he paid his debt with a Grover Cleveland—a one thousand dollar bill.

The Lindberghs moved back in with Betty Morrow at Next Day Hill. The images of the southeast corner window, the east side of the house, and the abandoned road where the kidnappers had parked the getaway car haunted Anne. To continue to live in her home "in freedom and sanity" was too painful to bear. "I shall always be trying to know just what happened in terror and curiosity and misery," she wrote in her diary. Then, in another entry made shortly before the Curtis trial in nearby Flemington: "I dread going to Hopewell. To live there in no hope, where I lived so long *just* on that."[10] Out for a drive to Princeton one evening, the Lindberghs came to the spot where the kidnappers had dumped their baby's body in the woods off the highway. Anne said, "It *isn't possible*," and Charles said bitterly, "It seems to be."[11]

Even in the protected Englewood mansion, however, the Lindberghs could not escape new dramas associated with the kidnapping. The evasiveness of Violet Sharp, twenty-eight, a dark-haired, slightly plump English maid on the Morrow staff, had raised the suspicions of detectives. Harry Walsh of the Jersey City Police took a lead role in the interrogations and, as historian Lloyd Gardner notes, pursued her with "tough questioning."[12] She claimed during her first interview that sometime before March 1, 1932, a man named Ernie had met her and her sister Emily and given them a ride to Englewood. The man took Violet's name, address, and phone number and promised to call. He phoned her at 7:50 p.m. on March 1 and picked her up at Next Day Hill around 8:30. Ernie introduced her to a couple in the back seat, but she could not remember their names. The group went to a movie at the Englewood Theatre, and Ernie took her home around eleven o'clock. Walsh pressed Violet for details, but she could not recall the name of the film— or anything about it.

At the time, Violet was dating the Morrows' British-born butler, Septimus Banks, who had first begun working for the family in 1919. According to a Bureau of Investigation report, Banks, who "had been discharged several times because of drunkenness and re-employed," did most of his drinking in a speakeasy in Yorktown, a German section of Manhattan. "He was very talkative and quite irresponsible when drunk," the report states. Banks often had to be put into a taxicab and driven back to Englewood. He told the police that he had been at the Sha-Toe, a speakeasy and "hangout for horseplayers" in Fort Lee, on the night of the kidnapping.[13]

Walsh puzzled at an item in Violet Sharp's room. A bankbook revealed a balance of over sixteen hundred dollars—four hundred more than her annual wages. "I'd feel quite comfortable," said the investigator, "if I had as much."[14] Violet admitted that a reporter with whom she had gone on three dates had offered her bribes to leak information about the Lindberghs, but said she have refused them.

Under further questioning, Violet confessed that she had lied about having gone to the movies with Ernie and his friends: the group had in fact enjoyed a few drinks and danced at a speakeasy near Newark called The Peanut Grill. She also acknowledged her awareness of the call at 10:30 a.m. on March 1 that had summoned Betty Gow to Highfields and of the Lindberghs' decision to stay another night at their new home.

On Friday, June 10, Betty Morrow's secretary told Violet that the State Police had called and that a detective was on his way to pick her up for another round of interrogation. Now there was suspicion that she might have tipped off the kidnappers that the Lindberghs would be at their new home on the night Charlie disappeared. Early in the evening of May 23, Walsh had grilled her in the presence of Lindbergh, and Colonel Schwarzkopf: "Will you explain why you told a lie about [going to see a movie]? . . . Are you in the habit of picking up strange men in the street? . . . Are you in the habit of going out with people you don't know and going and having a drink with them?"[15]

After receiving word that a detective was on his way to Next Day Hill, Violet ran to Septimus Banks. "Walsh wants to question me again," she said, "but I won't go! I won't! I won't!"[16] Violet ran upstairs and grabbed a tin of silver polish from a shelf in her bedroom closet. She spooned some crystals into a measuring glass and filled it with water. Lifting the glass to her mouth, she swallowed the mixture and staggered downstairs into the pantry. Members of the household and staff watched in horror as she gasped for air and collapsed. Only later would they learn that she had consumed cyanide of potassium.

The response to cyanide can be very rapid. The bloodstream begins delivering the poison to the cells. The cyanide inhibits cellular respiration and prevents ATP formation by the cells. Damaged physiologically, the cells begin to die from oxygen starvation.[17] As Sebastian Junger describes in *The Perfect Storm,* deprivation of oxygen to the brain causes "a sensation of darkness closing in from all sides, as in a camera aperture stopping down."[18]

Within minutes, Violet slipped into a coma. By the time medical help arrived, it was too late. Several hours later, Colonel Schwarzkopf issued a statement: "The suicide of Violet Sharp strongly tends to confirm the suspicions of the investigating authorities concerning her guilty knowledge of the crime against Charles Lindbergh, Jr."[19] As their daughter's body lay in the morgue, George Sharp and his wife received a cable in England from the New Jersey State Police: "Sorry to advise you daughter Violet passed away this morning; deepest sympathy."

"Ever since the baby disappeared, Violet was badgered and questioned until she did not know what she was saying or doing," said her sister, Emily, dressed in black as she addressed reporters. "She was driven nearly mad."[20] The tragedy exposed the New Jersey State Police to inflammatory criticism in the British press: In London, the *Daily Herald* accused the police of "venting their chagrin at their failure in the Lindbergh case on a poor English servant girl."[21]

It's always important, John Douglas and Mark Olshaker note, to examine the post-offense behavior. They believe it's "highly possible that Violet inadvertently tipped of the kidnappers" and that it is "difficult to imagine her committing suicide unless she either felt somehow responsible or thought the connection to the kidnapping would somehow ruin her life."[22]

Amid all of the turmoil, the Lindberghs, who were expecting their second child, sought to recover their lives. They were among the first to fall victim to out-of-control reporters in the new age of worldwide communications. Refusing to allow yet another media circus into his life, Charles held a ceremony of his own making to honor his son. On the fifteenth of August, newspapermen hovered around him as he prepared to climb into the cockpit of a Northrup test plane. Because it was his first time to take to the sky in months, they likely asked where he was going. If they did, perhaps he gave one of his typical responses: "Up." Decades later, he would write privately, "I distributed the ashes of my son over the Atlantic Ocean, some miles at sea."[23]

Although he refrained from displaying his tender side to the public, the love Lindbergh felt for his son could be seen in his kindness eight years later to his dying dog Skean, who had scampered in and out of Charlie's playpen as a puppy. Perhaps something of Charlie and that time in the father's life lingered in the sight of Skean. The night before the dog died, Lindbergh carried him on a quilt, put him in front of the fireplace, and held Skean's head in his hands for a long time. The following day, Lindbergh dug a grave and buried the dog in the garden. "It took an hour of hard work, but I felt much better doing it myself," he wrote in his journal. "It seemed an obligation that I, personally, must fulfill, and in which I could not let anyone else take part."[24]

As he was about to become a father again, Lindbergh saw no reason to continue to speak of the beloved firstborn son who had died. And as deeply wounded as they both were, he and Anne soon had to turn their attention to the new child they were expecting. What could more clearly mark the end of one time and the beginning of another than the birth of a new baby?

Twelve midnight had passed when, on August 16, 1932, the day after he had scattered Charlie's ashes, Anne began experiencing contractions. The Lindberghs had arranged for the medical team to meet them at the fifteen-bedroom Morrow apartment on East 66th Street overlooking Central Park.[25] On the ride from Englewood, as Anne looked at the billboards, newsstands, and milk wagons on the empty streets of the City, she felt "so strange (in the grip of something inevitable and tremendous, an iron hand)."[26]

Dr. Everett M. Hawks, the obstetrician, arrived with an anesthesiologist and a nurse. Unaware that she had begun to hemorrhage during labor, Anne gave birth by cesarean section to a seven-pound, fourteen-ounce boy. The infant had a nose like his mother's and a dimpled chin like his father's. Although the Lindberghs "had strong leanings toward *John*" for the name, they decided on *Jon*.[27] Jon Lindbergh would never hear his father speak of the child before him. "I saw nothing gained in discussing [the kid-napping] with my children," Lindbergh would write in 1968.[28]

For what had seemed an eternity until that moment, Anne's image of her murdered baby, accompanied by his dear and innocent remembered voice, had been a snare. Whenever she shut her eyes, memories of Charlie would come flooding back unbidden. Anne played her fingers through his curly, golden locks over and over in her mind. One day, she discovered his red mittens in the pockets of his little blue knitted jacket. "It was like touching his hand," she wrote in her diary.[29] Although Anne had realized that no other child would cause her to miss Charlie any less, the birth of her new baby filled her with "feelings of joy" and reborn faith.[30]

Through Colonel Breckinridge, Lindbergh issued a statement:

> Mrs. Lindbergh and I have made our home in New Jersey. It is natu-rally our wish to live there near our friends and interests. Obviously, however, it is impossible for us to subject the life of our second son to the publicity which, we feel, was in large measure responsible for the death of our first. We feel that our children have the right to grow up normally with other children. Continued publicity will make this impossible. I am appealing to the Press to permit our children to live the lives of normal Americans.[31]

Asking the press and the public for privacy was one thing, actually expecting it was another, and Lindbergh, as always, had made realistic preparations. Six weeks before Jon was born, the Lindberghs had visited the kennels of a breeder and trainer of German shepherds in Princeton. When Charles tried to befriend a large, handsome shepherd dog named Pal, the animal showed his teeth and growled. The breeder told how he had stopped to ask a policeman for directions one day. When the officer leaned into the open window, Pal lunged at him and tore a hole in his uni-form. Hearing this, Lindbergh knew he had found the perfect addition to the family. He renamed the dog "Thor" and trained him to protect baby Jon.

# 16

# "The Killers"

As the Lindberghs sought to move on, the hunt for the kidnappers intensified. The investigators continued to operate on the assumption that more than one man had taken the baby. References to the manhunt were usually in the plural. "We will do everything in our power to get the murderers," declared New Jersey Governor A. Harry Moore. "It is a perfectly horrible crime and we shall do everything in our power to find those responsible for it."[1]

"The city is in mourning that the Lindbergh baby was found dead and Colonel Lindbergh and his wife have the profound sympathy of New York," Mayor James J. Walker said in a radio broadcast. "It is a pledge that I make at this time over WOR that the 18,000 of our police will not be off duty but on duty, from now on, making every effort to run down what I consider to be the most miserable criminals and scoundrels in the annals of criminology."[2]

President Hoover issued a statement, also vowing to bring the "criminals" to justice: "I have directed the law-enforcement agencies and the several Secret Services of the Federal Government to make the kidnapping and murder of the Lindbergh baby a never-to-be-forgotten case, never to be relaxed until the criminals are implacably brought to justice. The Federal Government does not have police authority in such cases, but its agencies will be unceasingly alert to assist the New Jersey police in every possible way until this end has been accomplished."[3]

Under the headline GET THE LINDBERGH KILLERS! the *New York Daily News* called the kidnappers "damnable fiends" and "inhuman monsters" and urged the government to put its best men on their trail. "Until the killers are tracked down and brought to justice, the children of America will not be safe," the newspaper editorialized. "And the rest of the world will be able to point to this country and say: 'That is the country where criminals can persecute decent citizens in absolute defiance of the law.'"[4]

Because Lindbergh had refused to allow the police to shadow Condon at either of the Bronx cemeteries, the best opportunity to apprehend Cemetery John had slipped away. Pressure on Colonel Schwarzkopf to find the kidnappers grew as syndicated columnists and radio broadcasters derided the New Jersey State Police for its handling of the investigation. Representative Charles Adam Karch of Illinois made a speech inserted into the Congressional Record charging that "boneheaded police, from Norman Schwarzkopf on down, had bungled the Lindbergh case."[5]

Critics faulted the New Jersey State Police for lagging behind in modern investigative techniques and for their reluctance to cooperate and communicate with other law enforcement agencies eager to contribute their resources. Though the postmarks on the ransom letters indicated that the kidnappers lived in New York, Acting Lieutenant Jimmy Finn of the New York Police Department complained that he could learn as much from the newspapers as from his counterparts in Trenton.

As the feeling grew that crucial time had been lost, allowing the killers to get away, public opinion began to turn not only against Colonel Schwarzkopf but also against John Condon, who was receiving hate mail and threatening phone calls. Condon, who had vowed to spend the rest of his life tracking down Cemetery John and his accomplices, now believed himself unfairly assailed for having risked his own life to try to rescue the baby. Not long after Condon had vented his frustration to Breckinridge, the following letter arrived in his mailbox:

> My dear Dr. Condon:
>
> Mrs. Lindbergh and I want to thank you for the great assistance you have been to us. We fully realize that you have devoted the major portion of your time and energy to bring about the return of our son. We wish to express to you our sincere appreciation for your courage and cooperation.
>
> Sincerely,
> Charles Lindbergh

Notwithstanding the sharp criticism of the investigation, thirty men on the New Jersey State Police force had spent thousands of hours pursuing leads and questioning witnesses and suspects. Detectives had interviewed and obtained histories of the activities of all thirty-two members of the Morrow and Lindbergh staffs. More than one hundred members of the construction crew that had worked on the Lindberghs' new home had faced similar questioning. Acting on Schwarzkopf's order, Major Charles Schoeffel embarked on a trip to England to meet with Scotland Yard. He registered in hotels under assumed names, one of which was "John Condon" of Toronto; he derived this from his wife's maiden name and the name of one of her brothers. The backgrounds of the Whateleys and Betty Gow, Schoeffel discovered, revealed nothing of the slightest concern. He also met with J. E. Horwell, the inspector in charge of all of Scotland Yard's "forgery cases, extortion cases and blackmail cases and other crimes where the criminal has resorted to writing." According to Chief Inspector Horwell, the person who wrote the notes displayed "intelligence of more than average cunning and ingenuity." Considering the possibility that the crime could have been of a personal nature, the detectives of Scotland Yard suggested that the Lindberghs be contacted "to determine if they have any connection with outsiders who would wish harm to them."[6]

From England, Schoeffel traveled to Germany and Austria to continue his investigation. At the U.S. embassy in Vienna, he met with American Minister Gilchrist Stockton, who had an avid interest in handwriting. The men examined the ransom notes together for two days. Stockton immediately became convinced that the writing was that of a Southern German or an Austrian—not that of a Prussian or a Northern or Western German. He produced samples of letters written in English by Austrians applying for jobs at the embassy. Noting the "great similarity in the various characteristics in the [ransom] notes" to the writing Stockton displayed, Schoeffel concluded that a Southern German or an Austrian had authored the letters.[7]

To support the investigation of the New Jersey authorities, J. Edgar Hoover mobilized the cooperation of the U.S. Post Office Department, the U.S. Prohibition Bureau, the Coast Guard, the Customs and Immigration Services, and the Police Department of Washington, D.C. On June 1, a conference took place at the Training School of the New Jersey State Police. Joining Colonel Schwarzkopf and two of his lieutenants to field suggestions and solicit comments were Frank Wilson of the Treasury Department, Harry

Walsh of the Jersey City Police, and Lindbergh. The group concurred that the crime involved someone who possessed "vivid imagination," "a lot of ingenuity," "a great deal of nerve and courage," "calmness," and "foresightedness"—and who had an intimate knowledge of the Bronx.[8]

Schwarzkopf submitted the ransom notes to the foremost handwriting analyst in the nation, Albert S. Osborn. The seventy-four-year-old graphologist had appeared as an expert witness in cases involving documents under question. He had authored the books *Questioned Documents* and *The Problem of Proof*, copies of which he sent to Schwarzkopf with a cover letter: "I am pleased to have them in the hands of those who will be interested in them and who will find them useful."[9] The same person had written all of the ransom notes, Osborn concluded. The writer invariably had failed to dot *i*'s and cross *t*'s and had reversed *g*'s and *h*'s in words such as *lihgt* and *rihgt*. Many words such as *boad*, *mony*, and *singnature* were misspelled. The words *gut* and *aus* throughout the notes indicated that the author was German. "New York" was written *New-York*, and the dollar sign was placed after figures. What was more, the holes in the ransom notes lined up precisely.

The New York Police Department engaged a thirty-nine-year-old psychiatrist affiliated with Mount Sinai Hospital, Dr. Dudley D. Shoenfeld, to create a psychological profile of Cemetery John. John was confident, Dr. Shoenfeld asserted, that Lindbergh would accede to his demands. Twice the ransom notes had boasted "You have to come to us anyway." Even more compelling, John conveyed his feelings of omnipotence by referring to the kidnapping as a "world-affair." He was thrilled by the international attention his crime had aroused—attention that rivaled the acclaim Lindbergh had received for his flight to Paris. The kidnapper's own twisted thinking had convinced him that he was as courageous and talented as the great aviator.

Meanwhile, the Treasury Department used a map to plot the locations where Lindbergh ransom bills had turned up. The first to surface, a twenty-dollar note, had been deposited in a Manhattan bank two days after the ransom payment. Because of circumstances that Elmer Irey and his T-men had foreseen in their selection of the bills used to make up the package of ransom money, the note offered an opportunity to track down the kidnappers.

On April 5, 1933, just a month into office, President Franklin D. Roosevelt had exercised the power created by the Emergency Banking Relief Act. The presidential order required citizens in possession of more than one hundred dollars in gold certificates or coins to exchange or deposit all such money at a Federal Reserve Bank or at a member bank of the Federal Reserve System by the first of May. Just prior to closing time on the day of the deadline, a man with a deposit slip signed "J. J. Faulkner" turned in $2,980 of the Lindbergh ransom money at the Federal Reserve Bank of New York. The teller failed to check the bills against the master list.

Investigators looked into the history of the address on the deposit slip. A woman named Jane Faulkner had lived at the address—537 West 149th Street—in 1921. Because "only an absolute moron" would have given anything but an alias, the dead end did not surprise Special Agent Leon Turrou of the Bureau of Investigation's Lindbergh squad, which had little more than a few pins stuck in a map to show for all its efforts. "A better job of investigation, we sometimes thought, could have been done by a bright group of Dick Tracy Junior Detectives," Turrou would recall.[10]

A breakthrough in the case came after the New Jersey State Police sent fragments of wood removed from a wall of the Lindbergh house and from the kidnap ladder to the Forest Products Laboratory in Madison, Wisconsin. Founded in 1910, the laboratory was "an institution of industrial research of the Forest Service, an agency of the U.S. Department of Agriculture."[11] Arthur Koehler, the "No. 1 wood technologist in the government service,"[12] had written to Lindbergh after the kidnapping to offer his assistance.

During his two decades at the laboratory, Koehler had become an expert in wood science. In 1924, he published a textbook on the science called *The Properties and Uses of Wood*. Because of his expertise, he was called on to serve as an expert witness in criminal trials. His work had led to the conviction of the Yule Bomb Killer, John Magnuson. In 1922, Magnuson had fashioned a piece of wood into the hollow cylinder of a mail bomb mailed at Christmastime. Koehler's analysis proved that wood shavings from the killer's workshop had contained particles of elm of identical cell structure with those in the bomb fragments.

Colonel Schwarzkopf asked Koehler to conduct a study of the kidnap ladder. Koehler came to Trenton and returned to Madison with the ladder beside him in the aisle of a train. He disassembled it at the laboratory and numbered each piece of wood used in its construction. The rungs—ten of ponderosa pine, one of Douglas fir—showed no signs of wear which indicated that the ladder was undoubtedly made for the kidnapping job. Three of the rails were Southern Yellow pine, three of Douglas fir. The dowel rods used to connect the sections of the ladder were birch.

One particular piece of wood captured Koehler's attention. Four square nail holes driven through Rail 16 indicated its having served another purpose. The rail had no rust around the nail holes and showed no signs of having been weather-beaten. A piece of low-grade lumber that had been narrowed down from a wider board, the rail had been used for rough construction rather than for finish purposes. If a suspect were apprehended, Kochler advised, the police should search his attic and garage for clues.

Koehler observed that the two bottom rails bore distinctive power planer marks. A defective knife in the cutter head had made peculiar gouges on one edge of each of the rails. The recurrence of narrow cuts every 0.93 inches on the top and bottom of the pieces of wood and every 0.86 inches on their edges indicated the distance the lumber had passed through the planer per revolution of the respective cutter heads. Koehler's next challenge was to find the planer.

Having deduced that the Southern Yellow pine used in the production of the two rails had probably been milled somewhere along the Eastern seaboard, he wrote letters to 1,598 mill operators from New York to Alabama and asked whether they had a planer that matched his description. To increase his response rate, he indicated that the inquiry was in connection with a criminal case. Twenty-three operators replied in the affirmative. Koehler requested a sample one-by-four board from each. A lumber manufacturing plant in McCormick, South Carolina, the M. G. and J. J. Dorn Company, sent a board whose faces and edges bore the same planer spacings as the wood from the kidnap ladder. The Dorn customer list in hand, Koehler and a detective with the New Jersey State Police called on twenty-five lumberyards that might have taken delivery of the wood.

On November 29, 1933, they arrived at the National Millwork and Lumber Company in the Bronx. The search produced a one-by-four piece of pine with spacings and markings identical to those on the kidnap ladder. The company's customer list, Koehler concluded, would contain the name of the person who had built the kidnap ladder. But as usual, there was another obstacle. The store was a cash-and-carry business, maintaining no customer records at all.

# 17

# Capture

In 1991, Dr. Kim Rossmo, then a detective inspector with the Vancouver Police Department in British Columbia, Canada, developed the concept of geographic profiling, now an internationally used criminal investigative methodology. Geoprofiling analyzes the locations associated with a series of crimes to determine the most probable area of offender residence.[1] Now a professor at Texas State University, Dr. Rossmo applied his methodology to a cold case investigation of the Lindbergh kidnapping. He entered various locations connected to the crime into *Rigel*, a leading geoprofiling software system, which uses an algorithm to highlight areas where investigators could have focused their efforts. In addition to the locations of businesses (not banks) where six of the gold certificates surfaced, Dr. Rossmo inputted the addresses of the postal stations postmarked on the mailed ransom notes, the spot where taxi driver Joseph Perrone received a note of instructions to deliver to Condon, and St. Raymond's Cemetery, where Condon handed over the ransom money. All addresses were verified against a 1928 Rand McNally map of New York City.

The results show two peak areas where Dr. Rossmo would have advised investigators to concentrate their efforts. Both were in the same borough—one in the North Bronx, the other in the South Bronx. The Morrisania, Melrose, and Mott Haven neighborhoods in the South Bronx were known to have relatively large German populations and were clustered together. One of the area-based investigative strategies worth considering would have been the distribution, mailing, and posting of the

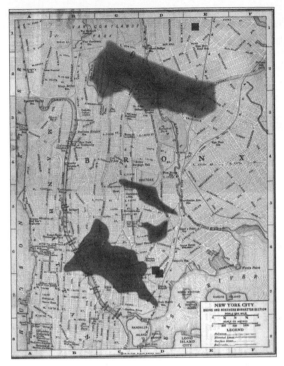

*The top geographic criminal profiler in the country, Dr. Kim Rossmo, ran this analysis of data points in the kidnapping. The results showed two peak area where the police would have been told to look for the kidnappers—one in the North Bronx, one in the South Bronx. The square in the North Bronx shows the location of Bruno Hauptmann's apartment. The two overlapping squares in the South Bronx represent the residence and workplace of John Knoll.*

description and police sketch of Cemetery John. The optimal approach would have involved "using the geoprofile, demographic data, land use characteristics, and proximity to Lexington Avenue line subway stations to create a final prioritization system."[2]

The presence of two high probability areas, Dr. Rossmo concludes, leads to three possibilities: (1) the offender recently moved; (2) the offender lived in one place and worked in another; or (3) more than one offender was involved in the crime. The third possibility provides a good operating assumption in the Lindbergh case: lookouts were seen at both of Condon's meetings with Cemetery John, and kidnappings often involve multiple offenders. Following this assumption, the geoprofile then suggests that one suspect likely resided in the North Bronx, the other in one of the German neighborhoods in the South Bronx.[3]

A friend of Dr. Rossmo uses an analogy to the game *Battleship* to describe geographic profiling: it's like being able to start the game having eliminated 90% of the squares where you know your opponent's battleship *isn't*. Geographic profiling would have drawn police attention into the general vicinity of both Bruno Hauptmann in the North Bronx and

John Knoll in the South Bronx. In the latter case, the posting of the police sketch of Cemetery John might have produced a suspect who bore
a much closer resemblance than Hauptmann to the drawing and who fit
every detail of Condon's description right down to the lump at the base
of his left thumb. Add in Knoll's handwriting that matched some of the
ransom envelopes, the evidence of sudden extra cash and attempts to
disguise his handwriting, a stamp collection to explain the unusual 10-cent
stamp on the package containing the baby's sleeping suit, and, as we will
see, a deli-clerk job to account for the stains of animal fats identified on
circulating ransom bills; with only these initial findings, the police would
surely have considered Knoll a person of interest. Investigators would
likely have put him under surveillance. What would have happened is a
matter of speculation, but it is certain that Knoll, by late 1934, had
enough money to afford first-class passage on a luxury liner back to Germany three and a half weeks before the man in the North Bronx, Bruno
Hauptmann, went on trial for murder.

As it is, sixty years before Dr. Rossmo began developing his concept
of geographic profiling, investigators of the kidnapping had to rely on
maps and pins. On the wall of his office in the Greenwich Street police
station, Lieutenant Jimmy Finn hung a large map of the five boroughs of
New York and used colored pins to designate where Lindbergh ransom
bills had surfaced. The detective began each day studying his map. In
Finn's pin scheme to indicate passed notes, black was for five-dollar
notes, red for ten-dollar notes, and a single green pin for the lone twenty-
dollar note recovered.

The authorities distributed 250,000 copies of the Treasury's ransom-
money circular during the first six months after the ransom was paid. Reading the booklet's tiny print was difficult both for bank tellers and retailers.
Yet by late 1933, a little more than a year and a half after the crime, Lieutenant Finn's map was covered with pins. Many were clustered along the
subway and streetcar routes in the northeast sector of the City along Lexington and Third Avenues in Upper Manhattan, in Yorkville, a district with
a high concentration of German immigrants, and in the Bronx.

The subway lines in the northeast sector of Manhattan and along
north-and-south-running Lexington and Third Avenues in Upper Manhattan offer convenient access from the Bronx. The Lexington Avenue

line has stops in Upper Manhattan at 125th, 116th, 110th, 103rd, and 96th Streets. Coming from the Bronx, the first stop in Manhattan after the subway tunnels underneath the Harlem River is 125th Street Station. Whoever had mailed the ransom note postmarked March 4, 1932, had likely ridden the Lexington Avenue line to Borough Hall Station in Brooklyn. It appears that the subway system—and the Lexington Avenue line in particular—were in his "comfort zone," in the vernacular of criminal profilers today.

Lieutenant Finn considered a reporter's suggestion that auto license applications bearing German-sounding names and Bronx addresses might include Cemetery John's or those of his accomplices. An investigator with the Treasury Department came up with the same concept, but his Special Intelligence Unit lacked the power to make the check; this was a job for the police. Finn approached his colleagues and described the strategy of wading through the New York Traffic License Bureau files at the Bronx County Courthouse. The idea was bandied about but withered on the vine; as the detectives figured, an application form contained too little information to make it worth the department's while to try to find a match.

On November 1, 1933, J. Edgar Hoover issued a statement that his organization had taken over all Federal aspects of the case. Meanwhile, Lieutenant Finn wrote to the major oil companies and asked them to provide their area gas stations with copies of the ransom-money circular and to be on the lookout for any customer paying either with a ten- or twenty-dollar gold note or with a twenty-dollar Federal Reserve note. He requested that employees write the license plate number of the suspect on the back of any such bill, then notify the New York City police immediately if the serial number appeared on the master list.

According to a Bureau of Investigation report, "a number of the ransom bills which turned up in November and December, 1933, apparently bore grease marks." Dr. Alexander O. Gettler, Chief Medical Examiner of Bellevue Hospital in New York City and a renowned toxicologist, conducted a chemical analysis of the bespattered bills. "The chemical analysis of the stains removed from the three bills which you submitted to me indicate that the stains are mainly of animal or vegetable fat," reported Dr. Gettler. "The consistency of the purified material indicates that it is composed of glycerine asters of the saturated fatty acids."[4]

Three ransom bills were passed at the United Cigar Stores chain: one in Queens on October 27, 1932; and two in Manhattan on December 21, 1932, and on March 1, 1933. On February 14, 1934, two men with German accents came to the Cross, Ireland and Austin Lumber Company in the South Bronx. The business was several blocks south of the 700 block of Jackson Avenue. The men selected a forty-cent piece of plywood and ordered it cut to size. One of them tried to pay with a ten-dollar gold certificate. The cashier, recognizing the bill as illegal, called for the foreman, whereupon the man snatched it away. As the men drove off, she jotted down their license plate number. Investigators would later determine that the vehicle was registered to Bruno Richard Hauptmann.

Six months later, as John Condon glanced out the window of a bus, he saw a man who resembled Cemetery John walking at the corner of Willamsbridge Road and Pelham Parkway in the Bronx. Condon leapt to his feet. "I am Jafsie!" he shouted. "Stop the bus!" By the time the driver could let him off, however, the man had disappeared.

On September 5, the National Bank of Yorkville in Manhattan alerted Finn to its receipt of a Lindbergh ransom bill. In the day's deposit was a ten-dollar gold note from a local grocer. The merchant told investigators that a man had given him the bill for a six-cent purchase of a few vegetables.

Three days later, the Chase National Bank on East Fordham Avenue in the Bronx reported that more Lindbergh money had turned up—a twenty-dollar gold note. The police traced the bill to a nearby shoe store. The clerk said that a man had given him the note the day before to pay for a pair of women's black suede shoes. A police briefing on the tenth of September revealed that several Lindbergh ransom bills had recently been recovered, and the press complied with a request to withhold the story until the authorities could make an arrest. With their supply of five-dollar notes depleted, the kidnappers were beginning to use more ten- and twenty-dollar notes.

At 10 a.m. on Saturday, September 15, 1934, a dark blue 1930 Dodge sedan with light blue striping and wire wheels pulled into the Warner-

Quinlan gas station at the corner of 127th Street and Lexington Avenue in Upper Manhattan. Walter Lyle, the manager of the station, and John Lyons, his assistant, stepped up to the pump.

"Fill her up, sir?" Lyle asked.

"No," said the man in a German accent. "Just five gallons of ethyl."

Lyons cleaned the windshield and checked the radiator while his boss pumped in the fuel.

"That's ninety-eight cents," Lyle said.

The man behind the wheel took out a ten-dollar gold certificate from an envelope in his inside coat pocket and handed it to the attendant. Lyle peered at the bill doubtfully. Warner-Quinlan had instructed its employees to be careful about accepting gold notes.

"They're all right," said the customer. "Any bank will take them."

"You don't see many of them anymore," Lyle said.

"No. I only got a hundred more left at home."[5]

As the customer drove off, Lyle penciled 4U13-41 N.Y. on the left margin of the back of the bill. After a passer of a phony bill had caused him to lose a third of his salary, he had resolved to record the license plate number of anyone who paid with "a bill bigger than a lousy five-spot."[6]

For two and a half years, Walter Winchell, thirty-seven, had been keeping America up-to-date on the Lindbergh case. By one estimate, two-thirds of the nation's 75 million adults either read the former vaude-villian's syndicated gossip column or tuned in to his Sunday night radio show. The sound of a telegraph key accompanied the "machine-gun-burst delivery" of the "Voice of America" as the sixth-grade dropout expounded on the news in his "rapid-fire, staccato way of speaking." "Good evening, Mr. and Mrs. America, and all the ships at sea," he would greet his audience.[7]

During his broadcast on September 16, Winchell groused that the kidnappers would have been caught long ago if the bank tellers responsible for scrutinizing gold certificates "weren't such a bunch of saps and yaps." He echoed the charge in his newspaper column. The authorities feared that the publicity might jeopardize their investigation. The next day, a customer of the Corn Exchange Bank brought a clipping of the *Daily Mirror* column into the Mount Morris branch at 85 E.

125th Street and showed it to teller William R. Strong. "Winchell says you're a sap," said the customer. "All bank tellers are, for not catching the passers!"

Strong, who also had read the column, had already determined to inspect the serial numbers of all 5's, 10's, and 20's more closely. The following morning, he sifted through a stack of checking deposits and came across two gold certificates. The serial number of the second note—A73976634A—matched that of one of the bills listed on the Lindbergh circular. Strong reported his discovery to his assistant manager, who telephoned the New York office of the Justice Department's Division of Investigation, as J. Edgar Hoover's organization had been renamed. Special Agent Thomas H. Sisk, the head of the Lindbergh squad, took the call and assigned Special Agent William F. Seery, a fourteen-year veteran of the division, to run down the lead.

For Seery, eighteen months of following up on ransom bill reports had seemed like trying to grab a ghost. Even earlier that day, at the Irving Trust Company, he had checked two gold notes that were untraceable. Seery arranged to meet Lieutenant Finn of the New York Police Department and Detective Corporal William Horn of the New Jersey State Police at the bank.

Strong greeted the three detectives and produced the bill. Horn observed the penciled notation in the margin. Finn requested to speak to the teller who had received the bill. The teller could not remember the customer who had given it to him but retrieved the day's deposit slips, which included three from filling stations. Finn recorded the names and addresses of each and left with Seery and Horn. The first stop was the Warner-Quinlan station, four blocks away. Finn fed Lyle "the usual story about counterfeit passers"[8] and pointed to the license plate number scribbled on the back of the bill. Lyle identified the handwriting as his own and described the customer's boast about possessing a hundred more gold certificates at home.

The investigators rushed back to the bank, where Finn called his friend Gus Reich at the New York Motor Vehicle Bureau and asked him to look up the license plate number. Moments after Reich put down the receiver, he came back on the line with information from the vehicle's registration card: the owner was Bruno Richard Hauptmann, a German-

born carpenter who lived at 1279 East 222nd Street in the Bronx. Hauptmann stood five-feet-ten and weighed 180 pounds.

Hauptmann lived in a five-room, fifty-dollar-a-month apartment with
his wife of nearly nine years, Anna, and their infant son, Manfred, whom
they called Bubi. After leaving Germany and settling in New York in
1924, Anna had landed a job cleaning the house of a Jewish family. An afi-
cionado of amusement parks, Hauptmann had taken her to Coney
Island during their short courtship. When Anna married her husband,
she did not know that his first name was Bruno.

The Hauptmanns' apartment was on the second floor of a two-story
frame-and-stucco bungalow. The home sat on a tiny corner lot at East
222nd Street and Needham Avenue in the northeast section of the
Bronx, one of the least densely populated districts in the borough. The
area was heavily wooded, and Needham Avenue was a narrow dirt road.
Hauptmann also maintained the exclusive use of a small frame garage
he had built on a lot owned by his landlord directly across Needham Avenue. According to neighbors, Hauptmann had erected the structure "a
few months after the kidnapping."[9]

Wanting to avert a shoot-out, Lieutenant Finn decided to arrest
Hauptmann outside his ordinary milieu—away from his family and
apartment—and ordered a stakeout. Finn deduced that the suspect
would be on the constant lookout for opportunities to exchange ransom
bills and would have one on hand, providing sufficient evidence for his
arrest. A dozen men in plain clothes converged on the home that night
and hid in and among the trees and tall brush. The arresting force parked
three black Ford sedans out of sight from the house. The plan was for
Finn, Special Agent Seery, and Detective Corporal Horn to ride in one
car; Lieutenant Buster Keaten of the New Jersey State Police, Special
Agent Thomas Sisk of Hoover's Lindbergh squad, and Detective Chester
Cronin in another; and Detective William Wallace, Detective Sergeant
John Wallace, and Trooper Dennis Duerr in a third. The remaining men
would keep vigil on the apartment.

As Finn sat in wait through the night, he had reason to brood on his
resentment of the New Jersey State Police for not being more forthcoming with information once the kidnappers had begun mailing ransom notes from New York and started spending ransom bills there. He

had taken a long, circuitous route to this nondescript, out-of-the-way frame house in the Bronx. For years, departmental politics at the Detective Bureau had spun him through a revolving door of demotions and reinstatements. During the previous two and a half years, his team of investigators had covered hundreds of thousands of miles in the manhunt. And now, his dream of making an arrest in the Lindbergh case—a watershed in his life—was so close it must have seemed impossible that it would not come true.

At five minutes to nine the next morning, a man emerged from the house, unlocked the garage, and drew open its windowed double doors. Finn trained his binoculars on a dark blue Dodge sedan as it rolled back into the driveway and came to a stop. Originally dark green, the car had been repainted after the kidnapping. The investigator tightened his focus on the black and yellow license plate: 4U13-41 N.Y. The man got out, locked the garage, stepped back into his vehicle, and headed west on East 222nd Street. For nearly twenty-five minutes, the caravan, spaced well apart to avoid raising the target's suspicion, trailed him until he reached the Fordham section of the Bronx. "We hadn't counted on the terrific speed he so rapidly picked up," Finn would recount. "The chase became wilder than expected. We had to do better than fifty to close up behind him."[10]

Detective William Wallace observed that a municipal sprinkler truck had blocked the Dodge as it approached East Tremont Avenue. Fearing the possibility of losing his man in the heavy cross-traffic, Wallace sped up, then slammed the brake to the floor and screeched to a halt alongside Hauptmann's automobile. With the suspect boxed in, Trooper Dennis Duerr jumped out of the front seat brandishing a pistol and shouted at him to pull over to the curb. Detective Sergeant John Wallace of the New Jersey State Police yanked open the right front door of the Dodge, slid into the passenger seat, and poked a gun into the driver's ribs. The detective seized Hauptmann's wrist, led him onto the sidewalk, and handcuffed him.

"What is this?" asked Hauptmann. "What is this all about?"

The eight men in on the arrest wouldn't say a word—instead they gaped as Lieutenant Keaten frisked Hauptmann and pulled a wallet out of his left hip pocket. Within seconds Keaten was clutching a twenty-dollar gold certificate. A quick check and yes—the serial number appeared on the Lindbergh master list. At this point the men began firing questions at the suspect: Where did you get this bill? How long have you had it?

Hauptmann explained that he had saved three hundred dollars in gold notes out of fear of the kind of runaway inflation he had witnessed in Germany. After he had realized that his worries were unwarranted, he began spending the money. This twenty-dollar bill was his last. Why, then, had he told the attendants at the Warner-Quinlan service station that he still had a hundred of them? Was that a lie, or was he lying now? Trapped, Hauptmann admitted that he still had a hundred of the notes in a tin box back at his residence. With that, the detectives shoved him into the back seat of a police car and sped back to his apartment.

# 18

# Interrogation

The police streamed into the Hauptmanns' apartment and searched the premises. The family's furniture, including a top-of-the-line Stromberg-Carlson radio, a walnut bedroom suite, and an ivory crib, seemed inconsistent with the modest exterior of the home. The radio cost four hundred dollars —the equivalent of nine months' rent for my grandparents' apartment on Jackson Avenue. The investigators began shoving furniture around, dumping out drawers, and heaping up the spoils of the search on the floor.

Finn ordered Hauptmann to produce the tin box with the money. The suspect opened a metal box with a combination lock and pointed to six twenty-dollar gold pieces. "There is the hundred or so," he said.

"No, no," said Sisk. "We want to see the gold certificates, just like the twenty-dollar gold note in your wallet. You bragged to the men at the gas station that you had a hundred of them at home. Where are they?"

"Gold is gold," Hauptmann said.

One of the men gave him a shove, and Hauptmann sat down on his bed. The questioning continued: "You extorted the bills from Charles Lindbergh, didn't you? Weren't the notes part of the ransom he had paid, thinking his baby would be soon returned to him and his heartsick wife?"

"I know nothing of the ransom payment."

Special Agent Seery walked into the bedroom and held up Anna's new black suede shoes, grabbed out of the closet. "Didn't you just purchase these shoes a week and a half ago with a twenty-dollar gold certificate?"

"Yes," Hauptmann nodded.

At this point Seery produced the ten-dollar gold note the suspect had used four days earlier to buy gasoline at the Warner-Quinlan station. "How is it that these two notes and the one we found in your wallet are all Lindbergh ransom bills?"

Hauptmann, floundering for something to say, contrived something about how the bills had come from many banks and stores. Maybe, he suggested, the people there could provide an explanation. After a while, a man in plain clothes ushered Anna Hauptmann into the apartment. Oblivious to the commotion inside, she had been in the backyard hanging her wash on the clothesline. Anna walked into her bedroom and saw her husband in handcuffs. "Richard, what is this?" she asked. There was no answer.

"Never mind," said one of the investigators. "You'll find out pretty soon."

"Richard, did you do anything wrong?" she asked.

"No, Anna."

"Tell me! Tell me if you did anything wrong!"

"Take that woman outside!" one of the detectives shouted.[1]

By this time, the men had found letters, lottery tickets, a hunting rifle, photographs of the Hauptmanns at parties and picnics, and several maps, including one of New Jersey. Downstairs, the police were interviewing Pauline Rauch, the elderly mother of Hauptmann's landlord. Eager to assist in the investigation, she fetched two gold certificates that her "sometimes abusive" tenant had used to pay the rent. Mrs. Rauch, a Jewish immigrant from Austria who had once called Hauptmann a Nazi to his face,[2] would describe the rancor that existed between them and would recount his complaints. "I don't give him enough steam," she said in a filmed interview. "I don't give him hot water."[3]

The search also produced a pair of Zeiss field glasses. Assuming that the suspect had spied through the expensive German-made binoculars into the Lindberghs' home, an investigator asked how he had used them. "I am a lover of nature," said Hauptmann, trying a long shot.

Instructed to get up, he walked over to a straight-backed chair by a bedroom window and sat down. The investigators hurled the blankets and sheets onto the floor and slashed open the mattress. Hauptmann sat expressionless as stuffing flew about the room. Then he threw a furtive glance out the window.

Out of the corner of his eye Sisk was watching the suspect. "What are you looking at?"

"Nothing."

Sisk went to the window. The only thing in view was the unpainted garage across the dirt road. "Is that where you have the money?"

"No," said Hauptmann. "I have no money."

Sisk called over two other men and described Hauptmann's suspicious look out the window. The detectives went outside and forced open the garage. Heavy eight-inch-wide planks splattered with oil covered the floor. The men pried up a couple of wobbly planks with a crowbar and spaded into the dirt below. A foot below the surface they hit a heavy metal jar. The men pulled off the lid and examined its contents: a few inches of water.

Anna Hauptmann stood on the front lawn clutching her baby as detectives came and went out of her apartment. Her husband had assured her he had done nothing wrong. Why, then, had the police arrested him and turned their home upside-down? Despite frantic pleadings for an explanation, her words hung in the air unanswered. At 12:30 p.m., two officers escorted Hauptmann down the front steps and put him into the back seat of a police car at the curb. Dumbstruck, Anna stared hollow-eyed at the departing taillights and watched the car disappear. She begged the detectives to tell her where her husband was being taken. "To the Greenwich Street police station in Manhattan," one of the men said.

The ride came to an end at the remote 2nd Precinct police station, a block away from the Hudson Street elevated tracks. The first kidnapping suspect ever caught because of the money he had spent, Hauptmann walked inside handcuffed to Captain John J. Lamb of the New Jersey State Police. As soon as word leaked out that the police had made an arrest in the Lindbergh case, a crowd formed outside the station house and packed its entrances on Greenwich and Washington Streets.

At 2:30 p.m., a group of detectives ushered Anna Hauptmann into an interrogation room in the station. In no time, they were grilling her: with her husband unemployed, where had he obtained the money to buy expensive furniture? They were savers, she explained, and her husband had made money on Wall Street. Did she not know that the cash he had been spending had come from the Lindbergh ransom? And that he had kidnapped the baby and extorted fifty thousand dollars from his father? In fact, her husband had been arrested with one of the ransom bills in his wallet.

Anna stammered and sobbed. Richard could not have done such a terrible thing. He was a loving husband and father—and they had a little boy of their own! Concluding that she knew nothing of the kidnapping plot, the police released her but told her to be ready for further questioning. A mob of nearly a thousand had formed outside the station. "Kill her!" someone shouted as she walked out of the building flanked by two detectives. Her apartment in shambles, Anna went to stay at the Bronx residence of her niece, Maria Mueller, and left Bubi in her care. To forestall the annoyance that the arrest might cause other tenants, the superintendent removed the Muellers' nameplate next to their unit's doorbell.

The search for clues inside the Hauptmanns' apartment intensified. The most crucial evidence was the ransom money, but the detectives also scoured each room for samples of Hauptmann's handwriting, paper and envelopes matching the ransom letters, and devices he might have used to create the signature-symbol at the bottom of each note. Investigators discovered a notebook that contained a penciled sketch of a ladder resembling the one abandoned at the crime scene. They also located Hauptmann's tool set, which was missing the standard three-quarter-inch chisel, a match to the one found near the ladder.

At the beginning, the accusation leveled against Hauptmann was extortion, but the hook needed on which to hang the charge—a large chunk of the ransom money—had yet to be found. Now the investigators were holding him responsible for the kidnap and murder of the Lindbergh baby. The case would have been easy to prove had Hauptmann's fingerprints matched those found in the nursery. The police, however, had discovered no fingerprints in the room, which appeared to the fingerprint specialist to have been wiped down.

The detectives asked if Hauptmann could provide alibis for three critical dates: March 1, 1932, the night of the kidnapping; April 2, 1932, the night that Cemetery John collected the $50,000 ransom at St. Raymond's Cemetery; and November 26, 1933, when a cashier at the Sheridan Square Theatre in Manhattan accepted a five-dollar ransom bill from a fidgety movie patron who had bought a ticket to a gangster film.

The police took Hauptmann to an interrogation room and sat him down in a wooden armchair. Over and over, he denied having any knowledge of the kidnapping. Hadn't he been near Hopewell, New Jersey, on the night of March 1, 1932? No, he was unfamiliar with Hopewell until news broke regarding the crime.

Hadn't he been inside the Lindbergh home while it was under construction to see how it was laid out? No, he had never even been on the property.

Why was he lying? On the night of March first, hadn't he been in the nursery? And taken the baby out of his crib? No. He had never seen the Lindbergh baby in his life.

He had heard of St. Raymond's Cemetery in the Bronx, of course? Sure, he knew where it was, but he had never been inside it.

And wasn't he familiar with Dr. John Condon? He knew who he was —as did most everyone in the Bronx. But he had never seen or met him.

Hadn't he gone to St. Raymond's Cemetery on the night of April 2, 1932, for the purpose of collecting the ransom payment from Dr. Condon? No, absolutely not.

Hadn't he written fourteen ransom notes to extort $50,000 from Charles Lindbergh? And isn't he the man who had called himself *John* in that first meeting with Dr. Condon? No, no, you have the wrong man!

Hadn't he gone to the Sheridan Square Theatre right here in Greenwich Village and paid for his ticket with a Lindbergh ransom bill? No. In fact, this trip to the police station was his first ever to Greenwich Village.

Was he sure? It was November 26, 1933. Wait, that was his birthday! His wife and a couple of friends had held a party for him that Sunday evening in their home.

At one o'clock in the morning, investigators forced Hauptmann to undergo a handwriting examination. Famished, exhausted, and sleep-starved from the marathon interview, and with no attorney present, the prisoner complied. Eager to submit the handwriting samples, Hauptmann furnished samples of his printing and his cursive. "I would be glad to write, because it will get me out of this thing," he said to Sergeant Thomas J. Ritchie.[4]

The Lindberghs were staying at the California ranch of their friends Will and Betty Blake Rogers at the time of Hauptmann's arrest. Quiet, private, and protected, the 300-acre ranch overlooked the Pacific Ocean and Santa Monica Bay and sat in the Santa Monica hills far out on a mesa above Sunset Boulevard.[5] Anne's sister Elisabeth and her husband of nearly two years, Aubrey Morgan, were also enjoying the refuge of the picturesque hideaway. Poor health, mainly chronic heart disease, had troubled Elisabeth for much of her adult life. Less than three months later, she would die at age thirty.

"Oh, God, it's starting all over again," said Anne after Colonel Schwarzkopf had called to inform them of the break in the case.

"Yes," said Charles, "but they've got him at last."[6]

For Charles Lindbergh, the nightmare that had begun thirty months earlier needed to come to an end. From her published diaries and letters, we know much about the emotional impact of the kidnapping on his wife.[7] Yet with "the extraordinary ability to hide his emotions" that he had inherited from his father, the impact of the tragedy on Lindbergh himself is harder to judge.[8] He was willing to meet personally with the kidnappers and thereby risk his life to save his son. As Dr. Mary Ellen O'Toole observes, Lindbergh internalized his grief and had no reprieve. He dealt with the sorrow in his own way, never talking about it. For parents of murdered children, Dr. O'Toole has found, there is *never* closure; in her work on child abduction and murder cases, one of the hardest things, she says, is telling parents that they will never get over their loss. Nor do parents even seek closure—they seek meaning.[9]

Forced to cut short their vacation by the news of Hauptmann's arrest, the Lindberghs flew back to New York, where Charles would have to face the suspect. Wanting to remain in seclusion, the couple retreated to Next Day Hill and refused to speak to the press.

"Things have been happening so fast, it is hard to keep up with them," Anne wrote her mother-in-law. "This is just a note at midnight to tell you that this man you read about in the papers is beyond doubt one of the right people."[10]

Harold Nicolson, a British author and diplomat who was conducting research for a biography on Dwight Morrow, was also staying at the Englewood mansion. Nicolson tried to make friends with the Lindberghs' German shepherd. Thor, he would recall, responded with "a deep pectoral regurgitation—predatory, savage, hungry"—the kind of noise "such as only tigers make when waiting for their food."

"You must be careful not to pass him," said Lindbergh. "He might get hold of you."

"By the throat?" Nicolson asked.

"Not necessarily," said Lindbergh with a straight face. "If he does that, you must stay still and holler all you can."

"By the time you get this," Nicolson wrote his wife, "I shall either be front page news, or Thor's chum."

Nicolson wrote in his diary that although the page one newspaper articles on the kidnapping seemed impossible to ignore, Lindbergh "never glances at them and chatters quite happily to me about Roosevelt and the air-mail contracts." It was the aviator's habit, the writer surmised, to ignore publicity. Sympathetic to the family's loss, Nicolson believed that the best course of action lay in "manifesting no curiosity" about the murdered child. But when he took up the newspaper each morning and found nothing but stories about the Lindbergh case, the author was hesitant to speak at the breakfast table.

"Things seem to be getting rather dangerous in Spain," he blurted out one morning.[11]

# 19

## "Not the Man"

Colonel Schwarzkopf described the evidence implicating Hauptmann to the Lindberghs. Because of the presence of a lookout at both Bronx cemeteries and the near logistical impossibility that one person acting alone could have carried out the crime, the police had from the outset referred to whoever was responsible for the kidnapping as a gang. And Schwarzkopf himself had concluded that the crime was the work of a team of amateurs. More than two and a half years after the kidnapping, with a suspect in custody at last, the entire focus of the authorities shifted to pinning the crime on the one man they had.

The morning after Hauptmann's arrest, a new group of federal agents and police investigators dismantled his garage. A detective with the New York Police Department removed a board nailed to two joists above the workbench and discovered two packets of ten-dollar gold notes wrapped in newspaper. The packets contained 183 Lindbergh ransom bills. Fearing the money would be inadmissible as evidence without a member of the household present, the men returned the bills to their secret hiding place, then "rediscovered" them in front of Anna Hauptmann. In an interview with the *New York Times*, Detective Sergeant John Wallace of the New Jersey State Police implied that the investigators had first discovered the bills in her presence.[1]

The detectives found a can of shellac on a hidden shelf behind a plank of wood. Inside, beneath some rags, were twelve packages of gold certificates—another $11,930 in ransom money. Also concealed was a loaded pistol. Shortly afterward the interrogators in Manhattan asked Hauptmann if he had stashed away any more gold notes. No, he told them three times. Then Wallace informed him of the discovery.

Caught in another lie, Hauptmann searched his mind for an explanation. Suddenly, the story came back to him in a flash of clear vision: his friend and former business partner, Isador Fisch, had given him several articles for safekeeping the previous December before he sailed home to visit his parents in Leipzig. Hauptmann had placed a shoebox Fisch had given him on the top shelf of a broom closet. After a leak in the ceiling had soaked the contents of the closet, he opened the box and, to his astonishment, discovered it full of gold notes. Because Fisch had owed him seven thousand dollars, he felt entitled to spend that amount. Circumstances did not allow his friend to corroborate what became known as "the Fisch story"; he had died six months earlier in a tuberculosis sanitarium. His family would inform the police that Isador had returned to Germany destitute. The Division of Investigation ascertained that in the spring of 1933, Fisch "was sleeping on park benches in New York City."[2] It is clear, moreover, that Fisch, a tiny, frail man, could not have been Cemetery John.

Hauptmann told the police that he had worked on a construction crew at the Majestic Apartments in Manhattan beginning on March 1, 1932, the date of the kidnapping. A follow-up on the statement revealed that March 21 had been his first day on the job. Was it a matter of coincidence that he had quit on the second of April, just hours before Condon handed over the ransom money?

As the interrogation continued, Joseph Perrone arrived at the police station. Over the previous two years, the nearsighted Bronx cab driver had identified several different men as the one who had hired him to deliver the kidnappers' note of instructions to Condon.

"Now Joe, we've got the right man at last," said Inspector John A. Lyons. "There isn't a man in this room who isn't convinced he is the man who kidnapped the Lindbergh baby."

At this point Hauptmann and two muscular police officers entered the room. Lyons asked if Perrone recognized the man who had flagged him down at 8:30 p.m. on March 12, 1932. The cab driver walked up to Hauptmann and rested his hand on the suspect's shoulder. "Yes," said Perrone. "That's the man." According to Special Agent Thomas Sisk, Lyons "practically coerced Perrone into identifying Hauptmann."

Meanwhile, a crowd of curiosity seekers descended on Hauptmann's residence and trampled his lawn. Scavengers rummaged through piles of junk tossed out by investigators in the hunt for evidence. "Two men always seemed to be working in the garage, and we never went near it,"[3] two children told a reporter from the *New York Daily News*.[4]

The suspect told the police that he had a clean record in his homeland. A check with German authorities uncovered, however, that he had spent four years in prison on charges of grand larceny and armed robbery. From the moment of his arrest, Hauptmann struggled to lie his way out of the growing mountain of evidence against him. With every new untruth they heard, the investigators became more certain of his guilt. The twenty-dollar gold certificate in his wallet was his last; after having bragged about possessing a hundred gold notes at home, he feigned confusion about the difference between gold notes and gold coins; when asked what he was looking at as he glanced at the garage containing the hidden ransom money, he said, "Nothing"; he said that he had not stashed away any more gold certificates; and now he claimed to have had no criminal record in Germany.

"Almost always [Hauptmann's] crimes revealed a lack of imagination," the *Detroit Evening Times* reported. Hauptmann had not worked alone in his previous crimes. In one episode, he and another confederate broke into the home of the mayor of Bernbruch by way of a ladder, a crime from which Hauptmann seized the larger share of the spoils. In another, he and a comrade smashed open a window of a neighbor's home and escaped with two hundred marks and a pocket watch. Seconded by an accomplice, Hauptmann aimed a pistol at two women pushing baby carriages and stole nine bread rolls and eight precious foodstuffs cards.

After his release, the police rearrested Hauptmann for a series of burglaries. This time, he escaped from prison. On the run, he failed twice to reach the United States as a stowaway on the SS *George Washington*. On his third try, on November 26, 1923, his twenty-fourth birthday, he succeeded and ambled down the gangplank of the SS *Hannover* with a fistful of forged papers—and began his pursuit of the American dream.

The police picked up John Condon in the Bronx and drove him to the 2nd Precinct police station. Condon arrived shortly after five o'clock and pushed his way through bystanders swarming about the entrance. "Jaf-SIE! Jaf-SIE! Jaf-SIE!" chanted the crowd. Condon ignored the attention as a pair of detectives escorted him inside, where reporters and cameramen were jamming the aisles and stairway. Escorted into a small anteroom on the first floor, he waited with Special Agent Leon Turrou of the Division of Investigation as the police prepared a lineup upstairs.

"If he's the fellow I met I'll know him. If I live a million years I'll know him," said Condon. Then, after a pause: "Now look here, describe this suspect you've got."[5]

Taken aback, Turrou explained that the purpose of a police lineup is to enable the witness to identify the criminal by himself.

"That's nothing but a fool notion," Condon said.

The lineup included a dozen policemen, all husky six-footers. Turrou would later recall that the suspect looked like "a midget who had wandered through a Turkish bath for two sleepless days and nights."[6]

J. Edgar Hoover, who had rushed up from Washington, said that the flimsy kidnap ladder probably could not have supported Hauptmann. Hoover added that it wouldn't be long before Hauptmann's accomplices were apprehended.

Inspector Lyons explained to Condon that the suspect was in the lineup. If Condon recognized the man whom he had met at the two Bronx cemeteries, he was to walk up to him and tap his shoulder. The assumption that he would point automatically in Hauptmann's direction infuriated Condon, who would grumble afterward that none of the policemen could have remotely been confused with Cemetery John.

"Ten-hut!" Condon barked out.

The policemen snapped to attention. Hauptmann, however, remained stoop-shouldered and spiritless, a picture of utter misery. Condon put the men through a series of drill maneuvers, left flanking and right flanking, until Inspector Lyons intervened: "Enough!"

"Can I eliminate several men?" Condon asked.

After he had selected Hauptmann and three of the officers, his mind drifted back to his long conversation with John on the park bench; he remembered the lump he had seen at the base of John's left thumb. Condon asked the four men to hold up their palms and inspected their thumbs. None had such a lump on either hand. In addition to the lump at the base of Cemetery John's left thumb, a "pointed chin" is a prominent feature of the description Condon had given the authorities. Hauptmann's chin was rounded. Yet like Cemetery John, Hauptmann had a high forehead and large ears, giving the two some degree of physical similarity—enough to cause Condon to speculate that they might have been brothers.

Condon turned to the suspect. "Did you ever see me before?"

"No, I never saw you before," Hauptmann said.

"How long have you lived in the Bronx?"

"Nine years."

"Nine years up there," said Condon. "You don't know me?" He was incredulous that a resident of the borough could be unfamiliar with him.

"We're tired," said Lyons, resting a hand on Condon's shoulder. "We want to go home and sleep. We deserve it. Now, do you know any of these men or don't you!"[7]

"I would not say he is the man," Condon said.

"You are not positive?"

"I am not positive."

Pressed again a few minutes later, Condon said, "[Hauptmann] is the one who would come nearer to answering the description than anybody I saw. You gave me no hint and I picked him out. He is a little heavier... I couldn't say he is not the man."

"But you cannot identify him?" Lyons asked.

"No, I have to be very careful. The man's life is in jeopardy."

After he had left the room, the detectives inside muttered and cursed.

"I won't identify him for those insolent morons!" Condon said.

"But have you seen him before, Doctor?" Turrou asked.

"No. He is not the man."

In a September 21, 1934, Bureau of Investigation memorandum, Turrou referred to Condon's statement that "Hauptmann appears to be much heavier, has different eyes, different hair, etc., and that he must be a brother of John." In another report dated October 5, 1934, Turrou would write that Condon complained that the police had attacked "his character, and particularly so since the time he failed to positively identify Hauptmann when confronted with him at the time of his arrest."[8]

Cameras clicked and flashbulbs popped as reporters swarmed around Condon. Voices begged for an answer: "Which one is John? Which one is John?" Meanwhile, the police transferred Hauptmann to another room and, according to one federal agent, "gave this fellow a real going over and punched him in the back and twisted his arms and legs and gave him

*This mug shot taken upon Hauptmann's arrest shows his rounded chin, not the pointed chin that Condon had earlier attributed to Cemetery John.*

hell."[9] Frustrated and irked by Condon's obstinacy, the police kept him at the station until midnight. "I guess you know that my life isn't worth five cents," he said. "Hauptmann's accomplices are going to kill me."

The September twenty-second edition of the *New York Daily News* reported that Condon had fielded questions about the lineup from his front porch. One journalist asked him whether Hauptmann was Cemetery John. "I can't talk. Really, I never said I was positive," said Condon. "All is in abeyance now. I did not identify Hauptmann. I didn't change my mind because it was never made up about him. I did say I'd know that voice anywhere—that's true. But I meant if I heard it under the same circumstances."

"Are you responsible for Hauptmann's arrest?"

"My, my, that's a mean one. That goes right into the roots of the case. Don't add to my conceit, please. I've worked two and a half years, day and night, on this, and it took all my courage. But conscience is above everything with me."[10]

Despite Condon's unwillingness to identify Hauptmann as Cemetery John, other evidence continued to mount against the suspect. Detectives found Condon's address written in pencil on the inside trim of one of Hauptmann's closets. Scribbled below the address was *SEDG 3-7154*, Condon's phone number before he changed it to a private listing. The police pried the door trim loose and showed it to the prisoner, who made no attempt to deny that the writing was his and offered a rather sheepish explanation: "I must have read it in the paper about the story. I was a little bit interest, and keep a little bit record of it and maybe I was just in the closet and was reading the paper and put down the address."[11]

Hauptmann's second-floor apartment led to the attic. A detective with the New Jersey State Police, Louis Bornmann, climbed into the attic through an opening in the ceiling of a linen closet. "Although the fact went unnoted at the time, the width of the kidnap ladder (14⅛") conformed to the irregular width of the opening of the door of this closet (14½")," said Kevin Klein, a New Jersey master carpenter who has built and performed stress tests on replicas of the kidnap ladder. "Also quite curious is the fact that the height of the ladder—6' 8¾"—was the same as that of the door opening. The ladder could have been used to get into the attic."[12]

One of the pine planks, Bornmann noticed, was eight feet shorter than the other boards. Wood scientist Arthur Koehler, carrying Rail 16 of the kidnap ladder, also went into the attic. The holes in the rail, he observed, lined up precisely with the vacant nail holes in the floor joist beneath. One of the nail holes in the rail slanted, and the corresponding nail hole in the joist had the same slant. On further study of wood patterns and other features of Rail 16, he concluded that someone had sawed off the board used to make the rail from a larger one in the attic. He had indicated in an early report that the rail had served some earlier purpose. A reticent, conscientious man described by colleagues as "flawless in his work," Koehler viewed his role as a reporter of facts—not as an interpreter of them.[13] To determine why an attic floorboard had been cut off and used—or whether or not Hauptmann had worked on the ladder in the attic—was not his concern. According to Klein, a shrewd student of the case, it appears that an electrician may have needed to saw off the board to lay electrical wire in a certain place in the attic. If so, he likely tossed the remnant onto a pile of scrap wood in the basement, where Hauptmann later found it.

The annual rings of the rail and board, Koehler would write, "were found to match perfectly as to width, prominence, and curvature." He also examined a hand plane found in Hauptmann's garage. The plane had nicks on the planing edge; as a result, when the plane was used, it left an irregular series of ridges on the planed surface. Testing revealed that the two edges of Rail 16 matched the pattern created by the plane.[14]

The analysis of the handwriting experts brought Hauptmann more bad news. Two months after the kidnapping, Albert S. Osborn had created a paragraph-long handwriting examination to identify the author of the ransom notes. Over a hundred suspects had taken the test since that time. Because the police did not want Hauptmann to be able to argue during a trial that he had not known what he was doing, an inspector informed him that he would be given a handwriting test to determine whether he had penned the ransom notes.

Exactly what happened during the test is unclear. What is clear, however, is that enough controversy surrounds the examination that the requested writings are not to be trusted. Those who administered the test may have dictated to Hauptmann how to spell particular words—or more accurately, how to misspell them as they had been misspelled in the ransom letters. By some accounts, Hauptmann was also ordered to copy or trace various words.

At first, Osborn and his son, Albert D. Osborn, noted much dissimilarity between Hauptmann's handwriting and the writing in the ransom notes. After the police informed the handwriting analysts of the discovery of ransom money in the suspect's garage, however, the Osborns realized they might look incompetent should they not tie Hauptmann to the ransom notes. Moreover, their firm, which would ultimately receive $11,100 in compensation for its services, would lose the lucrative, one-of-a-kind assignment and all the public relations exposure it would receive for its association with what would become known as the "Trial of the Century."[15] In a letter he would write to his mother, Hauptmann would describe the attitude of the handwriting analysts: "Whose bread I eat, his song I sing."[16]

Decades later, a colossal blunder of the younger Osborn would become famous. Having forged a set of documents he claimed Howard Hughes had written, author Clifford Irving used them as the basis for a biography on the reclusive business mogul. Engaged to analyze the documents, Osborn asserted that the writing was authentic.

As a film crew captured the moment, the elder Osborn read from a report: "I have examined a large number of writings by one Richard Hauptmann, including his automobile registration cards, and have compared this writing with the writing of the Lindbergh kidnapping notes, and in my opinion all of the kidnapping notes were written by Richard Hauptmann. I think the evidence is clear and unmistakable and sufficient in amount so that a most positive opinion can be given."[17]

# 20

# Homecoming

On September 26, 1934, Lindbergh testified before a grand jury at the Bronx County Courthouse. One juror asked whether he could identify the voice he had heard emanating from St. Raymond's Cemetery on the night of April 2, 1932—the voice that had called out to Dr. Condon. "I can't say positively," said Lindbergh. "It would be very difficult to sit here and say that I could pick a man by that voice . . . It undoubtedly was a very distinct foreign accent, the voice simply called to Dr. Condon, saying, 'hey doc' but there was a very distinct accent.

"Shortly after we first stopped the car out opposite the florist shop," Lindbergh went on, "a man walked by who I feel sure was one of the actual group of kidnappers or connected with them, he again came back on the opposite side of the street just before Dr. Condon returned after having paid the money."[1]

Hauptmann was indicted later that afternoon on extortion charges. Bail was set at $100,000. On recommendation of a friend Anna Hauptmann had hired James M. Fawcett, a lawyer with no experience in criminal cases, to defend her husband. The celebrated trial attorney Clarence Darrow told the press that he saw evidence to support Hauptmann's indictment for extortion, but none to implicate him in the murder of the Lindbergh baby.

The prisoner's fate rested in the result of a grand jury hearing on October 9, 1934, in the Hunterdon County Courthouse in Flemington, New Jersey. By terming the kidnapping a "burglary," the State could ask for the death penalty. Under New Jersey law, if a death occurred during the commission of a felony, the State could bring a charge of first-degree murder, punishable by death, even if the death resulted from an accident or by the hand of someone else. All the State needed to demonstrate was that Hauptmann had entered the Lindbergh home with the intent of "stealing the infant son in its clothing" and that the baby had died during the commission of the crime.

Dr. Charles H. Mitchell, the Mercer County physician who had performed the autopsy, testified that the child had died from a blow to the head. Hauptmann failed to prove in the hearing that he was not in New Jersey on the night of the kidnapping. The ransom note left in the nursery was a major setback for the defense; the Osborn father-and-son document examination team testified that Hauptmann had written the ransom letters, including the one left in the nursery.

A Sourland Mountains man named Millard Whited was eager to obtain reward and expense money. Whited testified that he had seen Hauptmann near the Lindbergh estate a week before the kidnapping. A Division of Investigation memo would characterize the witness as "a confirmed liar and totally unreliable."[2]

In Lindbergh's six minutes before the grand jury, he testified that his son had disappeared on the night of March 1, 1932, that he had identified his son's body in the morgue, and that the note left on the windowsill had in fact been a ransom letter. The wood expert from Wisconsin, Arthur Koehler, also appeared before the grand jurors to give testimony regarding the origin of the wood used to make the kidnap ladder.

Despite Fawcett's spirited fight to stave off his client's extradition to New Jersey, the testimony of the thirty-three witnesses heard by the grand jurors was too much to overcome. The foreman handed a bundle of papers to the clerk, and the State had its indictment. David T. Wilentz, thirty-nine, the Attorney General for the State of New Jersey, dismissed any consideration of searching for accomplices Hauptmann may have had in order that the trial might proceed in its simplest form. With the crime now construed for the first time as a "one-man job," Wilentz sought to convict Hauptmann of capital murder.

Late in the afternoon of October 19, 1934, the attorney general presented the sheriff with the court papers necessary to transfer the prisoner from the Bronx County Jail to Flemington. A few minutes before nine o'clock, a police car driven by Captain John J. Lamb of the New Jersey State Police and accompanied by a motorcycle escort reached the George Washington Bridge. In the distance to the south was Palisades Amusement Park, closed for the season. At 10:22 p.m., Hauptmann's ride came to an end. A crowd with lighted torches looked on as state troopers escorted the prisoner inside the Hunterdon County Jail.

The jail was a gray stone building with eighteen-inch-thick walls and green bars on the windows. During his escape from prison in Germany, Hauptmann had walked through an open gate and left his convict's uniform in a neat pile along with a note: "Best wishes to the police." As he examined his new quarters, however, he understood that the Flemington jail spelled the end of his game of escape: blowtorches, hacksaws, and drills would be useless in any attempt to breach the jail's case-hardened steel bars. Even Harry Houdini himself had turned down the opportunity to try to spring himself from one of the cells and win a $25,000 prize. Hauptmann refused the offer of any meal of his choice and looked about his cell, which measured six and a half by five feet and had a hole for a toilet. The naked light bulb suspended from the ceiling would burn twenty-four hours a day.

As Hauptmann sat in jail, Walter Knoll, John's twenty-five-year-old brother, was planning his wedding to Gladys Carmichael, a native New Yorker who lived in the Bronx and worked in the City as a stenographer. They would marry on June 22, 1935—what would have been the fifth birthday of Charlie Lindbergh. It was one of several happenings following Hauptmann's arrest when an odd confluence of events emerged in the Knoll family. At some point before the end of the year, John and his own new bride and second wife, the aviator Lilly, left New York. They moved in with his sister Agnes and her husband in Mt. Clemens, Michigan. The first of the three Knoll children to come to America, Agnes was known as the person in the family to go to in times of trouble. It's not known just how long he stayed, but it's quite likely that he saw picture postcards of Lindbergh in her home. She was, as her son Rudy remembered, a great admirer of the aviator.

Whatever John's difficulties were at the time, whatever his reasons for leaving the Bronx around the time of Hauptmann's arrest, they weren't financial hardships: he would soon head straight back to New

York City to board a luxury liner out of the country. Nor is it exactly clear when John moved out of the room he had been renting since 1926 from Emma Schaefer; all we know is that Emma had died at seventy-five in her apartment on the third of May. She had lived there with her daughter, Alice. Emma's son, Bill, forty-four, also had lived in the apartment from time to time. Twenty-two days after Emma's death, on May 25, 1934, the neighborhood learned that Bill had also died in that same apartment. My father recalled that the stated cause of death had seemed strange to him and to his parents: "acute indigestion."[3]

On October 2, 1934, less than two weeks after Hauptmann's arrest, the Knoll brothers' sister Elisabetha obtained a passport in Germany. A sister of the Dominican Order, Elisabetha, thirty-four, cast off from Hamburg on the *Bremen* and docked in New York on the twenty-sixth of the month. It appears to have been the first visit ever to the States for Elisabetha, who would live to age seventy-seven.[4] Also in October of 1934, the Knoll brother's sister Agnes, into whose Michigan home John and Lilly had moved, sailed from Germany to New York. As the Hauptmann trial approached, John Knoll purchased two first-class tickets for travel on the SS *Manhattan* from New York to Hamburg. Lilly obtained her passport on the fourteenth of November, less than a month before the voyage. Whether Knoll paid with gold notes is unknown. By then, however, any systematic search for the ransom money had ceased. John Douglas suggests that it's conceivable that a man with currency the police were looking for might think to convert it into German marks and then back again into U.S. dollars before returning to America, essentially dumping the ransom money in Europe.[5]

On December eighth, John and Lilly attended the *Manhattan's* Saturday evening gala dinner. As bright balloons rested on tables set with fine china and draped in white linen, a corps of waiters in tuxedos catered to the wishes of bankers, industrialists, and other first-class travelers whose fortunes allowed such indulgence five years into the Depression. A photographer making his rounds snapped a picture, capturing a souvenir for the Knolls. For most couples of their social status, traveling to Europe on a luxury steamship would have been unimaginable in such perilous economic times. Before his marriage to Lilly, John had been paying Emma Schaefer ten dollars a month for his rented room in the South Bronx. The cost of a pair of roundtrip tickets to Germany? Nearly seven hundred dollars.

*John and Lilly Knoll (seated in the back left) at the gala dinner aboard the SS Manhattan.*

Billed as the "Largest Ship Ever Built in America," the *Manhattan*, whose orchestral program included such numbers as *The Washington Post March* and *The Champagne Waltz,* supplied a romantic atmosphere. An attentive observer, however, would have suspected that the Knolls' relationship had gone adrift.

Lilly embraced the style of the day with her bobbed brunette hair and willowy, five-foot-ten frame draped in a black crepe dress. With the addition of a small pair of gold chandelier earrings and a sparkly sequined collar, her refinement rose to the evening's occasion. As the photographer focused his shot, Lilly turned to gaze at her husband, her expression a mixture of bewilderment and fear. A year and a half later, she would be on another ship to Germany, this time with her child in apparent flight from an abusive husband.

Coming ten years after his immigration to America, this voyage appears to have been the only trip back to Germany John Knoll would ever take.[6] He departed right before the Hauptmann trial, and would return shortly after Hauptmann's conviction. His first-class passage cost about five times the amount of his yearly rent in the Bronx—and probably not much less than a deli clerk's annual wages during the Depression. As Knoll looks straight into the camera, his eyes are cold and impassive, his lips clamped. He appears indifferent to his bride and out of his element.

The fastest cabin steamer afloat, the three-year-old *Manhattan* clipped along at twenty knots en route from New York to its final destination of Hamburg. In 1936, the ship would carry the U.S. Olympic team to Germany for the games hosted by Hitler in Berlin. Among the American athletes aboard the ship was long-distance runner Louis Zamperini. "Sailing on the SS *Manhattan* was a mind-blowing experience," recalled Zamperini. "It was like a floating city. The food was my gold medal: I gained twelve pounds on the way to Germany!"[7]

As the vacationing deli clerk John Knoll chose among such entrees as lobster *à la* Newburg, breaded veal chop *viennoise*, lamb chops *en papillote*, and mallard duckling with bread sauce, Bruno Hauptmann applied a paper spoon to his portion of liver pudding and paced the bullpen connected to his cramped jail cell.[8] The start of his murder trial in Flemington was but three and a half weeks away.

The *Manhattan* cruised up the Elbe, and the Knolls disembarked in Hamburg during the second week of December. From there, Knoll returned to Herxheimweyher and his two-story boyhood home at *Hauptstraße* 27. The story is still told within the family about his next stop, the small Catholic church across the street. Knoll entered Sankt Antonius-Kirche, walked to the rear of the sanctuary, and tugged on the ropes dangling from the three bronze bells high above the organ. In many European villages, the tolling of church bells was an alarm for fire. But on this occasion, the citizens who spilled into the *Hauptstraße* discovered that Knoll had rung the bells to herald the return of "Schah," as everyone called him, after a ten-year absence.

*"Ich bin zurück! Ich bin es!"*

With Hauptmann an ocean away, just about to face trial, it was an unlikely return to Germany for John Knoll, and not hard to understand his relief and even euphoria in shouting, "I'm back! It's me!"

# 21

# Trial of the Century

The namesake of an innkeeper and early settler of the area, Flemington was the Hunterdon County seat, the marketplace for the area's poultry farmers, and the host of an annual egg-laying contest.[1] And that, really, was about it—until the Hauptmann trial transformed the central New Jersey borough of three thousand into the epicenter of world news. Half the borough's residents rented rooms to the influx of visitors, bringing unexpected relief from the pressures of the Depression.[2]

Undeterred by the falling snow, vendors hawked fake rolls of ransom bills, photos of the Lindberghs with forged autographs, and wooden replicas of the kidnap ladder. The local notion store sold thirteen hundred of the ladders, two hundred autograph books, and two hundred "Room To Let" signs.

Five thousand requests for passes to the trial flooded into the offices of Sheriff John Curtiss from all over the world. Film stars, comedians, novelists, and society matrons competed for seats with the ordinary public. The sheriff enriched himself from under-the-table ticket sales to such customers as Wesley Lance, a Harvard Law School student and future New Jersey senator.

The four-story, red brick Union Hotel could lodge but a fraction of the visitors who begged for reservations. Designed in the late Victorian Eastlake gingerbread style, the hotel reserved its top floor for the jurors and let most of its other rooms to the press. The jurors, who received three dollars a day for fulfilling their civic duty, exercised on the top floor balcony but more often stayed inside, partly because of the freezing weather. The jury matron censored their mail, both incoming and outgoing, and police stood guard outside the jurors' rooms around the clock.

Offering on its specialty menu Hauptmann Stew, Lamb Chops Jafsie, Baked Beans Wilentz, and ice cream sundaes called "Lindys," the hotel served a thousand meals and two thousand drinks a day. Supposedly sequestered, the jurors ate in the dining room, separated from reporters only by a cloth screen that failed to block out lively conversation regarding the trial. Loud condemnations of "the Nazi monster" and "Hauptmann the baby-killer" penetrated the flimsy barrier.[3]

At the back of the hotel was a smoke-filled saloon where the press congregated at night to drink, shoot dice, and swap stories about the trial. One day, a reporter found a homeless mongrel on the steps of his boarding house and bought the hungry, shivering animal a steak and a checked coat. "Nellie" soon became the toast of the town, and the press called the saloon "Nellie's Tap Room." The hilarity at some of the more tipsy tables grew with the singing of a parody of the *Schnitzelbank* ditty for teaching children the names of objects. Because a *Schnitzelbank* is a woodworker's tool, the song seemed a fitting choice for the trial of a carpenter. With each stanza the raucous crowd sang louder and louder.

Because of the dearth of accommodations at the Union Hotel, male and female members of the press—married and unmarried—piled into rooms together and shared beds in a free-for-all. There were no reported complaints from the men. One morning, an overly proper, prudish AP reporter woke up and discovered an arrestingly beautiful woman with shapely legs sprawled out next to him; the legs belonged to thirty-one-year-old journalist, socialite, and future congresswoman Clare Boothe, who had flopped into his bed in the middle of the night. "I slept with Clare Boothe Luce at the Hauptmann trial," the reporter would reminisce decades later with his family.[4]

Technicians strung up telegraph and telephone wires about the snow-blanketed town in preparation for the trial. Most of the lines ran into the century-old courthouse, a two-and-a-half story Greek Revival building constructed of native stone. Western Union, with its 132 wires, had installed enough capacity to transmit three million words a day. The set-up was far more extensive than the preparations for coverage of the

World Series or the Olympic games. Meanwhile, many of the country's most famous celebrities, journalists, and authors came for the trial, and reporters hovered around the participants in the case.

On the morning of Wednesday, January 2, 1935, a shy radio reporter surveyed the press table in Supreme Court Justice Thomas W. Trenchard's courtroom and recognized the best-known journalists of the time. Gabriel Heatter was too timid even to say hello. The world's largest network, WOR, had offered him the assignment of a lifetime—three fifteen-minute segments a day, but with no guaranteed pay, to cover the first murder trial ever broadcast over the airwaves. Only if an advertiser were to sponsor the program would the station compensate Heatter beyond his fifty-dollar-a-week expense allowance. "Millions of people will drink in every word of that trial," Heatter's wife had advised him. "Better go."[5]

At ten minutes past ten o'clock, the clerk called for order, and everyone scrambled for their seats. "Oyez! Oyez! Oyez!" croaked the court crier. Judge Trenchard strode in from his chambers in his black judicial robe and settled into the chair behind his U-shaped bench. The courts had never overturned a verdict in a murder trial over which he had presided during his twenty-eight years on New Jersey's Supreme Court bench. Yet the judge himself opposed capital punishment—a conviction shared by the attorney general about to prosecute the case.

A heavy accumulation of snow during the Christmas holiday had whitened the rooftops of Flemington's gingerbread houses and covered the streets. Five hundred men and women, including a hundred and fifty members of the jury pool and an equal number of reporters, crowded into the courtroom. The thermometer registered five below zero outside, but the two fireplaces inside the courtroom, which was never meant to accommodate more than two hundred persons, went unused. Body heat sent the temperature in the room up to eighty degrees.

One of the great journalists of the day, Damon Runyon, would receive credit for having termed the event the "Trial of the Century." H. L. Mencken called it "the greatest story since the Resurrection." Reporters from around the world penciled their copy in "the Trenches" —the front rows of Judge Trenchard's courtroom.

Having decided to "do something" about the threat that kidnapping posed to the country, William Randolph Hearst had rung up his longtime columnist Adela Rogers St. John from his castle in California. No stranger to murder, celebrity, or the courtroom, she had often watched her father, famed criminal lawyer Earl Rogers, defend high-profile clients.

"Mrs. Lindbergh will require careful handling in this trial," said Hearst. "I hope you are free to be there for us."

"Oh yes indeed I am!" said Rogers St. John, who had waited by the telephone for Hearst's call like a "caged tiger."[6] For thirty-one days, the applejack-swilling reporter would churn out her column every day, sometimes twice a day. Her wardrobe for the trial—five Hattie Carnegie dresses of heavy slipper satin, in light and dark blue, beige, silver gray, and black, with matching fine woolen coats lined with soft moleskin and squirrel fur—were paid for out of her *New York Evening Journal* expense account. Hearst's policy was for his star reporters to sparkle in the height of fashion.

The *Daily Mirror*'s new editor-in-chief and lead columnist, Arthur Brisbane, a towering figure in journalism and longtime Hearst associate, had appointed Damon Runyon and Walter Winchell to complete the newspaper's three-man delegation to the trial. Runyon would provide on-the-scene reporting, Winchell human interest, and Brisbane point-of-view. In response to Winchell's commentary "that the circumstantial case will tighten around Hauptmann's neck,"[7] Brisbane wrote in his own column, "Winchell is probably right. But before executing Hauptmann, someone should be SURE that he is guilty."[8]

Brisbane had accused his colleague of nabbing every trial press pass allotted to the *Mirror*. Winchell fired back: he had obtained his tickets from the recently inaugurated governor of New Jersey, Harold Hoffman. Moreover, Winchell said, he had gotten seats for himself, Brisbane, and Dr. Dudley Shoenfeld, the psychiatrist who had created the psychological profile of Cemetery John and who was supplying "inside stuff."

In dark glasses and his trademark snap-brim gray fedora and blue serge double-breasted suit, Winchell was recognized in the courtroom at once. His signature style helped make him the celebrity he was. Few knew that he had invested in a closetful—literally dozens—of identical fedoras and suits.

Viewing the Lindbergh case as "the greatest news story in [his] time," Winchell, who had begun the 1920s as a soft-shoe vaudevillian and ended the decade as America's most popular columnist and radio commentator, saw the trial as the perfect stage to act out his transformation from a purveyor of gossip into a serious journalist. Yet the inventor of such words as "frinstance," "slanguage, " and "Cupiding" could not resist poking fun at the obesity of juror Verna Snyder, attributing the sound of a loud crash in the Union Hotel to her having fallen out of bed.[9] "I really hope to be a better reporter than I am—and I know I need practice," he wrote in his "Walter Winchell On Broadway" column after Hauptmann's arrest.[10]

"Never thought I'd ever get to the point where I didn't care a hoot about being on or seeing Broadway," Winchell would remark about his sabbatical from his column. "Don't give my regards to anybody."

# 22

# The State's Case

A thousand eyes fell on Bruno Hauptmann as he entered the courtroom wearing a grayish-brown, double-breasted suit. Because the courthouse was connected to the jail, the walk from his cell had been short. Three and a half years had gone by since my father had stood alongside John and Walter Knoll and a man called "Bruno" and heard them speak of "Englewood" outside Palisades Amusement Park. Having crossed the Atlantic eastward three and a half weeks before the trial, John Knoll could, if he wanted, still follow events through the German newspapers. The web of special lines installed in the courthouse included a direct wire to Berlin.

Hauptmann strode into the courtroom with a confident gait. A deputy sheriff in plain clothes and two state troopers in sky blue coats and dark blue trousers escorted him to his chair at the defense table. A rail separated the prosecution and defense tables from the spectators. Hauptmann shook hands with assistant defense counsel Lloyd Fisher, thirty-eight, a resident of Flemington, and sat down. Also seated at the defense table were assistant defending attorneys Egbert Rosecrans, an authority on constitutional law, and Frederick A. Pope, a country lawyer from nearby Somerville.

After James Fawcett had failed to prevent his client's extradition to New Jersey, Anna Hauptmann appointed Edward J. Reilly, fifty-two, a flamboyant Brooklyn lawyer whose best years were behind him, as her husband's chief defense counsel. The Hearst-owned *New York Journal* had paid Reilly's $25,000 legal fee up front in return for exclusive rights to Anna's story.

As was his habit, Reilly, who had spent but thirty-eight minutes with

his client, was lax in preparing his case. The Hauptmanns had no idea
that he was a womanizing alcoholic who hero-worshiped Charles Lindbergh and kept a framed photograph of the aviator on his desk. Just as
the trial was getting started, he was quoted as having wisecracked to reporters, "This will be a million dollars worth of fun!" After he had received a pile of mail of "an abusive nature" regarding the comment,
however, Reilly pleaded with Walter Winchell to tell the public that he
had been misquoted.[1] The attorney, whose nickname "Death House
Reilly" stemmed from his recent string of courtroom defeats, had confided to a Division of Investigation agent that he disliked Hauptmann,
was convinced of his guilt, and was anxious to see him get the electric
chair.[2] To respond to fan mail, Reilly ordered special stationery with a
sketch of the kidnap ladder drawn in red. With his bowler, white scarf,
striped trousers, and light spats, Reilly challenged Wilentz as the best
dressed man in the courtroom.

The lead defense attorney enjoyed the limelight and posed for news-
reel photographers and other cameramen. "Flemington is a very beautiful town," he said. ". . . I have been here only a short time, but I know I
should like to live here." Quipped Walter Winchell, "I'll bet he tells that
to all the girls—on potential juries."[3]

Ten tall, recessed windows flanking the judge's bench and another two
behind it allowed wintry sunlight to flood into the high-ceilinged courtroom. Lindbergh entered in a light gray suit that concealed a pistol in a
shoulder holster. His demeanor conveyed an attitude of studiousness, seri-
ousness, and self-control. It was clear he would not speak to the press. Lindbergh walked right past Hauptmann and took a seat at the prosecution table
inside the rail in front of the bench. Though the defendant sat but four seats
away, Lindbergh averted his eyes from him and observed the proceedings
with his arms folded or with his chin resting in the palm of his hand.

Remembering Elmer Irey's strategy to include gold certificates in
the package of ransom bills, Lindbergh had lauded the Intelligence Section of the Treasury Department: "If it had not been for you fellows being
in the case, Hauptmann would not now be on trial and your organization
deserves full credit for his apprehension." Incensed by Lindbergh's failure to give the Division of Investigation credit for Hauptmann's capture,
J. Edgar Hoover would later order a file to be kept on the aviator.

As the jury selection process began, Lindbergh jotted notes on a pad of paper and searched the faces of the members of the jury pool who took the stand. With a peculiar stare that had characterized his expressions since his arrest, Hauptmann also fixed his eyes on those questioned during the voir dire examination. Over and over, the defense asked potential jurors if Walter Winchell's radio broadcasts or his column in the *Daily Mirror* had influenced their opinions on the case.

Ten members of the jury were chosen from the fifty-seven candidates examined during the day's proceedings. All four women selected were mothers, one a grandmother. The last venireman under consideration was a farmer who claimed never to have heard of the Lindbergh case or the Hauptmann trial. Speaking for the defense, Fisher urged that the man be discharged for cause: "a total lack of intelligence."[4] Judge Trenchard disqualified him. The jurist also dismissed anyone with objections to capital punishment on religious or conscientious grounds. "You could see the look of disappointment on the face of those who were excused," radio broadcaster Gabriel Heatter would recall. "They would have had a ringside seat."

The judge remanded Hauptmann to his cell after the court was adjourned and ordered the constables to escort the jurors to the Union Hotel. Throughout the trial, mobs would unleash their hatred of the defendant whenever the jurors appeared on the street. There were cries of "Burn the Dutchman!" and "Put him in the hot seat!"

After two more men were put on the jury the next day, Judge Trenchard dismissed the dozens of remaining candidates. Because the sheriff could not hold back the crush of hundreds panting to see the action, the vacated seats were immediately seized. People squeezed together on the benches, clogged the aisles, crowded against the back wall, perched in windowsills, and hung over the balcony.

Wilentz, a short, wiry Latvian immigrant who liked cigars, horse races, and snazzy suits, addressed the jury first. He was about to prosecute the first criminal trial of his career. Wilentz had played a key role in helping elect Governor A. Harry Moore, the predecessor of the new governor, and for his efforts was appointed attorney general.

Anthony M. Hauck, Jr., the Special Assistant Attorney General charged with presenting the case against Hauptmann, joined Wilentz's veteran prosecution team. Also handpicked by the attorney general were Assistant Prosecutor Joseph Lanigan, who had worked under Hauck in the trial of the hoaxing shipbuilder John Hughes Curtis; Assistant Attorney General Robert Peacock, who had examined 315 documents and exhibits and checked the statements of 310 witnesses; and former judge George K. Large, a Flemington attorney and President of the Hunterdon County Bar Association.

Unlike his adversary Reilly, Wilentz maintained his professionalism throughout the Hauptmann trial, even refusing to obtain passes for relatives and friends. The attorney general vowed never to capitalize on his role as lead prosecutor in the trial through speaking engagements or other venues. He explained in his opening statement that a death resulting from the commission of a burglary is viewed under the law as first-degree murder.

"[Hauptmann] broke into and entered at night the Lindbergh home with the intent to commit a battery upon that child, and with the intent to steal the child and its clothing," said Wilentz. "And he did . . . Then as he went out that window and down that ladder of his the ladder broke. He had more weight going down than he had when he was coming up. And down he went with this child. In the commission of that burglary that child was instantaneously killed when it received that first blow."[5]

The attorney general laid out the foundation for the State's case: Hauptmann's scheme for financial enrichment, the reconstruction of the kidnapping as the prosecution team believed it had happened, findings at the crime scene, the two late-night meetings in the Bronx with intermediary John Condon, Lindbergh's identification of Hauptmann's voice at St. Raymond's Cemetery, the young father's futile search for his baby and the *Boad Nelly*, the gruesome discovery of the tiny corpse, the defendant's use of a floorboard in his attic to build the kidnap ladder, and a summary of Hauptmann's criminal past and extravagance before his capture.

"Let me just tell you, representing the State of New Jersey, that this State will not compromise with murder or murderers," said Wilentz. "We demand the penalty of murder in the first degree."[6]

# 23

# Sworn to Truth

A smattering of applause ensued as Wilentz concluded his opening statement. Reilly, alleging that the prosecutor had sought to "inflame the minds of this jury against the defendant before the trial starts," motioned for a mistrial. "The motion is denied," Judge Trenchard said.[1] The State called a surveyor and former county engineer to the stand. The witness pinpointed the location of the Lindbergh estate on a map and testified that the home was in Hunterdon County. The fact established the court's jurisdiction over the crime.

The next witness was Anne Morrow Lindbergh, who wore a black silk suit, a light pink blouse, a blue fox fur, and a black satin hat with a bow across the front. Spectators stood up and craned their necks to catch a glimpse of the victim's mother, whose approach to the witness stand was steady and brisk. Determined to impress her husband with her self-control, she explained the decision to keep her sick baby at their new home on the night of the kidnapping. The witness recounted how she had played with Charlie after his afternoon nap and described the frantic search of the house after his disappearance.

Anne identified a photograph of her son and the flannel nightshirt found on his corpse. She winced as she fingered the garment's rotted fragments. Wilentz laid a gray sleeping suit in her lap. "What sleeping suit is that, Mrs. Lindbergh?"

"It is the sleeping suit that was put on my child the night of March first," she said.[2]

Spectators dabbed their eyes with handkerchiefs as Anne smoothed out the wrinkles of the woolen garment. Hauptmann kept a steady gaze on her and showed no emotion. Given his turn to question the witness, Reilly said, "The defense feels that the grief of Mrs. Lindbergh needs no cross-examination."

At 3:30 p.m., Charles Lindbergh took the stand. Wilentz asked the witness to recount the history of the case. Until the court adjourned late that afternoon, Lindbergh described the events related to the crime. He began with his arrival home on the night of March 1, 1932, and continued up to his receipt of the second ransom note, the one postmarked in Brooklyn.

A cold wind was blowing when the court reconvened at ten o'clock the following morning. Anne Morrow Lindbergh did not accompany her husband to the courthouse. Her eyes blurred with tears, she wandered across the lawns of Next Day Hill.

Scores crowded against two walls of the courtroom, while others found places of vantage on windowsills, radiators, and the steps to the side of Judge Trenchard. In attendance were Al Reich, the former prizefighter who had driven Condon to Woodlawn Cemetery; William Allen, the trucker who had discovered the baby's corpse; Betty Gow, the baby's nursemaid; and Elsie Whateley, the Lindberghs' cook at the time of the kidnapping.

Not long into his second session in the witness chair, Lindbergh described his memory of the evening of April 2, 1932, when Condon had delivered the ransom money to Cemetery John. As Condon was crossing Whittemore Avenue, a man with "a foreign accent" had called out "Hey, Doctor" from within the cemetery.[3] Wilentz resumed his questioning for a while, then returned to the shout "Hey, Doctor" that Lindbergh had heard.

"Since that time have you heard the same voice?" Wilentz asked.

"Yes, I have," Lindbergh said.

"Whose voice was it, Colonel, that you heard in the vicinity of St. Raymond's Cemetery that night, saying, 'Hey, Doctor'?"

The witness swung in his chair and, for an instant, caught Hauptmann's eye. Adela Rogers St. John would later recall that she had never known a press box "so utterly silent and motionless."[4]

"That was Hauptmann's voice," said Lindbergh, his voice even and firm.[5]

*Charles Lindbergh testifying at the trial of Bruno Richard Hauptmann.*

"When people like the Lindberghs and the Morrows say something, you've just got to believe them," juror Howard Biggs would say after the trial. As Biggs would recall, the jury never doubted Lindbergh's identification of Hauptmann's voice.[6]

Lindbergh had heard the accented voice emanating from St. Raymond's Cemetery from a distance of at least two hundred feet, and more than two and a half years had passed since that night. To Division of Investigation Special Agent Leon Turrou, the witness's certainty seemed implausible. "Many, including myself, thought it remarkable that Colonel Lindbergh, sworn to truth, could recognize a voice heard for a few moments in a dark wood after a lapse of two years," Turrou would write in his memoir, *Where My Shadow Falls*. "It was all the more surprising since the colonel's accusation was not weakened by the slightest shade of doubt. I think his cold unhesitating recital loaded with stark drama convinced the jury more than anything else."[7]

Even Lindbergh himself had said during his grand jury testimony in the Bronx that one could not have expected him to make the identification. During cross-examination, Reilly failed to challenge Lindbergh and raise the possibility that he might have heard the voice of another German man. As A. Scott Berg notes in his biography of the aviator, Lindbergh had testified before the Bronx grand jury that he had heard "Hey Doc." As he remembered it in the Flemington trial, however, the phrase was "Hey, Doctor."[8]

More than sixty thousand tourists swamped Flemington that weekend. Among them was a young couple from Dallas and their two-year-old son. Jackie Carter climbed up the stone steps of the courthouse and asked, "Is this school?"

"No," said his father. "It's the theatre for the Crime of the Century."

"It's school," the boy insisted.

Five thousand visited the courtroom and lolled in the witness box, the jury box, and Judge Trenchard's high-backed chair. Volunteer tour guides from the American Legion answered the question on everyone's lips: "How can I get to see Hauptmann?" Signs labeled the chairs of the trial principals. Some abused the invitation, nabbing drinking cups and rifling wastebaskets for press dispatches. One man tried to steal the courthouse flag. "A guy just tried to carry off the witness stand," said the sheriff. "Lucky for us, it's bolted down."

Because the migration of visitors to Flemington seemed like an infestation, reporters called them "boll weevils." As a boy with a penknife prepared to carve his initials into a chair, a deputy sheriff stopped him and instructed him and his sidekick to leave town. The police discovered two men who had hidden in Judge Trenchard's library. Unwilling to tolerate further mockery of the hall of justice, the Hunterdon County Board of Chosen Freeholders announced that the courthouse would no longer be open to satisfy the curiosity of tourists.

Betty Gow had boarded the RMS *Aquitania* under the name "Bessie Galloway" and returned to the States from Scotland to testify. Pursued by cameramen upon her arrival at the courthouse, she shielded her face with her purse and fled inside. Her answers perfected by pretrial rehearsal with the prosecutors, Betty identified Charlie's sleeping suit and the tattered remnants of the undershirt she had sewn for him. The testimony validated Wilentz's claim that the kidnapper had committed a theft in taking the baby's clothes. Betty came across as a credible witness and a faithful servant to the Lindberghs who had adored their baby.

Reilly's repeated attempts to discredit her failed. Questioned about her association with Henry "Red" Johnson, the witness said that her relationship had been an innocent one with a good man who had done nothing wrong. When Reilly challenged Betty's acceptance of $650 from the prosecution, she explained that the money was a reimbursement for lost wages and her travel to America.

Exhausted after her three hours of testimony, Betty sank to the carpet in the courtroom library anteroom. Later, when informed that she had collapsed, Hauptmann smirked.

The following day, the State called eighty-seven-year-old retired security guard Amandus Hochmuth to the stand. A month before the trial, two state troopers had taken him to the Flemington jail to familiarize him with Hauptmann's looks.

"Where were you born?" Wilentz asked.

"I am here on and off on summertimes," said the witness. "I generally go to New York."

A few moments later, the attorney general posed another question: "On the first day of March, 1932, where were you residing?"

"I was standing on the porch."

The bespectacled, legally blind Prussian army veteran, who had cataracts in both eyes, testified that on that morning, he had seen a "dirty green" car skid into a ditch in front of his daughter's home, which was two miles from the Lindbergh estate. Inside the car was a ladder.

"[The driver] glared at me as if he saw a ghost," Hochmuth said.

"And the man that you saw looking out of that automobile glaring at you in the manner that you say, is he in this room?" Wilentz asked.

"Yes."

"Where is he?"

The lights in the courtroom flickered out just as the witness pointed a finger at Hauptmann. "It's the Lord's wrath over a lying witness!" roared Reilly.

When the lights came on again, Wilentz asked, "Would you mind stepping down and showing us?"

Hochmuth grabbed his cane, shuffled across the courtroom, and clapped the defendant on the shoulder. Hauptmann said to his wife, *"Der Alte ist verrückt!"* ("The old man is crazy!") Hochmuth's daughter would admit to reporters after the trial that her father had never seen Hauptmann.

Reilly failed to challenge the reliability of the octogenarian's enfeebled eyesight—even after Hochmuth claimed that his eyes were "all right." The old man acknowledged that a state trooper had guided him inside the courtroom the previous afternoon but refused to admit that anyone had pointed out the defendant to him.

The next witness called by the State was Joseph Perrone, the Bronx taxi driver who had delivered the kidnappers' note of instructions to Condon on the night of March 12, 1932. Wilentz asked the witness to indicate who had given him the letter that night. Perrone rose to his feet, walked across the courtroom, and stopped in front of Hauptmann.

Perrone's hand fell on the defendant's shoulder. "That is the man."

"You're a liar," Hauptmann said.

Upon cross-examination, Perrone said that the man who had run up to his cab wore a fedora that was turned up in the front. By Condon's account, however, the brim of Cemetery John's hat was turned down. Reilly failed to point out the contradiction.

## 24

## "Who Is John?"

The following morning of January 9, 1935, the courtroom crackled with excitement: the self-described "man of mystery," Jafsie was about to take the stand. Well-rested from a vacation in Miami, Condon wore a dark three-piece suit with a white handkerchief in his breast pocket and an old-fashioned watch chain draped across his vest. The witness interrupted his testimony with philosophical musings on life and embellished answers even to straightforward questions. When asked where he lived, the seventy-four-year-old Bronx native said: "In the most beautiful borough in the world." Fisher rose for the defense to object: "*Flemington* is more beautiful."

Condon relished his verbal sparring with the chief defense counsel and grinned at each landed blow.

"What am I, a heavyweight?" Reilly asked.

"You a heavyweight? May I look?" asked Condon, stepping down from the witness stand to examine the counselor. "This don't hurt you, does it?"

"Not a particle."

"Undoubtedly a heavyweight." The spectators laughed with gusto.

Deflecting questions about his earlier inability to identify Hauptmann as Cemetery John, Condon confounded the defense attorney with spurious logic and gibberish.

"In the Greenwich Street New York Police Station you said it was not the man, did you not?" Reilly asked.

"I never said it was or was not," Condon said.

"Because you know you are not sure!"

"Because I made the distinction between declaration and identification. The identification meant what I knew mentally. The declaration meant what I said to others. There isn't a man who breathes has ever heard me say that this was the man but one."

To Reilly this was patent nonsense. At one point, after the chief defense counsel had lost his temper, Condon lashed out at him: "Don't shout at me. I'm not deaf. I can hear you."[1]

During his opportunity to question the witness, Attorney General Wilentz brought up the matter of the ransom payment at St. Raymond's Cemetery. His left leg crossed over his right knee, Condon appeared confident in the witness chair.

"Who did you give that money to?" Wilentz asked.

"John," said Condon.

"And who is John?"

For Condon, this was his long-awaited moment in the public spotlight. Surely his response—the five words that would nail shut the prosecution's case—would not only wow the five hundred crowded into the courtroom, but would also secure his place in history. Lindbergh sat leaning forward in his chair, his eyes riveted to the man on the witness stand.

"John is . . ." began Condon. Then, wagging his index finger in Wilentz's direction: "Bruno Richard Hauptmann."

Before Condon finished his sentence, he looked away from Wilentz and dropped his eyes to the floor. Then the witness turned and glared at the defendant. Hauptmann, his arms folded, shook his head and stared back. No sooner had Condon finished his testimony than Walter Winchell jumped up from his chair to shake his hand.

After Lindbergh had identified Hauptmann as the man whose voice he heard at St. Raymond's Cemetery on the night of April 2, 1932, it was obvious that Condon would say that the defendant was Cemetery John. At the police station, with Hauptmann standing before him, Condon had told detectives "I would not say he is the man" and later more emphatically stated "No, he is not the man." But the knowledge that Lindbergh had identified the voice of Hauptmann with such confidence had, perhaps, a psychological influence on Condon, somehow easing the doubts he had so clearly expressed before. Nor can the other influences at work be overlooked. In his memoir *Jafsie Tells All*, he describes the privilege of having served Colonel and Mrs. Lindbergh as "priceless."[2] Condon might have been unwilling to jeopardize either his treasured association with his hero or his perceived chummy friendship with Henry Breckinridge, who had corresponded regularly with him and would continue to do so. In a letter to Breckinridge dated October 29, 1933, Condon had described his most recent efforts to find Cemetery John. "My dear Colonel," he began, closing with: "I shall be on the alert. Trust me, Stice."[3]

The testimony was no less important a victory for Condon, the recipient of dozens of mean-spirited letters and phone calls questioning his motives for entering the case, than it was for the prosecution. No reasonable person could now accuse him of having had a criminal hand in the kidnapping or profiting by it.

A cheer erupted as Condon emerged from the courthouse. The witness saluted the crowd, shook hands all around with strangers, and stepped into a chauffeured vehicle. Wilentz, bundled up with a white woolen scarf wound around his neck, climbed into the back seat and lit a cigar. The driver inched past the revelers surrounding the vehicle and headed for the Bronx.

Three days later, on January 13, Walter Winchell spoke on his Sunday evening radio program about Jafsie's refusal at the police station to identify Hauptmann as Cemetery John:

> Here is an observation . . . [that] shows, I think, that Dr. Condon's memory isn't muddled. In court last week he was confronted by a strange woman in green. 'Did you ever see her before' asked Mr. Reilly. Doctor Condon said he had—in 1932. 'Wasn't the lady with you that day named Mrs. Bush?' said Dr. Condon. The woman in green nodded yes. Therefore, if Dr. Condon—after three years, and after meeting Mrs. Bush and hearing her name once—could remember it—why then—couldn't Dr. Condon remember the voice and the face of the ransom man—with whom he talked twice and sat with the first time— for 70 minutes?[4]

Condon would take to the vaudeville stage to parlay his celebrity into a career as a self-professed crime expert. The Bronx Chamber of Commerce made him guest of honor at its 1935 annual spring banquet and dance and presented him with a large oil portrait of himself. A photograph of Condon appeared on the cover of the program. Condon lapped up the attention and sent a copy to Henry Breckinridge. It was autographed "Jafsie."[5]

The prosecution turned its focus after Condon's testimony onto its highly paid expert witnesses. Albert S. Osborn had testified before a Bronx grand jury that Hauptmann had written the ransom notes. Court attendants unrolled five blown-up photostats and displayed them against a wall rack near the jury box. Judge Trenchard had admitted the exhibits into evidence despite efforts by the defense to bar them.

Osborn, with his white hair, moustache, and wire rim glasses, took the stand. The witness described his efforts before Hauptmann's arrest to determine who had written the ransom notes. A comparison of the letters to the handwriting samples of over a hundred suspects had yielded no matches. A detective would dictate a test paragraph for the suspect to write three times, then each time take the paper away immediately. The process made it impossible for the writer to remember when and how he had disguised his writing.

The document examiner pointed to similarities between the handwriting on the ransom notes and the samples provided by the defendant. The same words were repeatedly misspelled—for example, *"Haus"* for "house" and *"gut"* for "good"—common mistakes for a German immigrant. Yet Osborn conveniently failed to distinguish between the handwriting taken from Hauptmann at the police station (the requested writing) and the examples of his handwriting found in his apartment (the conceded writing). The fast-moving presentation involved sleight of hand. For example, on multiple exhibits, two columns were presented, one under the heading "Ransom Notes" and the other under the writing "Hauptmann Writing." Samples under the Hauptmann Writing column, however, were not identified as being conceded or requested. Jurors found the testimony compelling.

With his large photostats showing the handwriting comparisons, Osborn's presentation must have looked, at that time, quite high-tech. As attorney Bob E. Lype wrote in a 1998 article in the *Tennessee Bar Journal*, the profession of handwriting experts has been "under a full-scale attack nationwide." Specifically, research and data have tended to show that "handwriting experts were not nearly as accurate or proficient as they claimed to be."[6] But what if technology available to us today, in 2012, could have been applied to analyze Hauptmann's handwriting and the ransom notes? I put this question to computer science professor Dr. Sargur N. Srihari, the same expert whose software demonstrated the 95% probability that John Knoll's writing appears on the ransom envelopes. Under Dr. Srihari's direction, the University of Buffalo's Center of Excellence for Document Analysis and Recognition (CEDAR) conducted an optical handwriting recognition (OHR) study of ransom notes number 9 through 15 as compared to known handwriting samples of Bruno Hauptmann—a short letter to a "Mrs. Begg" and a letter he wrote to Governor Harold Hoffman. It was important to use these later ransom notes because the writing appears to be more natural than the earlier ones—and thus less likely to have been disguised. "The analysis showed that the letters to Mrs. Begg and to Governor Hoffman were written by Hauptmann and that there is a very strong likelihood that the writing in these Hauptmann samples do not match the ransom notes," Dr. Srihari said. He added that CEDAR-FOX is designed to compare handwriting when disguise is not a factor.

On January 17, the twelfth day of the proceedings, the State summoned William Allen, who had discovered the baby's body in the woods, to the stand. The spectators were expecting a battle over the identification of the corpse, but Reilly sought to avoid inflaming the passions of the jurors in the event the prosecution exposed them to gruesome photos.

"We do not question that the body found on May 12, 1932, was that of Colonel Lindbergh's baby," Reilly said.

Fisher jumped to his feet and confronted his boss. "You are conceding this man to the electric chair!"

The eighty-seventh and final witness for the State, Arthur Koehler, introduced himself: "I am the expert on the identification of wood for the government." Arguing for the defense, Frederick Pope said, "We say that there is no such animal known among men as an expert on wood; that it is not a science that has been recognized by the courts."

"Well, of course, the term 'wood expert' is a broad term," said Judge

Trenchard. "Do you object to his qualifying as an examiner of wood and to finding out the history of that wood? Do you object to that?"

"Yes, certainly we do," said Pope, "and that he is not qualified to express an opinion."

"I think the witness is qualified as an expert upon the subject matter," the jurist said.[7]

Koehler described how, out of forty thousand mills and lumber companies across the country, he had identified the National Millwork and Lumber Company in the Bronx as the business that had sold the lumber used to construct the kidnap ladder. More than a year before Hauptmann's arrest, Koehler had interviewed employees at the store, where the German carpenter had been an employee and frequent customer.

The wood scientist explained that the nail holes in Rail 16 of the kidnap ladder lined up precisely with four nail holes in the joists in Hauptmann's attic. Koehler also showed using photographs that the grain of the wood in the rail matched "practically perfectly" that of the attic floorboard. Exhibit S-226. Rail 16 and S-226, he went on, were once part of the same piece of wood. Koehler also testified that Rail 16 had been planed down on both sides by one of Hauptmann's hand planes.[8]

"Intimate knowledge of wood . . . serves to show how technical experts along varying lines can often assist law enforcement agencies in tracking down and convicting criminals," Koehler would write after the trial.[9] Already having been strengthened by the damaging testimonies of Lindbergh and Condon, the clinical facts brought before the jury by Koehler and the other technical experts would give Wilentz's summary a final steeliness. As the trial headed toward its finale, the State rested, its case against Hauptmann nearing irrefutability.

# 25

# The Carpenter

Excited voices resounded in the streets on Thursday, January 24, as the jurors walked from the courthouse to the Union Hotel during a midday recess. Word was circulating that the defense's first witness might be Hauptmann himself. Egbert Rosecrans rose for the defense after the court resumed and addressed the bench. "If the Court please, I desire to make a motion for a verdict of acquittal."

Rosecrans said that the State had failed to prove that the crime had taken place in Hunterdon County, rather than in Mercer County, where the body of the Lindbergh baby had been found and where it could be presumed the child had received the fatal blow to the head. Moreover, the other actions attributed to Hauptmann—building the ladder, writing the ransom notes, and collecting the ransom money—had all taken place in New York and as such were outside the court's jurisdiction. Finally, the State had produced no evidence to demonstrate that Hauptmann had been in the baby's nursery on the night of March 1, 1932.

"Does the attorney general wish to be heard?" Judge Trenchard asked.

Wilentz was quick to puncture the argument. Not only was there ample evidence to support the charge, but the evidence of Hauptmann's guilt was overwhelming. The judge pondered for a moment, then denied the motion.

Fisher stepped up to the jury box and delivered his opening statement. The defense would prove that Hauptmann was not at the Lindbergh estate on the night of the kidnapping; that he was not in St.

Raymond's Cemetery when Condon paid the $50,000 ransom to John; and that on the evening of November 26, 1933, he was not at the movie theatre in Greenwich Village passing a five-dollar ransom bill as a ticket-seller had testified. Furthermore, the defense would show how the "so-called kidnap ladder" was a bungled piece of evidence that rendered all testimony concerning it of no consequence. With that, Fisher deferred to the lead defense attorney.

"Bruno Richard Hauptmann, take the stand!" boomed Edward Reilly.

Most of the country and many in the courtroom were already convinced of Hauptmann's guilt. Yet the defendant bore little trace of anxiety as he took the witness chair. Calling his client "Bruno," Reilly guided Hauptmann through a description of his background as a soldier who had been wounded and gassed during the war, as an inmate in the German prison system, and as an illegal immigrant. The attorney sought to establish his client's friendship and business partnership with the late Isador Fisch, who Hauptmann claimed had given him a box for safe-keeping and neglected to mention that it was full of Lindbergh ransom money.

Reilly turned to the kidnapping. "On the night of March 1, 1932, did you enter the nursery of Colonel Lindbergh?"

"I did not," Hauptmann said.

"—and take from that nursery Charles Lindbergh, Jr.?"

"I did not."

"On the night of March 1, 1932, did you leave on the window seat of Charles Lindbergh's nursery a note?"

"I wasn't there at all."

Reilly motioned for a court attendant to lean the three sections of the ladder found at the crime scene against the wall behind the witness chair.

"Did you build this ladder?" Reilly asked.

"I am a carpenter," said Hauptmann, evoking roars of laughter.

"Did you build this ladder?"

Hauptmann turned around and rose to inspect the crude-looking but rather ingenious device. "Certainly not. Looks like a music instrument."

As master carpenter Kevin Klein noted to me, it was a big break for the prosecution that the defense never tried to demonstrate how difficult the ladder would have been to operate alone. The jurors never even saw anyone attempt to connect the sections.[1]

The defendant denied that he had taken any wood from his attic to construct a ladder rail, that he had left a chisel on the Lindbergh grounds, and that he had written any of the ransom notes.

"On April 2, 1932, were you in St. Raymond's Cemetery and did you receive fifty thousand dollars from Dr. Condon?"

"I did not," Hauptmann said.

"When you were taken to the New York City police station, were you beaten by the police?"

"I was."

Reilly shifted his focus to the handwriting samples that the police had forced him to write. "In writing, did you spell the words of your own free will or did they tell you how to spell them?"

"Some of the words they spell it to me," Hauptmann said.

"How do you spell *not*?"

"N—O—T."

"Did they ask you to spell it N—O—T—E?"

"I remember very well they put an 'e' on it."

Hauptmann described how the police badgered him for hours after his arrest and deprived him of sleep. "You write," said the investigators, jabbing him in the ribs whenever he dozed off for a moment.

Reilly thanked Hauptmann, who appeared calm as the attorney general approached. Forty years after the trial, Wilentz, a short man, would remember the five-foot-ten defendant as "a very stolid sort" and as "cold, tall and imposing."[2] My father had remembered the man "Bruno" at Palisades Park as "fairly tall"—certainly taller than the five-foot-seven John Knoll. Because my grandfather stood only five-foot-four, Hauptmann would have seemed quite tall to my father.

Wilentz, attacking right from the start, began his cross-examination by asking Hauptmann if he stood by the story he "swore to before a court in the Bronx." Because the defendant kept deflecting the question, the attorney general had to repeat it three times. Hauptmann gave the same answer each time: "To a certain extent." Wilentz turned to the defendant's spree of criminal acts in Germany: robberies, broken parole, and the burglary of a local mayor's home, where he had climbed a ladder and entered through a second-story window. Within two weeks of being paroled after serving a four-year jail sentence, Hauptmann was arrested again. What was his explanation? "I was trying to sell some goods; later I find out it was stolen," the witness said.[3]

Just before the court recessed for the weekend on Friday, January 25, Wilentz asked, "Are you the Cemetery John that was in Woodlawn Cemetery?"

Over and over throughout the cross-examination, Hauptmann failed to answer the question put to him, prompting Wilentz to say, "I'm asking you about—" At other times, the defendant would remain silent in response to a question or would utter such comments as "I can't remember," "I guess I was honest," and "I really can't say yes or no about it." But when the attorney general asked him if he was Cemetery John, Hauptmann did not pause to ponder the question or hedge his answer. "Positively not," he said.

"Are you the Cemetery John who was in the other cemetery?" Wilentz asked.

"No," said Hauptmann, "I was never in the cemetery."[4]

When the defendant resumed the stand the following Monday, January 28, Wilentz went right back on the offensive, inflecting his voice and pounding the edge of his right hand into the palm of his left to emphasize his points. "Did you lie, or did you tell the truth?" he screamed. At times sarcastic and at others defiant and angry, Hauptmann never broke down. Nor did he confess to any involvement in or knowledge of the crime.

The witness admitted that he had lied to the police upon his arrest. The twenty-dollar gold certificate discovered in his wallet was not a hedge against the sort of inflation he had witnessed in Germany. Hauptmann had repeatedly altered his story. At the Bronx County Court, he had testified that he had written Condon's name and telephone number on a piece of wood trim in his closet. In their conversation at the Hunterdon County Jail in Flemington on October 24, 1934, Condon had asked the prisoner why he had written the phone number on the board.

"That's what I always do," said Hauptmann. "I was following up the case like everybody and I wrote the number on the board."[5]

Colonel Schwarzkopf, Attorney General Wilentz, and prosecutor Anthony M. Hauck, Jr., had all witnessed the conversation. On the witness stand, however, the defendant now claimed that the handwriting on the board belonged to someone else.

Emotions ran high as Wilentz turned to the subject of the ransom money. "You didn't collect the fifty thousand dollars, either?"

"No," Hauptmann said.

"You got part of it. Who got the rest of it?"

"Well, I don't know anything about it."

"You think you're a big shot, don't you?"

"No. Should I cry?"

"No, certainly you shouldn't. You think you are bigger than everybody, don't you?"

"No, but I know I am innocent."

"You're the one with will power. That is what you know, isn't it?"

"No."

"You wouldn't tell if they murdered you, would you?"

"No."

"Will power is everything with you, isn't it?"

"No, it is—I feel innocent and I am innocent and that gives me the power to stand up!"

"Lying, when you swear to God that you will tell the truth! Telling lies doesn't mean anything."

"Stop that!"

"Didn't you lie under oath, time and time again? Didn't you?"

"No, I did not!"

"Lies, lies, lies! But you're not smiling any more, are you? It has gotten a little more serious, hasn't it?"

All trace of bravura in the man in the witness chair had evaporated. He wiped his fingers with a handkerchief. "I guess," said Hauptmann, his voice trailing off, "I guess it isn't a place to smile."

"I am a carpenter!" said Wilentz.

"I am!"

"That was funny, wasn't it?"

"No, sir, there was nothing funny about it."

"You had a good laugh, didn't you?"

With that, defense attorney Frederick Pope popped up from his chair. "Well, I think this has gone just about far enough!"

At this point Judge Trenchard granted a recess. When the trial resumed, the prosecutor brought up the subject of Isador Fisch, who Hauptmann claimed had given him the shoebox full of Lindbergh ransom money. Wilentz cornered the defendant into admitting to more lies, including misrepresentations to Fisch's family in Germany. The prosecution confronted the witness with more incriminating evidence, including the sketch found in Hauptmann's ledger book of a ladder similar to the one abandoned at the crime scene.

The cross-examination lasted for eleven hours and resumed the following day, the twentieth of the trial. In a challenge to Hauptmann's earlier testimony that he and Fisch had begun their business partnership in 1932, Wilentz produced two letters that the defendant had written to Fisch's family. The letters revealed that the men had formed their partnership in 1933. Hauptmann also acknowledged that he had lied to Fisch's brother about $5,500 he said had come from a personal bank account. Wilentz told reporters afterward that the defendant had made a good witness, "considering the fact that he has told so many different stories and has had to admit both damaging truths and untruth."[6]

The next witness to take the stand, Anna Hauptmann, supported her husband's alibis on the nights of the kidnapping, the ransom payment, and the passing of a five-dollar ransom bill at the movie theatre. Wilentz was cordial but assertive with the witness, with whom he had exchanged friendly morning greetings throughout the trial. He reminded her that she had testified in the hearing in the Bronx that she could not remember whether she was with her husband on the night of the kidnapping.

The most credible witness called by the defense was handwriting expert John M. Trendley, who suggested that Hauptmann's handwriting resembled that of many German immigrants. The state had permitted Trendley only two hours to examine the ransom notes and the exemplars from Hauptmann's hand. With its unusual loop, the strange lower-case "k" found throughout the ransom notes never appeared in any of Hauptmann's handwriting—either in the handwriting found in his notebooks or in the tests administered by the police. In effect discounting the value of

Osborn's analysis, Trendley also maintained that any handwriting samples taken in a police station were not to be trusted.

A bizarre assortment of defense witnesses followed Anna Hauptmann on the stand. An amateur bootlegger named Louis Kiss testified that on the night of the kidnapping, he saw Hauptmann chatting with a waitress at the bakery where Anna worked. On his way to delivering two pints of rum to his friend Leo Singer, he had stopped for directions at the store. Kiss admitted in the cross-examination that he had manufactured the rum himself: he had purchased some alcohol and added flavoring.

"How long did it take you to make this rum?" Wilentz asked.

"Ten minutes," Kiss said.

That night, Nellie's Tap Room would hang up a new sign: "We Serve Kiss Rum: Aged 10 Minutes." When Singer testified, the attorney general asked whether Kiss had visited him on the night of March 1, 1932. "Positively no," the witness said.

Also called to the witness stand were a mental patient and a Bronx taxi driver. The cabbie, who claimed to have been at St. Raymond's Cemetery on the night of the ransom payment, was a surprise witness. To everyone's surprise, the man used the courtroom as a stage on which to showcase his impersonation of Will Rogers. With the testimony of each new defense witness, it was plain that the defendant's fate looked bleak.

"Where are they getting these witnesses from?" Hauptmann asked Lloyd Fisher. "They are hurting me."

# 26

# The Verdict

Tough and relentless, Hunterdon County prosecutor Anthony M. Hauck, Jr., took forty-five minutes to present the State's case to the jury. The prosecution had no obligation to produce a photograph of the defendant descending the kidnap ladder with the Lindbergh baby, he explained; the overwhelming evidence presented during the trial had demonstrated beyond a reasonable doubt that Hauptmann was guilty of murder.

"Judge not, lest ye be judged," said Edward J. Reilly, raising a Bible as he began his summation for the defense. "We must think about the real culprit—he must be somewhere in the world. There must be two or three of them still alive, because no one man could do this."[1]

The lead defense attorney suggested that any of a number of people could have conspired to kidnap the baby, including three who were dead: Isador Fisch, Violet Sharp, and Olly Whateley, the Lindberghs' butler, who had succumbed to peritonitis the previous spring. Reilly also included John Condon, Betty Gow, and Henry "Red" Johnson, her boyfriend at the time of the kidnapping, in his suspicions. And could not the police have tampered with and planted evidence? In particular, Reilly referred to the attic floorboard supposedly matching the rail from the kidnap ladder and the piece of wood trim from Hauptmann's closet with Condon's address and phone number written on it. At long last—but far too late—Reilly finally challenged Lindbergh's identification of the accented voice that had shouted "Hey, Doctor" from the interior of St. Raymond's Cemetery more than two and a half years prior.

In his summation the following day, Wilentz accused his adversary of "an old army game"—trying to intimidate, confuse, and befuddle the jury by planting seeds of doubt regarding the myriad of possibilities: What if someone confesses ten years from now? No one could have pulled off this crime alone—what if others were involved?

"Now, Mr. Reilly says for the defense that we have got to prove, in order to sustain this indictment, that Hauptmann did this job and did it alone," said Wilentz. "And I say to you jurors that is not the law. So far as Hauptmann is concerned he could have fifty help him; if he participated in this murder that's all you have got to deal with."[2]

The prosecutor said that no American gangster or racketeer ever sank to the level of killing babies and that "the most venomous snake in the jungle…would have passed that child without hurting a hair of its head." Wilentz called Hauptmann "a fellow that had ice water in his veins," "a fellow who thought he was bigger than Lindy," "panther-like," and "an animal lower than the lowest form in the animal kingdom."

The attorney general asked Colonel Schwarzkopf—the man who had been "pilloried around this State and around this Nation by ambitious newspapermen"—to stand up in response to the defense's suggestion that the New Jersey State Police had planted evidence in Hauptmann's apartment. "Does he look like a crook, a graduate of the United States Military Academy; a man who served his nation against his Fatherland, on the fronts in Europe?"

In contradiction to his opening statement, in which he had asserted that the baby was dropped from the ladder, Wilentz now claimed that Hauptmann had taken his chisel into the nursery and knocked the child "into insensibility right there in that room." Yet no blood was found either in the nursery or on the chisel, which investigators had discovered near the ladder.

The prosecutor attacked Reilly's efforts to pin the crime on the deceased Isador Fisch, Violet Sharp, and Olly Whateley and mocked the "pathetic" witnesses the defense had called to the stand. "The people he blames are physically dead; the people he brought here into this courtroom, most of them, are morally dead," Wilentz said. The attorney general said that Hauptmann had "disgraced Betty Gow," brought "unfair shame" on Dr. Condon, and caused panic in millions of homes across America.

"If you bring in a recommendation of mercy, a wishy-washy decision—yes, it is your province, I will not say a word about it," said Wilentz. "But it seems to me you have the courage, if you believe with us, you have to find him guilty of murder in the first degree."[3]

Judge Trenchard gave his charge to the jury the next morning: "If you find that the murder was committed by the defendant in perpetrating a burglary, it is murder in the first degree, even though the killing was unintentional. If there is a reasonable doubt that the murder was committed by the defendant in perpetrating a burglary, he must be acquitted.

"If you find the defendant guilty of murder in the first degree," he continued, "you may, if you see fit, by your verdict, and as a part thereof, recommend imprisonment at hard labor for life. If you should return a verdict of murder in the first degree and nothing else, the punishment which would be inflicted on that verdict would be death."

The judge stated that "every person convicted of murder in the first degree, his aiders, abettors, counselors and procurers shall suffer death"[4] unless the jury were to recommend imprisonment at hard labor for life. The jury filed out of the courtroom and entered the deliberation room at 11:16 a.m. Concerned that reporters might have planted listening devices in the room, the jurors searched beneath their chairs and behind draperies. Newspapermen had tried without success to get them to talk. As the jurors discussed the case, they kept their voices low to prevent eavesdropping. The twelve shared unanimous consent about the defendant's guilt. The debate shifted to the subject of punishment. Three voted for life imprisonment on the first ballot.

As long as the jury was out, Judge Trenchard confined the reporters in his chambers. During the long wait, Adela Rogers St. John would remember, a game of craps went on in one corner of the courtroom, a game of checkers progressed across one of the counsel tables, newspapermen sailed paper airplanes, and a practical joker mounted the judge's bench and rapped a gavel.

As a matter of tradition, the borough of Flemington rang the courthouse bell eight times whenever a jury had reached a verdict in a capital case. At seven o'clock, a church bell signaled the beginning of its Wednesday evening prayer service, causing confusion in the streets.

Inside the courtroom, a prankster imitating the deep voice of a guard cried out "Quiet, please," hoping to fool spectators into believing that the verdict was coming in momentarily. The first few times, the newspaper crowd fell for it.

At a quarter after ten o'clock, the foreman spoke a few words to the sheriff, who sent up an assistant to the belfry. As far as the eye could see from the top of the courthouse steps, a crowd of thousands stood massed in the icy streets. At 10:27 p.m., as the tolling began, menacing yells rocketed into the frigid night air: "Kill Hauptmann! Kill Hauptmann!"

A few minutes later, state trooper Hugo Stockburger, holding Hauptmann by the wrist, led the prisoner back into the courtroom; Hauptmann had refused his supper and had only eaten a piece of bread since the morning adjournment. Stockburger, a German immigrant and one of the guards in the Flemington jail, would recall decades later that Hauptmann, who had been placed on suicide watch, never once looked him in the eye.[5]

The jurors filed into the courtroom in a simple line. None made eye contact with the defendant as they passed him on the way to the jury box. As her husband stared straight ahead, Anna Hauptmann searched the faces of the jurors, then lowered her head.

"This is only the beginning, Richard," said Lloyd Fisher, draping an arm over his client's shoulder. "Don't show a sign."

At 10:45 p.m., Judge Trenchard took his chair behind the bench, rapped twice with his gavel, and asked the jury and the defendant to rise. Seated behind her husband, Anna Hauptmann trembled.

"Do you have a verdict?" the court clerk asked.

"Guilty," said the foreman, Charles Walton. "We find the defendant Bruno Richard Hauptmann guilty of murder in the first degree."

Messenger boys scrambled for the exit, but Judge Trenchard ordered them not to leave until the court had completed all of its business. One by one, each juror addressed the court and repeated the verdict: "I find the defendant Bruno Richard Hauptmann guilty of murder in the first degree."

"Do you wish to make a motion for sentence, Mr. Attorney General?" the judge asked.

"The State moves for immediate sentence," Wilentz said.

The judge asked the defendant to stand. "Bruno Richard Haupt-mann, you have been convicted of murder in the first degree. The sentence of the Court is that you suffer death at the time and place and in the manner provided by law."

The courtroom fell silent. Hauptmann had remained unflinching as he listened to the sentence. The jurors showed no emotion. Suddenly, a messenger boy poked his head out of a second-story window. On the streets, forty-two state troopers outside the courthouse fanned out to restrain the crowd. "Guilty—death!" shouted the boy. The mob hollered and whooped. Amid the commotion, Walter Winchell leapt to his feet and said, "I said that in October. I predicted he'd be guilty. Oh, that's another big one for me! Come on, fellas, put it in your stories. I was the first one to call it."[6]

Anna Hauptmann stared at the floor. At ten minutes to eleven, a constable and a state trooper led her husband out of the courtroom in handcuffs and deposited him in his cell. The condemned man buried his head into his cot and broke down. As men in plain clothes escorted Anna back to the little yellow frame house where she was staying three blocks away, she ignored the horde of reporters trailing her, including one who spoke in German and tried to persuade her to say something.

Colonel Schwarzkopf was visibly pleased with the outcome as he walked out of the courtroom. In Nellie's Tap Room, there were cheers and laughter and toasts and clinked glasses. At Next Day Hill, the Lindberghs, Betty Morrow, and her houseguest, Harold Nicolson, who had just returned from England to continue his research for his biography on her husband, were tuned in to coverage of the trial on the wireless. Although not present to hear the verdict, Lindbergh had spent each of the thirty-two days of the trial in the Flemington courtroom. After dinner, Nicolson retired to the library, where Betty interrupted him: "Hauptmann has been condemned to death without mercy."[7] The writer joined the family in the drawing room, where they listened to radio commentary, including one reporter's rants above the background noise of the delirious crowd: "Bruno Hauptmann now stands guilty of the foulest—"

"Turn that off, Charles, turn that off," Anne said.

After Lindbergh switched off the radio, the group retired to the pantry for a glass of ginger beer. "There is no doubt at all that Hauptmann did the thing," he said. "My one dread all these years is that they would get hold of someone as a victim about whom I wasn't sure. I am sure about this—quite sure. It is this way. . ."[8]

Lindbergh went through the case point by point. He commented that Hauptmann was "a magnificent-looking man. Splendidly built. But that his eyes were like the eyes of a wild boar. Mean, shifty, small and cruel."

"That howling mob over the radio—how incredibly horrible and bitter to realize that this has to do with us," Anne wrote in her diary. ". . . Incredible as that first night."[9]

The Lindberghs expressed no jubilation over the verdict. The life of their firstborn child had been taken, Hauptmann was guilty, and for them it was more a feeling that justice had been served. In their search to find meaning in the tragedy, they would give Highfields to the State of New Jersey for use as a home for troubled boys.

"Mr. Hearst took a poll of our reporters who had covered the kidnapping and the trial and those who had done editorial work on it at city desks and copy desks," Adela Rogers St. John would recount. "Without exception, we agreed that Hauptmann had not done it alone, that he should be kept alive to find the other guilty parties and to resolve the unanswered problems."[10]

Back at the Flemington jail, Hauptmann paced his cell and wept throughout the night. He was heard muttering to himself: "Little men, little pieces of wood, little scraps of paper."

# 27

# Arrival and Departure

On Saturday morning, February 16, 1935, a three-sedan procession carrying Bruno Hauptmann drove twenty-three miles from the Flemington jail to the New Jersey State Prison in Trenton. He had only nibbled at bread and potatoes since his conviction three days earlier. Five hundred of the curious and a cadre of fourteen county and State officers awaited the caravan. With just a hint of a smile, the prisoner turned toward a photographer who drew close to snap his picture. "I am innocent," he said.

After the vehicle carrying Hauptmann passed through, the prison gate, surmounted by eagles, winged monsters, and serpents, clanged shut. On the way to his cell, one of eighteen reserved for prisoners condemned to death, guards ushered him through the mess hall. Recognizing him at once, many of the six hundred inmates eating their midday meal jeered and booed him. The "pecking order" in the prison population of child killers is well known.[1] How would a man convicted of murdering the infant son of America's greatest hero have been treated, particularly if he were German? How long would he have managed to go unharmed? Hauptmann's quarters sat on the lower tier of the death house, a few steps away from the entrance to the "throne room," as inmates called the death chamber. The ten-by-twelve-foot cell had a cot, a sink, and a toilet. The prisoner requested a Bible, a picture of his wife and baby, and a box of cigars.

Hauptmann signed a petition to declare himself a pauper and asked the State of New Jersey for financial assistance to pay for an appeal. Meanwhile, the mayor of Kamenz received a letter from someone in Brooklyn suggesting that the town raise money to send Pauline Hauptmann to America to fight for her son's freedom. In a letter to Germany's Minister of Propaganda, the mayor said that the woman was in no position to declare her son's innocence and that he had no intention of conducting any such fund-raising. At the time, there was a swastika plastered on a bulletin board just a few steps from Pauline Hauptmann's front door, and the mayor had nothing to gain with Hitler's regime by coming to her son's defense.[2] Kamenz would later become the site of a Nazi extermination camp.

As Hauptmann began spending the last days of his life in the death house, John Knoll was sailing in grand style back to New York from Hamburg aboard the SS *Manhattan*, which had left Europe from Southampton.[3] The ship had cast off from Southampton on February 13, the day of Hauptmann's conviction.[4] When the *Manhattan* docked in the Port of New York, he was locked up in the New Jersey State Prison, about to be silenced forever.

No pictures of Knoll survive from this Atlantic crossing, and any cameras carried by his fellow passengers in first class were much more likely to be directed at a man whose fame truly did rival that of Lindbergh: Babe Ruth was on board, on his way back from Japan with his wife and daughter after a series of exhibition games.[5] Fans swarmed him on the ship to ask for autographs, and he was particularly obliging to his youngest fans. "The kidnapping of the Lindbergh baby horrified my father," Ruth's daughter Julia Ruth Stephens recalled in 2011. "Daddy so adored children and always made time for them."[6]

Knoll returned to the States alone: his bride Lilly, the one-time aviator, had discovered she was pregnant, perhaps soon after her arrival in Germany. She would remain in the country with her family for another four months and would return to America on the *Manhattan*, arriving on June 5, 1935.[7] It was during Lilly's stay in Germany that her parents helped lay her plan of escape from Knoll just as Hitler was laying plans to conquer Europe. At the time, the family was still grieving the loss of her grandmother, Margarethe Zorn Karg, who had died on August 19, 1934, the day that Hitler had become Führer. The Kargs sensed the inevitable heartache and trouble that awaited Lilly if she stayed with her husband.[8]

If John Knoll had moments of sullenness on his voyage to Hamburg before the beginning of the Hauptmann trial, he had reason to feel immeasurable relief during his two-month stay overseas. News from the Flemington trial had given no cause for worry. Lindbergh had identified Hauptmann as the man who had shouted "Hey, Doctor" from the interior of St. Raymond's Cemetery. Condon's sworn statement had assured all that Hauptmann was Cemetery John. The incriminating testimonies of wood scientist Arthur Koehler and handwriting analyst Albert S. Osborn had seemed to settle the questions of who had built the kidnap ladder and who had written the ransom letters. And, most importantly, there was Hauptmann's own testimony, in which he denied any knowledge of who had participated in the kidnapping. After the trial came yet another gift, when the various organizations that had worked to solve the crime all called an end to their investigations. The search for the kidnappers and the Hauptmann trial were estimated to have cost the government nearly $1,200,000—the equivalent of about $18,000,000 today.[9] With an obviously guilty man condemned to death, what was the point of going on and spending more?

Anna Hauptmann established a legal defense fund to rally the German community to her husband's aid. Before an audience of twenty-five hundred supporters in Yorkville, the center of New York's German-American colony, she walked onto the stage to thunderous applause. The mention of Charles Lindbergh brought hisses and jeers. A zealous crowd of fifteen hundred at Ebling's Casino in the South Bronx booed references to Judge Trenchard and "Wilensky," as one speaker called the New Jersey attorney general. Men hawked Nazi propaganda outside the auditorium. The beer and dance hall was less than a quarter-mile from the apartment on Jackson Avenue where John Knoll had lived before his move to Michigan.

Autograph seekers from across the country sent one-dollar checks to Hauptmann: his endorsement would make them collectors' items. Funds continued to arrive, but only in dribs and drabs. With Edward Reilly threatening to sue the Hauptmanns for nonpayment of additional legal fees, Lloyd Fisher, assisted by Frederick Pope and Egbert Rosecrans, took charge of the defense. "We were never able to sit down at one table with Reilly for more than ten minutes to plan defense strategy the entire thirty-two days of the trial," Fisher would recall.[10]

On June 20, 1935, the attorneys appealed to the highest tribunal in New Jersey to reverse the verdict in the Flemington trial. An expert in constitutional law, Rosecrans asserted that Hauptmann had not been tried by a jury in Mercer County, where it could be presumed the crime had taken place. Thus, as the defense had unsuccessfully argued before Judge Trenchard, the court in Flemington had lacked jurisdiction to try the case. Furthermore, there was no legal precedent for the State of New Jersey's charge against Hauptmann—"that he was guilty of murder during the commission of a felony in the crime of burglary." To argue that the baby's death had resulted from the commission of a statutory burglary defied a common sense approach to the law. The circumstantial evidence as to burglary was an inappropriate interpretation of the law, the charge being that Hauptmann had entered the home with intent to steal a sleeping suit of no demonstrable value and to commit battery upon the child. Furthermore, the return of the garment proved that there had been no intent to steal it.

Such an item of unproven value could not be regarded as proof of theft with the anticipation of convicting the defendant. Rosecrans did not concede that a burglary had been committed, but if it had, the theft was petty larceny. Therefore, the crime should have been considered a misdemeanor, not a felony, and thus the baby's death did not constitute first-degree murder.

The defense objected to the attorney general's injection into his summation that Hauptmann was guilty of a willful, deliberate, and premeditated killing of the Lindbergh baby—a new accusation to which the defendant was unable to answer. Wilentz had commented on facts not introduced into evidence and sought to influence the jury through inflammatory remarks.

Rosecrans also argued that Judge Trenchard's charge to the jury was improper and unfair: rather than acting as an arbiter, the justice had spoken as an advocate of the State's evidence against Hauptmann. In response to the defense's suggestion that the crime was the work of a criminal gang aided by servants of either the Lindberghs or the Morrows, Judge Trenchard had asked the jury, "Now do you believe that? Is there any evidence in this case whatsoever to support any such conclusion?"[11]

Other aspects of the trial were called into question, including the testimony of Lindbergh himself. How was it possible for a man to identify a voice he had heard two years before from a distance of two or three hundred feet away? What about the carnival atmosphere of the trial itself? How could the jurors not have been influenced by the spirit of mobs lusting for Hauptmann's execution, by newsboys shouting headlines, and by radio programs broadcast just a few feet away from their hotel rooms? And what did the constant presence of Lindbergh himself supply, a sympathetic figure for whom the masses were demanding justice? For all these reasons, Rosecrans asked the court to reverse the verdict. Full of vigor and sarcasm, Wilentz rose to reply: Hauptmann had been rightly convicted, and he deserved the death penalty.

On October 9, 1935, in a unanimous decision, the New Jersey Court of Errors and Appeals upheld the verdict of the Flemington court. The evidence, although circumstantial, was overwhelming and left no room for reasonable doubt. Fisher delivered the news to his client. Hauptmann stared at a photograph of his wife and child on the wall of his cell. It was the eve of his tenth anniversary.

Determined to resolve unanswered questions regarding the possible involvement of accomplices in the kidnapping, Governor Harold Hoffman ordered the superintendent of the New Jersey State Police to renew the investigation. In a letter to Schwarzkopf dated January 30, 1936, Hoffman wrote: "I am not satisfied that the execution of Hauptmann will be a complete punishment for the crime. There are many indications that more than one person participated in the activities which led to the kidnapping of the Lindbergh baby and his death. To let any one of these persons escape trial and punishment would be as grave an offense against justice as would be the punishment of any person not guilty."[12]

Schwarzkopf, who disliked the governor and resented the directive, refused to comment to the press. Hoffman, a Republican, had also carried on a running feud with David Wilentz and with another Democrat on the attorney general's prosecution team, Anthony M. Hauck, Jr. Neither Wilentz nor Hauck, whom the governor called "an errand boy," had investigated the possibility that multiple kidnappers had participated in the crime. Hauck fumed that he was "sick and tired" of Hoffman's meddling and criticism of the State's handling of the case.[13]

An opponent of the death penalty, Clarence Darrow sent a telegram to the governor. "It seems unprofessional to demand immediate death of Hauptmann," wrote Darrow. "In face of such widespread public disapproval Hauptmann should be entitled to retrial. This with sincere desire for fair play."[14] Out of similar conviction against the death penalty, and to urge the use of lie-detection methods to get Hauptmann to name his accomplices, the aviator Amelia Earhart also sent a plea to Hoffman. "Whether or not it affected the sentence of the man in the New Jersey State Prison," she wrote, "it would still demonstrate to the world American sincerity and American belief that no stone should be allowed unturned in the search for justice."[15]

The *Detroit Free Press* reported that Lindbergh had complained to friends about Hoffman's "belated attempts in Hauptmann's behalf" and "the vacillation of law enforcement and the sentimentality over Hauptmann."[16] As the execution date approached, the Lindberghs received crank letters and warnings of danger. One note carried a threat to their three-year-old son if his father did not "come to the defense of Hauptmann before it is too late."[17] One day, as Jon's nurse was driving him home from nursery school, an automobile crowded the car to the curb. Men with cameras jumped out and snapped photographs of the terrified child. This was not the first time such an incident had occurred.[18] By this point, the Lindberghs were convinced that a normal life for them in the United States was impossible.

Shortly before midnight on Saturday, December 21, 1935, a 7,500-ton freighter, the SS *American Importer*, cast off from a deserted Manhattan pier with only three passengers: Charles, Anne, and Jon Lindbergh. So secret was Lindbergh's planning that not even the captain knew who would be aboard. As the ship left the harbor, the aviator saluted the Statue of Liberty. And unlike John Knoll leaving on the *Manhattan* a year earlier, it would be a long time before Lindbergh saw that statue again. To the forces that had made life in America untenable—the press, the ubiquitous crowds, and madmen threatening further harm, only one answer was possible: a self-imposed exile to England, whose people,

Lindbergh believed, set the standard for civilized behavior. It was a rough crossing. One night, a wave crashed through the window and flooded the Lindberghs' cabin, soaking Anne and Jon.[19] The family spent Christmas on the high seas, and on New Year's Eve, Charles carried his tousle-haired son down the gangplank in Liverpool.[20] Although Charles had spoken of leaving America for over a year, the speed with which the family departed left Anne feeling confused and worried about the future. "I want silence and peace," said Lindbergh to a reporter in Wales. "I want to be forgotten, even my name."[21]

"We were very happy in England and France," Anne would say more than forty years later. "It was so marvelous to go out without being mobbed, to have our privacy."[22] Some in America, however, failed to understand the reasons behind the family's sudden departure. On January 1, 1936, the *New York Daily News* criticized Lindbergh in an editorial. Neglecting to take into account the aviator's determination to protect his second son and his displeasure with how "difficult, disagreeable, and dangerous"[23] life had become for his family, the newspaper claimed that Lindbergh had invited trouble and acted "hoity-toity and surly almost every time he appeared in public . . . like a prima donna on parade."[24]

Four members of the Morrow family—two siblings and a brother-in-law of the late Senator Morrow and a sister of his wife, Betty—spoke to the media but asked not to be quoted. "There has not been the slightest change in the conviction held by the Lindberghs and members of their family that Hauptmann is guilty," wrote the interviewer. "It was admitted, however, that he might have had accomplices and that reprisals by them are a source of fear."[25] Indeed, even in Anne Morrow Lindbergh's diaries and letters, she referred to whoever was responsible for the kidnapping in the plural. "I don't want to get any nearer to his murderers, to see their faces, the weapon they killed him with, the place where he was killed," she wrote in her diary. "It must be discovered, but not by me."[26]

Hoffman told the press that he had little to say about the impact of his own actions on Lindbergh's decision to leave America and said that the flier "must have had sufficient reason for taking this action."[27] As editorials called for the New Jersey Legislature to impeach the governor, political pundits agreed that this latest chapter in the kidnapping saga would doom his ambition to secure the Republican vice presidential nomination in the 1936 election.

Many aspects of the Lindbergh case troubled Hoffman, including the "truthfulness and mental competency"[28] of some of the witnesses called by the State and Condon's refusal in the Manhattan police station to identify Hauptmann as Cemetery John. As historian Lloyd Gardner describes the scene, Harry Walsh of the Jersey City Police had led Condon "along a narrow path near a precipice" atop the Palisades Cliffs to frighten him.[29] Only after having been subjected to such intimidation did Condon change his position; he was reminded that he was the only person who had dealt with Cemetery John and was threatened with indictment as an accessory after the crime if he failed to say that Hauptmann was Cemetery John. The month after the baby's body was discovered, Walsh told Condon that he was "firmly convinced beyond any reasonable doubt" that the go-between knew who the kidnappers were.[30] The governor also reflected on the words of Dr. Condon, whose testimony had proved crucial to the prosecution: "I am still convinced that more than one person is involved in this crime."[31] In a letter dated March 3, 1938, to Henry Breckinridge, who "occupied an elevated throne in [his] mental sphere," Condon would decry the "scurrilous, libelous and vituperative articles from the hands of Pudgy Harolf [sic] Hoffman, his Ex-Excellency, and Lloydie Fisher" in *Liberty* magazine.[32]

Files on the Lindbergh case that the FBI would release in 1977 under the Freedom of Information Act reveal that the organization's chief agent in the inquiry, Thomas H. Sisk, had argued after Hauptmann's arrest that a strong likelihood existed "that there [were] others connected with this case." Sisk suggested that Hauptmann, who had weighed 180 pounds at the time of the kidnapping, "would have had difficulty going through the window." He also cited the presence of another man "giving signals at each of the cemeteries" during ransom negotiations and contended that Hauptmann "had a lot of help in the passing of the money."[33] Despite these lingering doubts, however, the highest levels of law enforcement abandoned the investigation. Hauptmann was their man, and the matter was settled.

# PART III

# 28
# Silence

On the evening of April 3, 1936, fifty witnesses with nontransfer-able invitations entered the execution chamber at the New Jersey State Prison. The room was small and brightly lit and had white-washed brick walls. Thirty reporters, men from the governor's office, and a collection of state legislators and police officials, including Colonel Schwarzkopf, filled several rows of folding chairs. Signed by the warden, each pass read: "You are hereby invited to be present at the execution by electricity of Bruno Richard Hauptmann, #17400."

Under a moonlit sky, prison officials had escorted the witnesses across a courtyard to the squat brick building housing the execution chamber. Each invitee was frisked beforehand. At the execution of Ruth Snyder at Sing Sing in 1928, a spectator who had smuggled a camera in-side the death chamber snapped a picture as the current streaked through the murderess. The photograph created a national front-page sensation. The warden overseeing Hauptmann's execution had resolved that no such antics would occur on his watch.

The door to the execution chamber opened and Hauptmann walked in. He was pale and the life was gone from his face. During his final weeks, the prisoner had received comfort from the Scriptures and from the Lutheran pastors who visited him. His private writings reflected an attitude of for-giveness toward David Wilentz, who had humiliated him and called him "a snake" and other hateful names during his summation; from all appear-ances, Hauptmann went to his death holding a grudge against no one.

Hollow-eyed and dazed, Hauptmann shuffled forward toward death in a pair of bedroom slippers and continued past the electric chair. He was about to collide into a physician when a guard nudged him out of his trance and maneuvered him into the seat. His right pants leg slit to allow his bare leg to come in contact with the lower electrode, he was fastened into the chair, which had two straps for each arm. Straps also secured each leg at the ankle and the waist, head, and chest. Hauptmann gripped the arms of the chair and stared straight ahead. He made no final statement.

The man appointed to throw the switch, Robert G. Elliott, had dreaded this assignment "more than any other."[1] For weeks, reporters had hounded the executioner, who had received a constant stream of letters from autograph seekers, issuers of threats ("If you give B.R.H. the juice, you will be sorry"),[2] and anonymous hurlers of insults ("You should blow your brains out, if you have any").[3] During his career, Elliott, whose home was bombed after he had executed the Italian anarchists Sacco and Vanzetti, would usher three hundred and eighty-seven to their deaths.

With his gray hair, wrinkled skin, and gaunt, cadaverous face, the executioner looked far older than his age, which was sixty-two. In repose he could appear agonizingly sad and grim—almost haunted. "Even pictures of me have been retouched so I would resemble something akin to Mr. Hyde," he would write in his memoir, *Agent of Death.*[4]

The executioner fastened an electrode to Hauptmann's shaved head and drooped a delicate black cloth hood over it. With an almost imperceptible movement, the man in the electric chair shook his head. Two ministers read in German the ritual of the Lutheran Church.

At 8:44 p.m., the warden gave the signal. Elliott twisted the wheel on the generator's control panel. "I believe in one God the Father Almighty," began one of the clergymen, but the humming of the current drowned out his voice. Hauptmann's muscles tensed up as he received the first of three shocks of 2,000 volts. Although the need to listen for the heart was a formality, six physicians approached the body with stethoscopes. At 8:47 p.m., the prison doctor broke the silence: "This man is dead."

Sam Blackman, the AP man who had been the first reporter to arrive at the crime scene on the night of the kidnapping, was among the witnesses. "I was absolutely positive that Hauptmann was guilty," he told his daughter Carolyn many years later. "But it was horrible to watch." He could not bear to elaborate.[5]

Shortly after the execution, Lloyd Fisher's secretary went to Anna Hauptmann's room in the Stacy-Trent Hotel in downtown Trenton and delivered the news. "*Ach, Gott, mein* Richard!" cried Anna, dissolving in tears and clasping her head in her hands. A crush of cameramen and reporters, some of whom had been grinning in the corridor moments before, pushed their way inside the room and began snapping photographs of the widow and asking her for comments.

In the Hotel Hildebrand, Fisher, who had always believed in his client's innocence, sat slumped in an armchair and wept. The lawyer had visited Hauptmann three hundred times in the Flemington jail and the prison in Trenton. Fisher would call the execution "the greatest tragedy in the state of New Jersey."

"Time will never wash it out," he said.

"They think when I die, the case will die," Hauptmann had said as the day of his execution drew near. "They think it will be like a book I close. But the book, it will never close."

Gabriel Heatter, who had covered the trial for seven weeks, spoke on the air without interruption for fifty-five minutes. As he signed off, Heatter abandoned his signature "There's good news tonight" slogan. "Bruno Hauptmann is dead," he said. "Good night."

The Lindberghs declined to make a statement. An ocean away from the publicity that had forced them to keep their home and grounds under armed guard "as a protection from criminals, lunatics, reporters, and photographers,"[6] they had entered into a two-year lease of Long Barn, a fourteenth-century country home in the village of Sevenoaks Weald, Kent. The Lindberghs lived quietly in England, bothered only "by American tourists."[7]

Lindbergh would travel to America only once during the next four years. After "giggling high-school girls, silly boys, and older people who should have more consideration" hounded him for autographs on a train ride to Washington, he wrote in his journal, "I certainly miss the privacy and decency of Europe. . . Impossible to do anything."[8]

In Kamenz, Pauline Hauptmann, who had been hoping for another reprieve for her son, received the news:

078 TELEGRAM                                      6.4.1936 8, 15

RICHARD DIED RECONCILED WITH GOD HE WAS INNOCENT
MAY GOD COMFORT YOU

ANNY AND PASTOR WERNER

The following day, a Lutheran minister who had spent time with
Hauptmann at the New Jersey State Prison wrote his mother a letter:

Dear Frau Hauptmann,

I did what I could to get everyone to believe he was innocent but they
would not believe so we have to live with this decision under God's
hand. It is a great pain for every one of us. I met with Richard over the
past six months and learned to love him. He lived as a Christian and
died as a hero. This appears fantastic but it is the truth.

My dear Frau Hauptmann, you will soon have the wish to go to
Heaven. Richard is there. If I can say that someone is in Heaven, then
Richard is there for sure. During his last days on earth, he learned
about the Word of God and he learned to love it. He learned much
about the Bible. In his last days, he prayed often and very earnestly.
He knew how to speak to God. His last minutes were passed in prayer
and in the reading of the Word of God.

He was prepared to die and all of us who were standing around
him saw that God does wonders right now. He is in God's hands. The
people may have killed his body, but his soul has gone home to God,
who created him.

So you, dear Frau Hauptmann, may wish that the day comes soon
when you may be with your son in Heaven. We who are alive have
promised him that we will care for his wife and child as best as we can.
Also we will take care that the shame will be erased from his name.

Now, dear Frau Hauptmann, I pray that God will look at you and
take you home, where there are no trials or prisons, where you can
praise God forever. We will all meet in Heaven, and we will speak of
these things that happened on earth—whether they are happy or not.

We wish God's blessing on you. It goes through a fight to victory,
through power to light, and through the Cross to the crown. A greeting to you from here.

J. Matthieson, Pastor

Pauline Hauptmann's health declined after her son's death. Her hands shook so badly she could not write. A neighborhood girl helped her open a package from Anna and wrote letters for her. "Pauline Hauptmann could not bring herself to say that her son had been executed," recalled this girl, Gerda Hartmann, many years later. "She told me that he had died as the result of a very bad illness."[9]

The *Kamenzer Tageblatt* reported on the execution and incorrectly described Hauptmann as a naturalized U.S. citizen. The newspaper did not try to absolve its town's most infamous citizen of blame but said that American public opinion became more an issue than the legal facts, calling the trial a dark moment for the U.S. justice system.[10] Rather than express indignation at the jury's verdict, the *Tageblatt* had reported objectively on stories after Hauptmann's conviction, including Governor Hoffman's demands for further investigation into the kidnapping.

The governor called Schwarzkopf responsible for "the most bungled case in police history"[11] and continued to pursue the case. "If Hauptmann had been kept behind prison bars for a reasonable time, there would have been an opportunity to answer many of the unanswered questions, particularly those involving an accomplice or accomplices," Hoffman would say sixteen years after the execution. Two years later, in 1954, the former governor would die in a New York hotel just as he was about to be indicted for embezzlement. The man assigned to the investigation was Colonel Schwarzkopf.

The media had maligned Schwarzkopf for his handling of the Lindbergh investigation, but his conclusion that the kidnapping was the work of a small gang of amateurs had been right all along. Even a member of Wilentz's prosecution team, George Large, doubted Hauptmann's role as the lone kidnapper. During a recess one day, Large had invited his nephew Edwin, a law student at Columbia, to join him for lunch with Lindbergh and Schwarzkopf. "My uncle was an experienced prosecutor, and he never doubted that the verdict was right and that Hauptmann was guilty," Edwin K. Large, Jr., would recall. "But he also thought that other people were involved and never caught."[12]

# 29

# Last Chance

In Washington, D.C., society matron Evalyn Walsh McLean, a mining heiress and the owner of the Hope diamond, sympathized with the Lindberghs and wanted to help them. Her own son, who had himself been the target of multiple kidnapping threats, had died at the age of eight in an accident involving a Tin Lizzie. After a con man who had convinced her he was in touch with the Lindbergh kidnappers had scammed her out of $104,000, the society matron asked her friend Charles Curtis, former vice president under Herbert Hoover, to arrange an introduction to Governor Hoffman.

When the governor came to her mansion a few days later, she urged him to continue the reexamination of the Lindbergh case. Convinced that the kidnapping was not the work of one man, she hired one of the country's foremost criminal defense lawyers, Samuel S. Leibowitz, to head her own investigation. Leibowitz expressed confidence that he could persuade Hauptmann to confess and name his accomplices. "It was a blustery night and only a crazy fool would have planted that ladder against the wall without someone to steady it," he would recall years later.[1] On February 13, 1936, Leibowitz met with the prisoner in his cell. It was the one-year anniversary of his conviction. As usual, Hauptmann protested his innocence. The following day, and again on February 17, the attorney came to talk more about the kidnapping. Each time, the conversation went in circles. Point by point, Leibowitz reviewed the arsenal of evidence that had led to the guilty verdict. "*Dot's* not so," Hauptmann said over and over.

"What was the most damning evidence?" Leibowitz asked.

"That handwriting is the *worst* thing against me," Hauptmann said.

Leibowitz painted a ghastly picture of the execution chamber and of the equipment that dominated the room. He warned the prisoner that he was bound for the electric chair unless he confessed. During their third meeting, Leibowitz leaned a miniature ladder against a cardboard replica of the east side of the Lindberghs' home. "What theory have you developed about the kidnapping?" he asked.

"Me? Why, none," Hauptmann said.

"Oh, you haven't thought about it at all. During all the time you've been in jail in peril of your life, you've never thought of it, eh? You've never tried to figure out how it might have been done."

"No."

"Who else would have had to figure it out?"

A long silence. Then: "The one who did it."

"But suppose you had figured it out, what would be your theory? How would you have done it?"

"I would have got somebody through the front door."

The lawyer turned to the subject of the baby. "How was he killed?"

"By accident," Hauptmann said. He added that anyone who had wanted to take revenge on Lindbergh would have murdered the child.

"And if they did, they'd have left the body right there in the house."

"That's right."

Leibowitz suggested that as the man inside the nursery was transferring the baby to a second man at the top of the ladder, the baby was dropped, and the second man fell from the ladder.

"There must have been two men," Hauptmann agreed eagerly.

"Two, three, four," said Leibowitz. "It makes no difference. The point is you agree that the baby must have been taken down the ladder."

"Yes."[2]

Leibowitz's technique—a cerebral chess game in which he pretended to be clueless and asked the criminal to imagine what might have happened rather than how he had done it—would become a standard FBI interviewing technique decades later.

"Guys like Hauptmann love to stroke you and fool you," said retired special agent Ed Sulzbach. "He had no idea Leibowitz was fooling him."[3]

The attorney believed that he would have wrung a confession out of Hauptmann had the prisoner not assumed that the governor, who had already issued one thirty-day reprieve, could continue to rescue him from the electric chair. Knowing that Hoffman had no such authority, he gave up. In recounting the conversation decades afterward, Leibowitz said, "Hauptmann never confessed. I wish I had been able to persuade him to. What a great victory for justice it would have been if those who helped in the kidnapping of this little child had faced the electric chair as Hauptmann did."[4]

On the witness stand, Hauptmann had said to Attorney General Wilentz, "I feel innocent." And earlier, at his extradition hearings: "I never murdered," a carefully couched remark that has been overlooked ever since. In his mind, because he hadn't dropped the baby, he bore no responsibility for the tragic result. And thus, he was no murderer.

As Lloyd Gardner tells the story, Hauptmann's original attorney, James Fawcett, asked him, "Did you murder the child, Charles Augustus Lindbergh . . ."

"No," interrupted Hauptmann.

". . . on March 1, 1932, or any other time?"

"I never murdered," Hauptmann said.

Given his turn to question Hauptmann, Wilentz asked, "Didn't you build a ladder and put it up against the Lindbergh house? And didn't you go up that ladder into the house and murder the child?"

"No!" Hauptmann shouted. As Gardner observes, "It was his only outburst in five court appearances."[5]

"The State's witness, Dr. Condon, when he visited me in Flemington, said to the prosecutor that he could say nothing against me," Hauptmann wrote in a letter dated December 27, 1935, to his mother in Kamenz—a letter never mailed by the warden and official censor of inmate mail at the New Jersey State Prison. "But why he changed his opinion up to the time of the trial is a riddle to me. Dear mother, to write down here his phantastic statements would only be wasting paper . . . How this 70-year-old man can still sleep with peaceful conscience, I truly cannot understand."

In the letter, Hauptmann referred to a piece of evidence that cast doubt on Condon's identification of him as Cemetery John: the impression of a footprint taken by the police at St. Raymond's Cemetery. "A man by the name of John" who had received the $50,000 ransom payment from Condon, asserted Hauptmann, had made the footprint.

"When I was arrested on the 19th of September, 1934, the police seized, among many things, all my shoes. At that time I could not imagine what for," he wrote. "Why did not the Prosecutor produce at the trial the impression of which they had cast a model? Why? They cannot say that my foot has become larger or smaller . . . My shoe certainly did not fit."[6]

The warden stashed away the letter in his files, where it was discovered decades later. In the letter, Hauptmann expressed his shock and hurt at Wilentz's "vile language" during the trial. In his summation, the attorney general had referred to him as a "wild animal, snake, tiger, lowest being of the animal kingdom."

Neither the governor's willingness to commute Hauptmann's sentence to life imprisonment nor the Hearst syndicate's offer to put $100,000 into a trust fund to provide for his wife's financial security could persuade Hauptmann to admit to any participation in the kidnapping. To receive life imprisonment instead of the death penalty, he would have had to tell his wife that he had misled her ever since his arrest—in short, that his entire life was a lie. Instead, he held fast to his story, leaving Anna and their baby boy nothing. When Hoffman inquired about the existence of accomplices, Wilentz replied that Hauptmann would never name them: to do so would incriminate himself, something he had resolved never to do. "Hauptmann knew that if he had admitted his role in the kidnapping, his reputation in the eyes of his family, friends, and fellow countrymen would have been destroyed," said Mark Olshaker.[7] John Douglas points out that Timothy McVeigh, after his conviction for the Oklahoma City bombings, never gave up "John Doe Number Two" before his execution. The profiler observes that a convicted criminal, even one sentenced to death, may be unwilling to name his accomplices.

Dr. Sally C. Johnson was the court-appointed forensic psychiatrist who interviewed Theodore J. Kaczynski, better known as the Unabomber. As an expert on forensic psychiatry, Dr. Johnson has studied the many stories of John Knoll's life and analyzed both his personality and Hauptmann's. Noting Anna Hauptmann's "unwavering allegiance to her husband," she views him as "a man who possessed a powerful ability to charm others and get family members and others to believe him."

"I don't believe that Hauptmann was as dumb as many considered him," said Dr. Johnson. "That he never ratted on anyone shows that he wasn't so dumb. A simpler man would have caved."[8]

David Wilentz would live to age ninety-three. For the rest of his life, he rarely discussed the case. In the fall of 1981, he opened up to his respected friend Brendan T. Byrne, the New Jersey governor who would issue Executive Order No. 110, which required the Superintendent of the State Police to make the 250,000 investigative files, records, and exhibits within his custody on the Lindbergh kidnapping case available to the public. Still protesting her husband's innocence forty-five years after the trial, Anna Hauptmann had sued Governor Byrne and Wilentz to release the information.

"Wilentz told me he could have indicted Mrs. Hauptmann as her husband's accomplice in the kidnapping," recalled Governor Byrne. "Not wanting to complicate the process, and wanting to be sure that he could convict Hauptmann, he decided not to do so."[9] Governor Byrne has long believed that Hauptmann was guilty, but that he had worked with accomplices. "I wanted to take Anna Hauptmann's deposition and was eager to do the job myself," said the former governor. "But when I mentioned taking her deposition, Wilentz got hysterical."[10]

Governor Byrne and Wilentz discussed the Lindbergh case at Morven, the New Jersey Governor's Mansion in Princeton. Don Linky, an attorney and advisor to the governor, sat in on the meeting.

"General, do you really believe that Bruno Hauptmann was guilty?" Governor Byrne asked.

Here, Linky would recall, "a long silence of at least thirty seconds" followed as Wilentz contemplated his response.

"Brendan," said Wilentz, "let me put it this way: If Hauptmann didn't do it himself, he went to his death knowing who did."[11]

Until her death at age ninety-five, Anna Hauptmann fought to clear her husband's name, and in October 1991 even returned, for the first time, to Flemington. Leaving the Union Hotel, as the *Hunterdon County Democrat* described the scene, "Mrs. Hauptmann never looked across

Main Street at the historic courthouse. Before turning toward the driveway next to the hotel, she said that, while she was afraid to come back to Flemington, she was reassured when she saw all the people. 'It's not 1935 anymore.'"[12]

Her death in 1994 left only Manfred, who as a baby, Anna recalled in Flemington, used to fall asleep to the sound of his father playing Brahms's Lullaby on a mandolin. After their son's birth, Hauptmann said to his wife, "Honey, I'm the happiest man in the world."[13] It's doubtful, of course, that Manfred Hauptmann had ever described himself in such terms, and I knew when I went to see him that the odds were against a long conversation.

On a clear October evening in 2010, I drove to his home in a small Pennsylvania town. I figured he must have encountered many people before me, materializing at his door with their various theories. I seriously doubted he would have any interest in hearing my father's story, much less in telling his own. But I decided it was worth a try, just in case Manfred Hauptmann was willing to speak with me. Maybe *this* story would ring true to him, as it had to various students of the case such as former Governor Byrne. Maybe he could supply little-known facts about his father that, added to the John Knoll story, suddenly took on new relevance.

My father had believed that Bruno Hauptmann, recognizing John Knoll's cunning nature, had gone to the electric chair closemouthed in order to protect his own baby son from harm. There's no way of telling if this is true, of course. But if it is, my father's conclusion would have been consistent with the faith and the model of forgiveness Hauptmann displayed at the end of his life and also with the theory that his denials would at least spare the son from the burden of knowing for sure that his father was guilty. As I reflected on Hauptmann's situation, I knew that my own father would have laid down his own life for me without hesitation. Believing there was a chance my father was right, I wanted to share his perspective with Manfred. And so I asked him to give me a hearing.

Outside his house, the light was fading as I arrived a little after seven o'clock. Manfred opened the door. Nothing was memorable about his appearance other than his trimmed white beard. He left the door ajar and leaned against the doorframe as we talked on the front porch. When

I told him that my father had grown up in a German neighborhood in the Bronx, he seemed curious. Then I showed him the photograph of John Knoll aboard the SS *Manhattan*.

"This man was responsible—"

Just when Manfred realized that the purpose of my visit involved a discussion of his father, he brought the exchange to a quick end. Very politely, he turned away and closed the door. I could understand why, from his standpoint. So many years after the grief that changed so many lives forever, his life almost as much as any, knowing more, even if there was more to know, wouldn't change a thing. He didn't want to hear it, and who could blame him?

# 30

# Justice Delayed

Even at the time, many shared prosecutor George Large's belief "that other people were involved and never caught." Because Hauptmann had remained silent to the end, however, there wasn't much to go on other than that haunting insistence that it wasn't he who collected the ransom at the cemetery but rather "a man by the name of John." With those words, and with Hauptmann's confident assertion that his shoe would not match the footprints found at St. Raymond's Cemetery, the doomed man seemed to be going as far toward implicating others as his own code of honor would allow.

There had been the lookouts observed by Al Reich and by Lindbergh himself at the two cemeteries as Condon was meeting with one kidnapper; the pair of German men seen driving off in a car together after trying to pass a gold note at a lumberyard in the South Bronx; and Condon's adamant reaction at the police station that Hauptmann was "not the man" he had spoken to for more than an hour on a park bench. These and other facts of the case left grounds for strong suspicion at the time that Cemetery John was Hauptmann's accomplice and not Hauptmann himself. But it was undirected suspicion, centering on no particular figure or evidence, and the only person who could put a name to it didn't make the connection until decades later.

As is usual in history's great crimes and tragedies, there are a few "might have beens" in the Lindbergh case, and one of them is how much better justice might have been served had one teenager in the South Bronx followed the story more closely and remembered earlier the day he had seen "Bruno" with John and Walter Knoll at Palisades Park, speaking in German about something going on in "Englewood." He just didn't; he didn't think much at all about his former neighbor in the years afterward except to puzzle now and then at the variation of handwriting on the self-addressed envelopes that Knoll had given him. Doubtless my father's indignation at the thought of John Knoll getting away with the murder of a baby was mixed with a sense of regret.

After Hauptmann went to the electric chair, Gene Zorn saw his former neighbor only once more. After my father graduated from college, one of his sisters heard that John Knoll had returned from Michigan and opened his own delicatessen in an Irish-Catholic neighborhood in Yonkers. He also operated a pub called Emerald Isle at the same location. Because Knoll was frugal, it's possible that he could have saved the money to open up two businesses, even without a sudden infusion of cash. It's just another of those facts that catches our attention once we know the rest of John Knoll's story. The name he gave the Emerald Isle pub falls into the same category—for some reason, as family members recall, Knoll often told people he was Irish.

My father and his family stopped by to see Knoll one Sunday afternoon in 1940. Nothing particularly memorable happened during the visit. My father had just bought his first car, and it's likely he showed it to Knoll and they chatted about it. Some time later, Knoll opened another deli near the train station in Scarsdale.

In 1942, the U.S. Army drafted Knoll, sent him to Panama, and put him to work as a cook. Perhaps not wanting to represent himself as a German immigrant, he lied on his induction form and put down that he had been born in Poland—a minor fib, but a serious offense under U. S. law.[1] During his absence, his third wife, Ida, ran the family business. Like his first two wives, she was a German immigrant. In later years, he would refer to Ida, a short, round former nanny seven years his senior, as "the old lady." Her lack of common sense exasperated him, especially when she used valuable stamps from his collection to pay bills. Yet by every measure, the marriage certainly seems to have gone much better than his first two. In a sympathy letter to her recently widowed sister-in-law Agnes, Ida would write that she would not know what to do without John; according to the note, she was under the impression that his feelings for her were the same.[2] Unlike Paula and Lilly before her, Ida served a practical long-term purpose for her husband by taking on a lot of chores. She labored endless hours to help run his stores, both during and after the war.

Despite the country's pressing need for men in uniform, Knoll received an honorable discharge from the Army in September 1943, after just one year of service. Many years later, he would tell relatives that he had gotten into trouble during the service for disobeying orders: he claimed to have given food that he was supposed to have thrown away to hungry children, giving the story a positive gloss. It doesn't square; the idea that military authorities would punish such an act seems as far-fetched as his claim to have done something of such compassion. Because his military records were destroyed in 1973 in a fire at the National Personnel Records Center in St. Louis, little information is available regarding his service.

Photographs of Knoll during his Army days are typically offbeat. One shows him with a black eye swollen shut and a black monkey in his arms.[3] In another, several servicemen are laughing—apparently at Knoll rather than with him—as he stands beside a tall, slim Panamanian engaged in a dance routine. Knoll does not seem to be enjoying himself—or to be fitting in. Dressed in a white suit and top hat, the entertainer wears one white glove and taps a cane. As Knoll dangles a cigarette out of the corner of his mouth, a tiny white dog peeks its head out from what appears to be a pouch. Neither photo is exactly *Stars & Stripes* material. I showed the pictures to John Douglas and left it to him to pronounce judgment: "Weird."[4]

While Knoll served in Panama during the war, his second wife, Lilly, still lived in Nazi Germany, where she had moved with their infant son in 1936. She worked at the American consulate. In honor of her father, Robert Karg, Lilly called the baby "Bobby."

Bobby Knoll, as family members described him, grew into an adventurous boy. Ignoring his mother's protests that he was too young, he joined the water brigade, which rushed to put out fires caused by Allied bombing raids. Before the age of ten, he was already nearly as tall as some of the men running alongside him. He would reach six-foot-eight, thirteen inches taller than his father. Bobby pleaded with his mother to let him join the Hitler Youth, but she forbade it.

Their beautiful two-story home in Ingelheim destroyed by enemy bombs, Lilly's family lost everything during the war. Once a prominent scientist and *Syndikatsdirektor* with a thriving career and future pension, her father led his family on foot to Mainz; the Kargs stuffed all their surviving possessions into backpacks and carried them for twenty kilo-meters. The only one of the Kargs' four daughters to leave Germany, Lilly returned to New York in 1946 with eleven-year-old Bobby. She would never discuss with her son—or with anyone else in the States—what had happened in her marriage to John Knoll. During the rest of her eighty-nine-year-long life, she would never remarry. Bob Knoll had his mother's ashes buried in a family plot in Kempten im Allgäu.[5]

Unable to provide a home for her son upon their return to America, Lilly put Bobby in the Wartburg Orphans' Farm School in Mt. Vernon, New York. She found work as a live-in nurse in the City and cared for the children of well-to-do families, many of them Jewish. Every so often, she could afford to rent a hotel room and spend a weekend with her boy. In the difficult early days after the war, she took great joy in these occasional visits. The orphanage was located in the same county where John and Ida Knoll were living comfortably in a lovely home with cedar shake shingles in the wooded Grassy Sprains area of Yonkers. A sign at the entrance to the subdivision said "Grassy Sprain Knolls." Although Bobby was nearby, his father offered no financial support.

In 1962, Bob Knoll, by then twenty-six, was living in California. Bob, by all accounts, was a soft-spoken, kind, and unassuming person with a repu-tation for integrity, decency, and selflessness. He is remembered as a won-derful family man. An ardent railroad fan since his teenage years in Arizona, he had figured out how to turn his passion for trains into a successful career in the transportation industry. In his later years he would produce two mag-nificent books of photo essays, *Bob Knoll's Southern Pacific: The Southern Pacific Railroad Photos of J. R. Knoll* and *Steely Trains*.

In the early 1960s, John Knoll owned a delicatessen in Yonkers that did double duty as a grocery store. One day soon after Bob Knoll had met his future wife, Adrienne, he called his father long-distance. The young man, as Adrienne tells the story, wanted to share the details of his romance. "Dad, I've met the love of my life," said Bob. "I'm engaged!" Uninterested and dis-missive, John Knoll offered little reply, and didn't attend his son's wedding.[6]

Walter Knoll and his wife, Gladys, whom he had married on what would have been the Lindbergh baby's fifth birthday, moved to the Detroit area in the 1950s and lived for a while in a flat above his brother-in-law's butcher shop. The Knolls purchased a home in Macomb Town-ship but eventually returned to New York, where Walter opened his own delicatessen in Yonkers. A self-proclaimed financial guy who speculated in the stock market but never achieved significant wealth, he liked to go to Radio City Music Hall and the chariot races at Yonkers Raceway.

Gladys Knoll was a slim and perky blue-eyed blonde who stood five feet tall. "Scottie," as people called her, was the daughter of a trainman from Newfoundland and his Scottish wife. At five-foot-eleven and 149 pounds, Walter was a faintly handsome man with a broad smile.[7] After the war, he and his wife suffered the loss of a stillborn boy to be named Robert. For years afterward, they refused to speak the name.

Walter Knoll, a heavy smoker, died at fifty-three of lung cancer. The June 21, 1962, edition of *The Herald Statesman*, a Yonkers newspaper, printed his death notice: "Knoll, Walter A. Beloved husband of Gladys. Dear brother of Leo and John Knoll, Agnes Breiling, Barbara Diehlman, Anna Schlachter and Sister Leoba. Reposing at Cuccia Funeral Home, 23 Lockwood Avenue, Yonkers. Mass at St. Eugene's R.C. Church."

Walter was buried in Woodlawn Cemetery. John Knoll was there as his brother was laid to rest one mile from the spot where Cemetery John had leapt over the fence on the night of his first meeting with Jafsie thirty years earlier.

From that point on, John Knoll seems to have led a fairly ordinary life. Professionally, he had gone from deli clerk to deli owner, and, in his home life, from wives who got out fast and never spoke of the marriage again to a wife who found him at least companionable. Family members recount stories of mundane events given an odd twist when Knoll steps into the scene, as on one occasion when he drove from New York to Michigan to visit his nephew Rudy and his wife, Sharon.[8] No sooner did Knoll come rolling up the driveway than he built a tepee of leaves, twigs, and brush in the backyard. A few minutes later, Sharon, standing in the kitchen, smelled smoke. As she looked out her sliding glass door, she saw a man fanning a big blaze in her backyard. Terrified, she took a closer look. Then: "Rudy! Uncle John's here!" It was a habit of Knoll's to build fires in his own backyard, and at Rudy's house this was his way of announcing his arrival. Knoll's preoccupation with fire-setting was a warning flag to the criminal profilers who listened to the stories about him. In the first meeting with Jafsie on the park bench, Cemetery John had asked if he would "burn" if the baby was dead.

As a houseguest, he seems to have called on the patience of relatives, who remembered or passed along stories of occasional outbursts such as when Knoll told a nephew, "I'll drive you into the ground without sharpening you! Then I'll whack you so hard that for forty days you'll be chasing the street-car!" One evening, he proposed a quiz to his niece Sharon at the dinner table. "Hey Blondie, you know what you do if you have a burglar?" Sharon had no answer. "You invite him to tea. Then you throw boiling water into his face."[9]

Another "Blondie" figures into an oft-told story about the time Knoll entered the home of a new acquaintance uninvited and grabbed a can of beer out of the refrigerator. Believing she had heard her husband come home, the man's wife came downstairs into the kitchen to greet him. Stunned, she stared at the intruder, who took a swig of his beer. "Hello, Blondie," he said.

The alcohol consumption doesn't seem to have abated since his twen-ties, when Knoll and Oscar Rietschel got together in the Bronx for some of Oscar's homemade specialty. Knoll was a heavy drinker, and didn't let his var-ious health problems interfere with the evening routine. On one of his visits to Michigan, his nephew Lud, a doctor, checked him into a hospital. The facility specialized in the treatment of mental health, but according to his family, Knoll entered the hospital because of a heart problem. One evening, he got dressed, snuck out of his hospital room, and walked half a mile to a bar.

In the end, though, it wasn't drinking that was responsible for killing John Knoll. He had an accident that occurred, as it happens, less than two months after my father had shared with me his theory about Bruno Hauptmann and the Knoll brothers. We were on a vacation in March of 1980, and my father started off with a warning: "Bob, after you hear this, you may think your old man's off his rocker, but—" I was startled by this, partly because he was a highly educated and a slightly formal person who had never referred to him-self as my "old man." Nor had he ever said anything to me I'd considered the slightest bit crazy. I listened to his story intently. As he brought the story to a close, he mentioned that John Knoll, having retired from the deli business in 1972, was living in Toms River, New Jersey—an hour and a half drive from where I lived on the University of Pennsylvania campus in Philadelphia.[10]

My impulse, which grew stronger the more I thought about it, was to show up on the doorstep of this John Knoll and confront him. At night, as I lay awake in my dorm room, an imaginary encounter turned over in my mind: Cemetery John—Cemetery John *Knoll*—once the target of the country's greatest manhunt since the twelve-day chase of John Wilkes Booth, opens his front door to see a student born a quarter-century after the "Crime of the Century" took place. The old man has succeeded in escaping justice for forty-eight years. I introduce myself as the son of his former Bronx neighbor Gene Zorn. Knoll invites me to come inside and offers me a seat on the living room couch.

I didn't know at the time, of course, about the handwriting match to the ransom envelopes, the lump on the thumb, the Kamenz connection linking Knoll to Hauptmann, or any of the rest of the evidence tying him to the crime. So, as I pictured the scene, all I'd have said was, "John, my father told me about Palisades Park." And then, leaning toward him, looking the man square in the eye: "You kidnapped the Lindbergh baby, didn't you?"

That meeting, however, was not to be. Just weeks later, on May 4, 1980, John Knoll died. Bob Knoll received the news by phone in California. He, naturally, would be expected to make arrangements, which he did without delay. Three of John Knoll's nephews from Michigan drove seven hundred miles to attend the funeral. When they arrived at their uncle's home in Toms River, Bob told them that there would be no memorial, no service, or anything else. His father's body had already been cremated. Not knowing what to make of this statement, Bob's three cousins looked at one another as John's wife Ida sat mute in a living room chair, her eyes glued to the television. "I was shocked," said John's nephew Rudy Breiling.[11] Rudy's mother Agnes and his wife Sharon did not accompany him  and his two brothers to New Jersey.

So much for mourning—Bob's father was dead, and that was that. As Adrienne remembers it, Bob didn't waste time in giving away or otherwise getting rid of his father's possessions, stamp collection and all. Other than some old photographs, she could not think of anything else his father left behind that Bob had kept.

At age seventy-five, John Knoll had still been collecting stamps, growing vegetables in his garden, and working on outdoor projects—which is how he came to grief. He had died in the hospital with heart complications shortly after suffering a terrible mishap at his home. The manner of death was so stunning, so perfect in its way, that I had to hear the story from three different family members—one of them a physician—before I accepted it as true. John Knoll had fallen off a ladder and hit his head.

# 31

## Cemetery John Knoll

The criminal attorney Sam Leibowitz who interviewed Hauptmann on three separate occasions in the New Jersey State Prison probably uncovered the truth when he suggested that an intruder inside the nursery had handed the baby to someone waiting at the top of the ladder. Hauptmann seemed to signal that this is what happened, and the great weight of evidence suggests that Governor Hoffman and others were correct in asserting that Hauptmann had worked with accomplices.

Dr. Mary Ellen O'Toole has worked on many high-profile cases of abduction and mysterious disappearance, including those involving Elizabeth Smart, Polly Klass, and Natalee Holloway. Dr. O'Toole, who has long been fascinated by the Lindbergh case, puts it bluntly: "The kidnapping was not a one-man crime."[1] This was the assumption in the very hours after the crime, when an investigator spotted two sets of footprints leading from the kidnap ladder to the abandoned road.

Imagine a flimsy ladder leaned up against the home and positioned to the side of the second-story window. The top rung falls two or three feet short of the window, and no one is there to secure it. It is cold and dark outside. The intruder had to open the window then get into the nursery without disturbing a beer stein on the windowsill or any items by the window—all of this without leaving muddy footprints on the floor. The child weighed about thirty pounds, roughly the weight of two bowling bowls. If we assume one kidnapper, we have to imagine Hauptmann dragging the child from the crib, squeezing back through the window with the child, and maneuvering to the appropriate rung amid darkness and heavy winds, again while leaving all the objects near the window undisturbed. Assuming he didn't kick over the ladder, then he would have had to descend with the baby and carry him to the car. Trying to imagine how anyone could have done all this, John Douglas and Mark Olshaker concluded after they visited the crime scene that a handoff of the baby from the window was the most likely scenario.

Two or more kidnappers was also Condon's surmise when Cemetery John mentioned the ransom note "left in the crib," when it had, in fact, been left on the windowsill. It was Lindbergh's impression when he observed a man covering his face with a handkerchief and lurking about St. Raymond's Cemetery as Condon was about to meet with John. It explains why the police demanded that Hauptmann tell them where the rest of the Lindbergh money was; the bills discovered in his garage had amounted to less than a third of the total ransom. All of these facts, and many more, pointed to a conspiracy.

As John Douglas sees it, Hauptmann participated in the crime but did not accomplish it alone; moreover, he was not necessarily the leader of the gang. Douglas suspects that someone in the German community recruited Hauptmann into the scheme, partly because of his skills as a carpenter. Yet when he and Mark Olshaker wrote about the kidnapping in *The Cases That Haunt Us*, they had no way of knowing the recruiter's identity. There were gaps throughout the case, but no clues to where the missing pieces might be. As we'll see after we examine the results of a forensic study conducted on the wood evidence, no serious student of the crime can deny that Hauptmann was involved. Yet if Hauptmann doesn't fit the description of Cemetery John, who collected the ransom money? The question has been asked many times in eighty years, but without my father's testimony no credible lead has materialized.

A collaboration in the crime is the most plausible explanation, and John Knoll is the most plausible collaborator. Although much of whatever evidence existed eighty years ago has long since vanished, Knoll nonetheless left behind significant clues to be discovered. But other than my father, no one knew where to look. If this new figure is added to the story of the Lindbergh kidnapping, the missing pieces begin to line up like the nails in the piece of wood traced back to Hauptmann's attic. In addition to the fact that John Knoll is long dead, he was never suspected by authorities and left few records, surviving family members, or acquaintances necessary for the collection and analysis of evidence. A crucial distinction exists, however, between standards of criminal evidence and standards of historical evidence. Whether all that we know about John Knoll would be enough to indict him, in some hypothetical grand jury trial, is a complicated question and, of course, moot. But to prove a historical case, and draw conclusions about guilt or innocence, it is enough to use our common sense, by applying standards less strict than juries are instructed to use, but based on a reasonable weighing of probabilities. And the more surviving evidence points to guilt, the more evidence would have been found eighty years ago.

Applying Ed Sulzbach's observation about how "life is just not that coincidental,"[2] to rule out John Knoll, all of the following, and more, would have to be pure coincidence. To review the evidence:

### PHYSICAL CHARACTERISTICS

Unlike Hauptmann, who had a rounded chin, John Knoll strongly resembles the suspect in the police sketch, and he matches Condon's descriptions of the weight, the build, the light complexion, the prominent forehead, the pointed chin, and large ears, as well as the fleshy lump at the base of the left thumb. This final feature, visible in pictures and verified by a noted hand surgeon, appears exactly where Condon saw it on Cemetery John when they were sitting together on a park bench in enough light to observe such details. Bruno Hauptmann did not have such a lump on his thumb. That's one reason why Condon, after having studied Hauptmann in a police lineup and examined his hands, said, "No, he is not the man."

Moreover, in three different photos of John Knoll smoking, he dangles his cigar or cigarette out of the left corner of his mouth. In the same photo that shows the abnormality on his left thumb, he is holding his infant son with his right arm, leaving his left hand free. Knoll appears, therefore, to have been left-handed. This connects with another feature of the crime: because the ladder was positioned to the right of the nursery window, the climber of the kidnap ladder was probably left-handed.

### EYEWITNESS TESTIMONY

At Palisades Park in New Jersey, my father heard John Knoll talking to a German man he called Bruno about the city in New Jersey where the Lindberghs lived at the time. The kidnappers repeatedly stated in their ransom letters that the crime had been planned for a year. The meeting my father witnessed outside the amusement park took place nine months before the March 1, 1932, Lindbergh kidnapping.

### SELF-IDENTIFICATION

The kidnapper who met with Condon at the two Bronx cemeteries identified himself as *John*. Thereafter he never used the name "John" and never signed any of the ransom notes "John," suggesting it was not an intentional pseudonym but his real name, revealed in that first encounter when Condon surprised him with a direct request for a name. Indeed, a line in the ransom note that came with the baby's sleeping suit—*"We will note allow ouer man to confer in a way like befor"*—suggests that Cemetery John regretted speaking carelessly with Condon.

### GEOGRAPHIC FAMILIARITY

The kidnappers responded within hours to the *Bronx Home News* article outlining Condon's offer to assist in the kidnap negotiations. The first ransom note he received was mailed right from the South Bronx neighborhood where John Knoll lived and worked. Geographic profiling, an investigative methodology developed by Dr. Kim Rossmo and employed by law enforcement worldwide to determine the most probable area of offender residence, was applied to the Lindbergh case. After Dr. Rossmo entered specific locations associated with the crime into a leading geographic profiling software program, the algorithm generated a map that drew attention to two high probability regions where investigators could have focused their efforts. The peak areas identified were the North Bronx, where Bruno Hauptmann lived, and the South Bronx, where John and Walter Knoll lived.

### PERSONAL INTERESTS

Students of the case have long wondered why the package containing the baby's sleeping suit carried a 10-cent stamp when very few people used them in those days. John Knoll was a stamp collector. Additionally, the kidnappers' signature-symbol resembles a stamp collector's cachet, just like those on the First Day Covers Knoll collected. The size of a cachet, the signature-symbol would fit perfectly in the lower left-hand corner of an envelope. The various locations from which the ransom letters were mailed reveal an understanding of postmarking practices such as a stamp collector would possess.

In addition to marrying a flier, Knoll had a strong interest in aviation that may have bordered on being a fetish. Among the collectibles he gave my father were eight that pertain to flying. The gifts included a "Lindbergh Airmail" stamp and a cachet commemorating the five-year anniversary of Lindbergh's flight to Paris.

### HANDWRITING

In the first-ever application of advanced handwriting recognition software to the Lindbergh case, the CEDAR-FOX system compared John Knoll's writing to the handwriting on the ransom envelopes. The results indicate a 95% probability that Knoll's writing appears on the ransom envelopes. Moreover, Knoll's self-addressed envelopes, given to my father, show an attempt to disguise his handwriting after the baby's body was discovered, most notably the *J* in *John* and the *K* in *Knoll*. According to the CEDAR-FOX analysis, someone else's handwriting other than Knoll's appears on some of the commemorative envelopes he gave my father, indicating that he was at times hesitant to address the envelopes in his own hand.

The CEDAR-FOX system also analyzed the handwriting of Bruno Hauptmann in two reliable samples, including his letter to Governor Harold Hoffman. In a comparison of Hauptmann's handwriting to the ransom notes, the result generated was "Identified as different."

### FINANCIALS

Three weeks after Condon delivered the ransom money to Cemetery John on April 2, 1932, John Knoll began making generous contributions to my father's stamp collection. Four First Day Covers and one commemorative cover Knoll gave my father all bear an April 22, 1932, postmark. In February 1934, two men with German accents tried to pass an illegal ten-dollar gold certificate at the Cross, Ireland and

Austin Lumber Company, and the car in which the men drove off was later traced to Bruno Hauptmann. The business was one mile away from John Knoll's residence. Among the many ransom bills recovered, one turned up at a bank in the South Bronx. The bank was a five-minute walk from John Knoll's residence on Jackson Avenue and from the deli on Westchester Avenue. Three ransom bills were passed at United Cigar Stores, and John Knoll, like Hauptmann, often smoked cigars: A mid-1930s photo of Knoll shows him standing on a porch and puffing on a stogie.

### FORENSICS

A renowned toxicologist, Dr. Alexander O. Gettler, detected animal fat on some of the circulating ransom money. In addition, the baby's sleeping suit sent by the kidnappers was wrapped in the same kind of paper used to wrap deli foods. John Knoll and his brother Walter worked at a delicatessen.

Catherine J. Sporer has over twenty years of experience in chemistries related to surfactants with such organizations as Abbott Laboratories and Stepan Company. "The glycerol asters referred to by Dr. Gettler indicate the presence of animal fats on the grease marks," said Sporer. "Such grease marks are typical of the type of stains that would have been left on the bills by delicatessen workers such as John Knoll who handled meat."[3]

### ACCENT

When Condon asked the kidnapper on the telephone where he was calling from, he answered: "Westchester." Knoll worked at Woltmann's on Westchester Avenue, and the store had a phone. My father also remembered a particular accent of John Knoll's when he referred to the subway as the *supway*, the same way that the kidnappers spell the word in a ransom note. In the trial transcript, Hauptmann's use of German words in English sentences and his German pronunciation of certain English words are written as he pronounced them. For example, he is quoted in his testimony as having said, "living mit two friends," "farder vest" ("farther west"), "like dat" ("like that"), "I don't tink so," ("I don't think so"), "mitout" ("without"), "dem bundles was mostly mesh up" ("those bundles were mostly messed up)," "cardon" ("cardboard"), and "slippy" ("slippery"). Yet the word "subway" in his phrase "Bronx Park subway" is written with a "b," not a "p."[4]

### CONNECTION TO HAUPTMANN

After he came to America, Hauptmann was known to look up and visit people from his home town of Kamenz. The German immigrant who rented an apartment in his home to my grandparents, Oscar Rietschel, knew John Knoll, and they could often be seen together. Not only was Rietschel also from the same small town as Hauptmann, but also the Rietschels' home in Kamenz was only 125 yards away from the Hauptmanns' doorstep.

### VERACITY

In 1973 Knoll misstated the year he had moved to the Bronx by a full six years, thereby placing himself elsewhere during the planning of the Lindbergh kidnapping. Though he claimed to have arrived in 1932, his Petition for Citizenship proves that he had, in fact, lived in the Bronx since December 16, 1926.[5] Knoll also lied to the military upon his induction into the Army in 1942. By doing so, he failed to disclose that he had been born in Germany, the primary adversary in the war.

### FLIGHT

At the time of the manhunt, John Knoll left the Bronx and moved in with his sister Agnes in a suburb of Detroit. After she had examined the evidence contained in this book, Agnes's daughter-in-law, Sharon Breiling, told me about a puzzling comment Agnes had once made to her. "As we were standing in the kitchen one day, Agnes told me that John had a way of getting into really serious trouble," said Sharon. "She said this very somberly and with a faraway look in her eye." For the first time, she understood why Agnes, who herself had made a round-trip to Germany right after Hauptmann's arrest, had said these words: Sharon realized that they provided a clue to the existence of a very well-kept family secret.

Shortly before Hauptmann's trial, John Knoll left Michigan for New York and promptly boarded the SS *Manhattan* to Hamburg. On the very day the trial ended, after all witnesses and Hauptmann had testified and just hours before the jury delivered its verdict, the *Manhattan*, with Knoll aboard, left Southampton and sailed to America.

On that trip to Hamburg, Knoll and his wife Lilly traveled on a luxury liner. From the wages of a deli clerk, a renter paying ten dollars a month for a room in the Bronx, he somehow came up with nearly seven hundred dollars for two first-class, round-trip tickets on the *Manhattan*. Knoll's voyage back on the same ship appears to have been his final trip abroad except for military service in Panama. Fifty-four years living in America, just one trip abroad on immigration records, and it just happened to occur at the time of Hauptmann's trial for murder.[6]

Suppose that someone, having all of this information when Hauptmann was about to go to trial, could have informed the police that a male, working-class German immigrant named John, a deli clerk who lived in the Bronx, matched the police sketch of Cemetery John, matched the physical description by Condon, matched the deformity on the left thumb, matched the handwriting, matched the precise accent of certain words, matched the mailing pattern of the ransom notes, and not only had been seen with Hauptmann in New Jersey but was, at that very moment, on a luxury liner bound for Germany with his aviator wife and a pair of boarding passes costing nearly seven hundred dollars. What might the police have done with that information? When he disembarked from the *Manhattan* either in Hamburg or in New York after the Hauptmann trial, John Knoll in all likelihood would have been followed by detectives, kept under constant surveillance, and in due course arrested on suspicion of complicity in the abduction and murder of Charles A. Lindbergh, Jr.

# 32

# An Uncommon Criminal

What would the authorities have made of their second suspect, once John Knoll was in custody? How would they have sized up Knoll as they began looking into his past to assess whether he was capable of such a crime? John Douglas has developed a pattern in his mind of "what sort of crime is committed by what sort of person."[1] Yet even long before the days of modern criminal-investigative analysis, detectives assigned to the Lindbergh case had patterns of their own formed by experience.

Their conclusion about Hauptmann is clear, and Douglas and most experts today hold the same view: he was "a common criminal."[2] For him, the kidnapping seems to have been a more audacious version of his criminal partnership to burglarize the home of a bürgermeister, and the motive for the two crimes was the same: money. He was a product of the economic devastation in Germany after the First World War, the veteran of a beaten army who couldn't find work and turned to a life of crime. Nothing in his behavior and personality—intensively studied at the time and in the years since—suggests a motive any deeper or more subtle than a desire for instant wealth. "Possessing a criminal bent," observes Sulzbach, "Hauptmann was the type who could have fallen prey to the get-rich-quick scheme of a persuasive leader. An examination of his life uncovers no evidence that he wanted to deal a blow to Lindbergh or was obsessed with him—or that he had any aspiration to create a 'world-affair.'"[3]

To determine the type of person who would commit a certain crime, Douglas says, we must understand the motive, and "the key to that is in the victimology." Why was the victim targeted? Did the perpetrator make "a careful and deliberate choice"?[4] How was the crime perpetrated, and how was the body treated? In physics, the best-known equation links energy and mass: $E = mc^2$. In behavioral analysis, the Douglas equation supplies the links: $Why + How = Who$. Was it possible that the kidnapping was a crime of opportunity, with Charlie Lindbergh simply one of thousands across the country who fell prey to the snatch racket? After all, money was a clear motive of the perpetrators. Or were the victims—the most famous child in the world and the most famous and admired couple in America—targeted at least in part because of who they were?

The type of criminal who could be enlisted as an accomplice in the plot to steal the child of the most famous man in the world is not the type who would conceive it. To understand the difference, consider all the targets the kidnappers might have selected instead of the Lindbergh baby in the second story of a house sixty miles from the City. Even during the Depression, many prominent families lived within easy driving distance from Manhattan. Far wealthier men than Lindbergh—among them the partners of J. P. Morgan and Company and of other investment banking firms—lived in constant fear of the "snatch racket." It was common knowledge, moreover, that because he had spurned the opportunity to make millions in endorsements and in motion pictures after his flight to Paris, Charles Lindbergh did not achieve the enormous wealth he could have. The victimology suggests that many wealthier but less famous targets would have made a far more strategic choice if the planner's motive had been purely financial.

Kidnapping for ransom, moreover, is challenging enough to carry out without making a "world-affair" of it and inviting the global attention and unprecedented manhunt that were certain to follow. This particular kidnapping was logistically high-risk, involving entry into a second-floor room with five adults in the home followed by the escape, the handling of the baby, the mailing of the letters, the negotiations, and the collection of the money. Why go to such elaborate lengths, assume so many avoidable risks, and incur the rage of the public and the law, when a simpler plan against a less visible target could bring an even bigger ransom? The crime required, among other traits, imagination, and Hauptmann hadn't even prepared a simple, consistent story in the event the police ever questioned him.

Profilers study the "high points" of a crime, and one of the first to emerge in the Lindbergh kidnapping is the thrill-seeking element, at least for the one who planned it. Disregarding the long odds against success, he seems to have thrived on the excitement and intrigue such a daring crime would provide. One imagines Hauptmann, the common criminal, saying "Let's get out of here!" when the kidnappers saw Lindbergh himself pull up the driveway. Whoever was in the lead that night, however, apparently was not deterred in the least, and perhaps the presence of the famous aviator made the kidnapping an even greater thrill.

Dr. Mary Ellen O'Toole detects a strong bullying behavior in the ransom notes: "We warn you . . ." . . . "We have warned you . . ." . . . "We warn you again . . ." . . . "We warn you not to set up any trapp . . ." . . . "You are willing to pay the 70000 note 50000 $ without seeing the baby first or note . . ." . . . "ouer program is . . ." . . . "If there is any trapp, you will be responsible what will follows" . . . "If you don't accept den we will wait untill you agree with ouer deal. we know you have to come to us any way . . ." . . . "if [Lindbergh] keeps on waiting we will double ouer amount" . . . "have the money in one bundle we want you to put it in a sertain place . . ." . . . "If there is a ratio alarm for policecar, we warn you. we have the same equipment."[5] As Dr. O'Toole remarks, the leader of the kidnapping gang could just stand back and "watch" the Lindberghs squirm. And any emotional pain he could inflict on Lindbergh would have been particularly thrilling to him.[6]

There are two ways to look at the kidnappers' decision to hold the late-night meetings with Jafsie at cemeteries. On the one hand, a cemetery is a quiet, isolated place where it's unlikely others will be encountered on a cold, dark night. This is how some experts see it—the choice of cemeteries was solely a logistical consideration, and the signature-symbol simply served the purpose of enabling the men who stole the baby to identify themselves as the bona fide kidnappers. On the other hand, Dr. O'Toole observes, a cemetery is also a perfect place for "a super-secret spy game." In her opinion, the mastermind—the creator of the elaborate signature-symbol with interlocking circles and three holes—was a game-player.

This latter interpretation, the planner as game-player, coincides with the sheer audacity of the plan. That night, not only did the kidnappers take from the Lindberghs the most important thing in their lives, but they did so right in their own home with the mother and father themselves just steps away. It is generally assumed that the kidnappers were surprised to find Charles Lindbergh himself arrive at the house that night, and it is likely they were. But why, since he was there, didn't they back off and return at a more opportune time some other evening? Dr. O'Toole notes that the kidnapping was an "arrogant crime"—one that was unrealistic and unlikely to be successful. "Thinking you could get away with it was arrogant," she said. "Not only were there people at home, but the crime involved a famous and wealthy target who probably would have taken precautions and had security. The kidnapping would guarantee a strong response, and it was sure to bring down the wrath of God."

With that extreme egotism in mind, Dr. O'Toole describes how she would have conducted an interview with the planner of the kidnapping. Playing to his egotism she would have flattered him by remarking on the unique skill and daring of the crime. What was one man's flight across the Atlantic in a tin can compared to this amazing feat at Hopewell that had gained the attention of the world? Criminals of this kind do not see their offenses as shameful, but on the contrary crave recognition for what they see as stunning achievements.

It's just possible, Dr. O'Toole adds, that the Lindbergh kidnapping was also "personal in nature." As she sees it, the motive behind the crime was unconnected to any cultural issue such as anti-German bigotry, and something else might have factored into the human equation. Strange as it may seem, she explains, the tiniest perceived or imagined slight, can develop into an obsession, which in turn can lead to a retaliation of monumental proportion and catastrophic consequences. In one of her cases, a woman who believed that she had been "screwed over" by a bank because of money related to an inheritance orchestrated a plot to rob the bank—one that involved the detonation of a bomb.

Could the planner of the kidnapping have had some similar grievance against Lindbergh? "Something personal may have been going on here that started an obsession," says Dr. O'Toole. "It could have involved an attempt by the offender to shake Lindbergh's hand on the street or a request for an autograph that was turned down," she observes. "In any case, it would have been something very minor. If you were to have asked Lindbergh about it, he would have said, 'I never met the guy!'"

Thus, the man who stole and killed the baby could have been one face in the many crowds that Lindbergh had encountered, a troubled figure who'd had some brush with Lindbergh that *he* remembered, some unintended slight that wounded a fragile psyche and who directed vengeance on the aviator and his family. Dr. O'Toole believes that the kidnapping may have been what could be referred to in the FBI's Behavioral Science Unit as an "in your face crime."[7] If so, then the crime was meant to make a "statement" as well as to collect riches. The leader could have wanted to settle a score, to bring down Lindbergh and elevate himself. And how would it be possible to hurt a man more deeply than to make him feel that he had failed to protect his own child, and a first-born son at that, sleeping in a crib under his own roof?

This impression of an "in your face" crime is actually not so different from the original personality profile prepared for the police by Dr. Dudley D. Shoenfeld long before Hauptmann's arrest. As George Waller, the author of *Kidnap,* summarizes the report, Dr. Shoenfeld concluded that Cemetery John was "elated by the international attention his feat had aroused." This "world-affair" of his own creation gave him a "feeling of omnipotence."[8] In other words, the kidnapper was an envious, frustrated nobody with a grandiose sense of self, striving to achieve something large and memorable in the fashion of the most shocking and dramatic crimes in history. To Cemetery John, kidnapping the Lindbergh baby was his equivalent of the Orteig Prize. And for his magnificent feat he perhaps considered himself entitled to demand twice the $25,000 Lindbergh had received.[9] The great crime would make him not only wealthy but also the most talked-about man in the world overnight.

The problem, here again, is that Hauptmann doesn't match this psychological personality profile of Cemetery John any more closely than he meets the details of the physical profile, a disconnect that explains why the Shoenfeld study was rarely mentioned again after the arrest of a suspect. Hauptmann was a recruit with both a criminal history and carpentry skills. Someone talked him into the scheme. Who was doing the talking?

We have, at the very least, a plausible candidate in John Knoll—a man who, at so many turns in his life, seemed to be saying "In your face!" to anyone he pleases. What kind of kid, growing up in a small German village, earns the nickname "Schah," or "shah," and upon his return as an adult alarms the whole neighborhood by ringing church bells and shouting "I'm back! It's me!"? Indeed, if we assume his complicity in the crime, that voyage on the luxury liner back to Germany, just as Hauptmann was about to go to trial, might reasonably be interpreted as an "in-your-face" farewell to law enforcement: the docket in Flemington for Bruno, the dining room of the *Manhattan* for John. And even if we don't assume Knoll's guilt, there's still something about the voyage that looks bad: A humble wage earner employed at a deli, in the middle of the Depression, is paying what would today be about $12,000 for first-class tickets. We can believe that this working man's fortune constituted all of his life savings, slowly built up in years of toil—and that this frugal man spent it all on one extravagant trip. Or we can surmise that Knoll could spare the seven hundred dollars because, somewhere, there was a lot more hidden away. Either way, that shipboard photograph of a sullen man and his uneasy wife trying to blend in with the moneyed and powerful offers pretty good evidence of foolish grandiosity.

Then there's Lilly herself and that curious background. Not too many deli clerks in the Depression-era Bronx ended up marrying aviators. This is a fact about Knoll that just hovers silently above the whole story with a very peculiar feel to it—like the fact that Lilly was a nurse, and Cemetery John assured Condon that the baby was being cared for by a nurse on a boat. From a psychological-profiling angle, it seems to say something about what he was thinking and fantasizing about. Throw in the Lindbergh-themed stamps and envelopes he bought, and it's not a leap to speculate that he had some fixation about aviation. It seems even odder because Knoll most likely didn't even know Lilly before the crime was committed, but met her only after the kidnapping. Lindbergh, the hero of the age, marries Anne and trains her to fly. Then comes the shocking crime, with all of the intense and sympathetic coverage it brings to the couple. The next couple to enter the picture, after the ransom is paid, is John Knoll and his aviator wife, off on a spare-no-expense holiday across the Atlantic. If an envious, resentful, thrill-seeking game-player wanted to prove something—to say "Look at me, I'm greater than Lindbergh!"—that might be one way to do it.

The more we follow John Knoll through the years, in any event, there's always the feeling that something was just not right. Why did those first two wives, the showgirl and the flier and nurse, leave him so quickly, and rarely if ever speak of him again to family members? What did they learn about him that was so bad it couldn't be shared? In the case of Lilly, who escaped with their infant son in 1936, what was so awful that life in Hitler's Germany seemed preferable to life in America with the boy's own father?

John Knoll comes across as a man capable of extreme egotism, arrogance, and—as Lilly's niece Brigitte Geiger put it—"unpredictability." We find him in his teenage years taking great personal risk by spitting and urinating on the French troops in his family's tobacco barn; in his twenties again engaging in dangerous behavior by swimming in the treacherous waters of the East River; and, in his later years, setting fires to announce his arrival at the home of relatives. So many incidents in between have the same odd ring—surprising people in their own homes, throwing around crude nicknames, and demeaning others even while snapping at the least sign of disrespect, as when he rebuked a nephew who called him "John" with a sharp "That's *Uncle* John!" A few of these stories would be one thing, but with him they just keep coming, the pattern invariably to shock, manipulate, draw attention to himself, and doubtless to conceal the kind of deep insecurity that such conduct usually suggests. John Douglas observes that "most violent offenders [have] two warring factors within them": "a feeling of superiority, grandiosity" and an "equally strong feeling … of inadequacy."[10] Both of these factors, he and Mark Olshaker agree, were present in John Knoll.[11]

As for human empathy, perhaps the best witness on this count would be Bob Knoll, the son he never bothered to visit or help even when Bob was in an orphanage a few miles away. What kind of man, in the apparent estimation of his only child, doesn't even merit a funeral service, but only an immediate cremation and a brisk disposal of his possessions?

There are a few good stories to tell about John Knoll, particularly his helpfulness to neighbors toward the end of his life. For the most part, though, without the Lindbergh connection his life would be tale after tale of secretive, self-centered, boorish, and abusive behavior to the point of monotony. Were we dealing with anyone else, we could readily accept the verdict of his father-in-law, that he was "a bum," and leave it at that.

But in the story of the Lindbergh case, John Knoll is not just anyone. He is the first real person of interest to emerge in the seventy-eight years since the arrest of Hauptmann, and the question is whether his psychological profile fits the picture as well as the physical profile. Every crime involves multiple motives, Dr. O'Toole reminds us, and clearly money was a motive both to Hauptmann and to his accomplices. Even so, if John Knoll's psychological profile is a match to someone who would steal the infant son of the world's most famous man, the case becomes that much stronger, and we're left with one more reason to conclude that he was Cemetery John.

One element missing from the whole profile is a detailed history of criminal activity. Lilly, her niece Brigitte Geiger said, worried that John was "at the edge of the law." Yet we don't know if, in fact, Knoll ever crossed over the edge of the law before 1932 or afterward other than falsifying information on his military induction form. This, however, is not surprising. "Most psychopaths have no formal criminal history," Dr. Toole said.[12] In any event, John Knoll mellowed later in his later years, as many criminals do, and his life became more conventional. He committed the "Crime of the Century," escaped justice, grew old, and stayed out of trouble. He was the most uncommon criminal of all—the one who never got caught.

# 33

# March 1, 1932

For two generations, the Lindbergh case was largely ignored, just as Lindbergh himself wished. Though suspicions lingered that Hauptmann had worked with unknown accomplices and the details were occasionally debated, for the most part the matter was left alone as a settled piece of history. Then in the 1970s, the era of Watergate and of conspiracy theories about the Kennedy assassination, writers and film producers took a fresh look at the kidnapping, among them opponents of the death penalty who argued that an innocent man had gone to the electric chair. The "Trial of the Century," with its elaborate cast of characters and intricate subplots, provided rich material for an indictment of overzealous prosecutors and a corrupt American legal system: The police beat Hauptmann after his capture, much of the testimony used to convict him was questionable, and the trial itself was conducted in a circus atmosphere. Leading the charge to criticize the verdict was a tabloid writer named Anthony Scaduto, author of *Scapegoat*.

Scaduto's case for Hauptmann's innocence rests on the testimony of Murray Bleefeld, an ex-con who claimed to possess knowledge that a disbarred attorney—whom he himself had kidnapped and tortured in the basement of a home in Brooklyn—had murdered the Lindbergh baby. Bleefeld said that his story would make a terrific movie and that Walter Matthau should be cast in a starring role. Scaduto goes on to argue that the body discovered in the woods did not belong to Charlie Lindbergh. In 1977, the year after *Scapegoat* came out, the New Jersey Crime Laboratory's reexamination of the garments and hair follicles found on the corpse provided scientific validation of its identity. Dr. Alan T. Lane, the senior forensic chemist at the West Trenton Laboratory, concluded that the cloth-ing found on the corpse matched the blue thread and flannel cloth Betty Gow had used to make the baby's undershirt; moreover, the bits of cloth fit together like pieces of a jigsaw puzzle. Dr. Lane also compared the hair follicles found at the wooded gravesite with samples of Charlie Lindbergh's hair and determined that they had come from the same person.[1]

Over and over, Scaduto tries to discredit Arthur Koehler, the wood scientist whose testimony had solidified the State's case. "Worthless bums," writes Scaduto, quoting a lawyer friend's opinion of expert wit-nesses. Referring to Koehler and to his methods and conclusions, the author chooses the epithets "charade," "distortion," "falsification," "glossy misrepresentation," and "reprehensible."[2] But did Scaduto ever inter-view former colleagues of Koehler, a man respected by his peers for his knowledge and integrity, to determine if such "reprehensible" actions were consistent with the scientist's reputation?

Missing between Rail 16 and the attic floorboard was a sawed-off, inch-and-a-quarter-wide piece of wood. As Koehler pointed to his ex-hibits, he made it easy for the jurors to see how the rail and the floor-board had once been part of the same piece of wood. Yet Scaduto tries to muddy the waters: " . . . we must 'imagine' the manner in which the grain traveled across the missing piece."[3]

In a three-year study completed in 2005—the most comprehensive forensic examination of the wood evidence conducted on the Lindbergh case since the 1930s and one involving a number of leading wood scien-tists and other experts—researcher Kelvin Keraga tested Koehler's conclusion about the link between Rail 16 and the floorboard in Haupt-mann's attic. As Keraga writes, "accusations have been made of police coercion, planted evidence and false testimony."[4]

Hauptmann's defenders have charged that a detective with the New Jer-sey State Police, Lewis Bornmann, colluded with Koehler to fabricate evi-dence and that the police replaced the original Rail 16 with a substitute board. A picture of the ladder taken by press photographer William B. Springfield the day after the kidnapping proves, however, that the current Rail 16 is the same rail found on the device at the time of the crime. Keraga's next task was to determine the relationship between Rail 16 and the attic floorboard, known as S-226. He focused on six areas of comparison: "milling characteristics; general natural characteristics; knot patterns; surface grain patterns; relationship between end grain and surface grain; and end grain comparisons."[5] In each area of comparison, Keraga's analysis demonstrates that Rail 16 and S-226 were once part of the same board. Among the wood scientists who reached this conclusion was Dr. Alan Drew of the State University of New York College of Environmental Science and Forestry (SUNY-ESF), who performed a regression analysis of the thickness of the tree rings.

"It is highly unlikely that these two boards came from separate trees," wrote Dr. Drew. "How unlikely is that? Quantitatively, if you sampled 1 million trees where their growth rings showed the same degree of complacency/sensitivity as R16 and S-226, you might find that in one of those trees you could conclude that the two end views were not from different trees. Even that may be too conservative a figure, given the conditions."[6]

Keraga also discovered new evidence: marks left on Rail 16 caused by defects in a planer blade match defects on S-226 and other boards from Hauptmann's attic in size, shape, spacing, and location. Thus, his three-year forensic study settles the matter, proving that a piece of wood used to build the ladder came from Hauptmann's attic and that, therefore, Hauptmann must have been involved in the kidnapping. "The wood has always spoken the truth," Keraga said.[7]

On October 28, 1980, my father phoned Anthony Scaduto and described his suspicions about his former Bronx neighbor John Knoll.

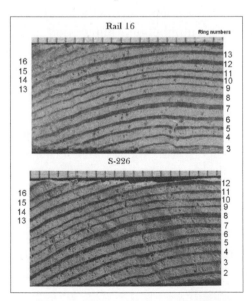

The author recognized the incompatibility of my father's theory with his own that Hauptmann had played no role in the kidnapping—that each witness who had testified against him had either been mistaken or had committed perjury, that the police had tampered with every piece of physical evidence used to convict him, and that the

*Comparison of the growth rings of Rail 16 of the kidnap ladder and of S-226 (the floorboard of Hauptmann's attic)*

police, Betty Gow, and Lindbergh had all misidentified the dead baby discovered in the woods.

A few minutes into the conversation, Scaduto expressed his indifference ("I could spend all my time pursuing leads") and declared his unwillingness to discuss the matter further.[8] My father realized that Scaduto—and others who followed his lead—wanted the German carpenter to be innocent and refused to consider any evidence that contradicted this position.

In addition to the "Hauptmann was framed" books, there were two others involving theories suggesting that Lindbergh had staged a kidnapping. As one would expect, the authors offer no evidence to support their positions and rely entirely on speculation.[9] Ed Sulzbach shakes his head at such far-fetched theories, especially when basic facts of the case contradict them. He taught agents in his profiling classes at the FBI Academy to use common sense. "If you have a pasture full of polo ponies," he told them, "don't go looking for unicorns."[10]

Though skeptics of Hauptmann's guilt remain, and some—to get an obvious pun out of the way—will doubtless dismiss my father's story as the "grassy Knoll theory" of the Lindbergh case, too many incriminating facts point in John Knoll's direction to let him go, at least from the judgment of history. "There's never been a stronger candidate for Hauptmann's accomplice in eighty years,"[11] Mark Olshaker said. Knoll, not Hauptmann, was Cemetery John, and a final test for this conclusion is to figure out how they carried out the kidnapping together.

A couple of years before his death in 2006, my father and I discussed John Douglas's unique perspective on the Lindbergh case—that Hauptmann was guilty, that he was not necessarily the leader of the kidnapping gang, and that someone in the German immigrant community had likely recruited him into the plot because of his skills as a carpenter.[12] Furthermore, a man who had stolen inside the home had likely made a handoff to an accomplice waiting at the top of the ladder. Of the many theories developed about the kidnapping over the years, it was the only one that made sense to my father and that fit with the special knowledge that only he possessed.

With so much evidence pointing to John Knoll, previously unknown to students of the case, how might he and Bruno Hauptmann have carried out the kidnapping? To begin with, it is highly likely that Knoll had a second accomplice, given the logistics of the crime, including the need for a third man to hold the ladder. My father's clear recollection places Walter Knoll in the company of his brother John and Hauptmann as the men were discussing "Englewood." Although Walter is the obvious candidate, nothing in the case against John Knoll depends on that assumption. He might have known of the plan but wanted no part of it or been party to the conspiracy but backed out when things got serious. We don't know. Beyond his presence that day at Palisades Park, we know little about Walter Knoll. He died fifty years ago and left no children to tell us more about him. It does appear, however, that the Knoll brothers' sister Elisabetha, a sister in the Dominican Order, was summoned to the States from Germany right after Hauptmann's capture, and it's unlikely that John would have felt such a desperate need to reach out to his sister the nun for comfort or guidance.

As John Douglas told me, there are always aspects of a crime that don't make sense. Consequently, we can never be certain of all that happened the night of the kidnapping. Piecing things together as much as possible after eight decades, though, and assuming Walter's involvement, here is how I believe the crime unfolded:

On the night of Tuesday, March 1, 1932, three German immigrants—John and Walter Knoll and Bruno Hauptmann—drove from the Bronx to the Lindbergh estate outside Hopewell, New Jersey. John Knoll was the ringleader, the man who conceived the scheme and had the bluster, force of personality, and an ability to manipulate others. He had met Hauptmann through a mutual connection with my grandparents' landlord, Oscar Rietschel. From Rietschel, or from Hauptmann himself, Knoll had heard about Hauptmann's use of a ladder in a burglary back in Germany. That crime either planted an idea in Knoll's mind or completed an idea already taking shape. His carpentry skills and other assets made Hauptmann an ideal partner. He was a risk taker. He owned a car. He could devise and build a three-section kidnap ladder that fit into a sedan. And, as he would go on to prove, Hauptmann could be trusted to keep his mouth shut.[13]

The original plan was to kidnap the baby from Englewood. The three men surveyed the Morrow estate on the day of their rendezvous at Palisades Park. The surveillance operation made it clear that they would have to wait until the Lindberghs had moved to their much more vulnerable home near

Hopewell. On the drive to the Lindbergh estate on the night of the crime, they had no difficulty following the winding rural roads for the last several miles. They knew the area because they had been to the house before—and perhaps even inside it. The newspapers had published details regarding the layout of the home, making the location of the nursery public knowledge. The house had not been made secure during construction, and one of the kidnappers could have appeared one day under the pretext of looking for work. A quick survey of the interior would have revealed the ease of slipping in through the front door and reaching the nursery within seconds.[14] Because the new home had no curtains or shades, anyone could spy inside. On that same reconnaissance mission, one or all of the men had waited nearby to observe when the lights went off in the nursery, giving them an estimate of when the baby was usually put down for the night.

The plan called for an evening when Lindbergh would be away from home. After months of waiting, John Knoll decided to put his plan in motion after he had read in the newspapers that the aviator would be giving a speech in the City on the evening of March first. What a shock it must have been as the three men were waiting in the darkness when headlights suddenly appeared in the distance followed by the sound of an engine, the crunch of gravel, and a black Franklin sedan driven by Charles Lindbergh himself.

Huddling together as the car disappeared into the garage, the kidnappers conferred. As his younger brother and Bruno Hauptmann whispered second thoughts about proceeding, John Knoll said that there was no turning back. "It is the greatest shot of adrenaline to be doing what you want to do so badly," Charles Lindbergh himself once said. "You almost feel like you could fly without the plane." The men watched the house closely. After a while, Hauptmann, with field glasses, crept up for a closer look. Inside, supper was ending, and the parents were retiring to the living room in front of the fireplace. Olly Whateley was reading a magazine in the servants' sitting room downstairs. Moments later, the lights came on in the Whateleys' quarters on the second floor. The nursery was dark and the baby asleep. It was time.

The man who made the ladder was not the one who climbed it. Hauptmann, heavier than Knoll by fifteen pounds, was given the job of sneaking into the house, putting the baby into a burlap sack, and handing it off to Knoll out the window. Directly below the nursery was the library. The kidnappers did not want anyone inside the library to be able to see the ladder through the southeast corner window. Because Knoll, left-handed, needed to reach up to his left and receive the baby from Hauptmann, they needed to position the ladder to the right of the window and set it against the exterior wall. Having connected the two lower sections with a dowel pin, John and Walter maneuvered the ladder into a vertical position and stuck it into the ground about three feet from the wall. The imprints of the ladder show that it had been set into the ground in a vertical position, then gently leaned up against the house. Against fierce winds, the wobbly ladder was unwieldy even with just two of the sections connected. Standing with his back facing the house, Walter reached up high and grabbed the top section to keep the ladder from hinging as he and John tilted it and set it against the house.

Hauptmann, standing at the northeast corner of the house, signaled to John and Walter that the vestibule was clear and that he was going in. With that, John began his climb as Walter steadied the ladder and kept an eye out for signs of activity. Hauptmann, leaving his shoes on the flagstone court, opened the front door a crack and, after one last peek into the tiled vestibule, slipped inside and made his way into the entrance hall. At that juncture, Lindbergh and his wife, sitting on a couch on the other side of the living room wall, were only fifteen feet away. The dog, asleep on his bed in the kitchen, heard nothing.

The staircase was to Hauptmann's left, a few steps from the entrance hall. Clutching a handgun and the burlap sack, he tiptoed in his socks up to the second floor. The nursery sat at the top of the staircase just to his left. As he opened the door, the half-light from the hallway revealed the silhouette of the four-poster crib. He stuck the gun into his coat pocket and pulled out a flashlight.

He closed the door behind him, switched on the flashlight, and looked down at the blond, curly-haired baby boy. As exposed and fearful of capture as Hauptmann was at that moment, he was a man who had broken into homes before. He had the nerves for the job, and quickly went to the window at the southeast corner of the room across from the crib.

The shutters were unlatched, and Hauptmann leaned out the window to see the face of John Knoll. Both men at that moment must have felt at least slightly panicked: The top rung of the ladder was three feet below and to the right of the window; the handoff would be more difficult than either had imagined. Had they elected to use the third section of the ladder, the baby might have lived and the story might have ended differently. But the third section had been constructed for a backup plan in case the front door was locked. They would have then positioned the ladder directly in front of the nursery window, risking visibility from the library below, and climbed inside to take the child.

Hauptmann set the burlap sack on the floor and spread it out, then returned to the crib, twelve feet away. He took the baby out of the crib and walked over to the window. Working quickly, he opened the mouth of the sack and slipped him inside. The child thrashed about and cried out as Hauptmann grabbed the mouth of the sack, lifted it into the air, and carried it to the thirty-inch-wide window. Then he leaned over the chest in front of the window and transferred the sack to John Knoll, who grabbed it with his left hand as he held onto the ladder with his right.

As Knoll began his descent, Hauptmann placed a blank envelope with a ransom note on the one-foot-wide windowsill. He would forget to tell Knoll where he had put it. Cemetery John would later mention to Condon the letter "left in the crib"—because he hadn't left it there himself nor even been in the nursery that night.

Closing the door behind him, Hauptmann exited the nursery and made it as far as the first landing, four steps down, when he heard the sound of one piece of wood hitting another with tremendous force. As Lindbergh looked up, wondering what it might be, Hauptmann stood just feet away, frozen in place with a gun in his hand. Against his usual instincts, Lindbergh decided not to investigate, and Hauptmann hurried down the remaining twelve steps and out of the front door.

It was John Knoll who dropped the baby. Misjudging where his foot would land on the next rung of the ladder, he began to lose his balance, let go of the sack, and grabbed the ladder with his left hand. We can only imagine the frantic scene that ensued as John scrambled down the ladder after the baby's fall. After John reached the ground, Walter, panicking, lost control of the ladder, which scissored and made the loud sound that Lindbergh and Hauptmann had heard. As John grabbed the sack and the unused section of the ladder and began heading for the getaway car, Walter followed his brother carrying the two connected sections. After seventy-five feet the combined weight of the baby and the spare ladder section—about forty-four pounds—was too much for a man in flight. John Knoll dropped the section he was carrying, Walter abandoned the other two, and they were gone, leaving two sets of footprints.

The rails of the top of the two connected sections cracked. This likely occurred either when the ladder scissored or when Walter tossed it to the ground. (If the rails had cracked on the climber's descent, the terrific pressure on the joint would likely have resulted in much more collateral damage to the ladder.) In March of 2012, Kevin Klein, a master carpenter in New Jersey, conducted a stress test of a replica of the kidnap ladder. "It held over 250 pounds with no sign of failure," Klein said.[15] Incidentally, the famous Rail 16, the most convincing piece of evidence there would ever be to implicate Hauptmann, belonged to the third section of the ladder. It had not been needed.

It is possible sometimes, during full-immersion research of the story of the Lindbergh kidnapping, to feel occasional stirrings of pity for Hauptmann, who would be left to stand alone and answer for the crime of three, and weep alone in his cell after the sentence of death was read—muttering about those "little men, little pieces of wood, little scraps of paper." At such moments, all one has to do is recall what they did next that night, four miles from the crime scene. With Hauptmann driving, it would have been John Knoll who opened the burlap sack to see if the baby showed any sign of life. Finding none—or perhaps finding the child still breathing but mortally injured—he carried the sack fifty feet into the woods and dumped the body of Charlie Lindbergh.

Even though his kidnapping had now become a murder, John Knoll disregarded any inner voice that might have warned him not to go on with the extortion phase of the plan. This grim determination to continue, despite the heightened risk, reveals that the kidnapping was about more than just the ransom.[16] And if any of the three conspirators was in the least bit remorseful about the fate of this little boy who had been sleeping innocently in his crib just minutes earlier, it didn't stop them from trying to get the money, from tormenting the child's parents in their extortion notes, or from using the ransom money for pricy

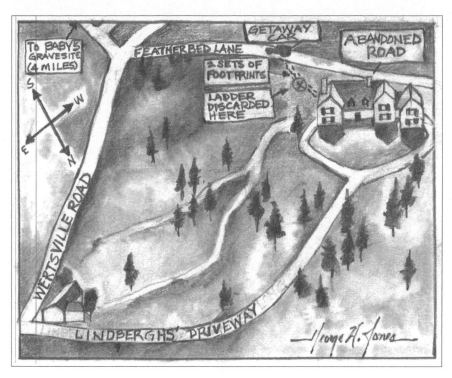

*The layout of the 425-acre Lindbergh estate near Hopewell, NJ*

new furniture (including, in Hauptmann's case, an expensive ivory crib for his own baby) or for prized stamps and first-class tickets to Germany. None of the kidnappers, even now, warrants much sympathy— and least of all the one who would fall from a ladder again, as an elderly man, forty-four years after death should have found him at the New Jersey State Prison.

# 34

# The Archivist

My grandfather's responsibilities in the 1930s included working ten hours a day, six days a week as the manager of the J. Kindermann & Sons storage warehouse in the Bronx. For his work he made forty-three dollars a week. My grandfather also cared for a wife and five daughters. He regretted that he couldn't devote more time to my father, but they did go to baseball games together at Yankee Stadium and the Polo Grounds.

Unlike my grandfather, Knoll had plenty of free time to spend with my father. There's something suspicious, observes John Douglas, about a grown man who hangs out with a fifteen-year-old boy. As he examined photographs of John Knoll and thought about the nature of this attachment, Douglas began to see a pattern: Knoll with a cat on his lap; Knoll carrying a tiny white dog in a pouch; Knoll, during his military days, with a black eye swollen shut and a monkey in his arms; Knoll going places with a boy half his age and giving him valuable gifts. Douglas had the familiar conviction that he was studying a manipulator. For decades he has studied the inner workings of personalities of criminals whose main goals in life are to "*manipulate, dominate,* and *control.*"[1]

The story of John Knoll really begins when he lived down the block from my father. What can we make of my father's experiences with him, and what clues does Knoll's behavior reveal about his mindset? Was he, at best, a somewhat kind, generous man with a dark side, a reluctant criminal who conceived the kidnapping scheme as a means of hitting it big in the middle of the Depression? And if this was the case, was Knoll genuinely interested in the companionship of a fifteen-year-old boy, and did his seeming generosity to the boy emanate from pure motives? How did he view my father? To determine at this point if any of the conspirators involved in the Lindbergh kidnapping had any sort of psychological disorder is almost impossible—and unimportant. Yet researchers of these disorders, forensic psychiatrists, and profilers who have spent years hunting and studying violent criminals all have thoughts on the subject.

Psychopathy, as Dr. Mary Ellen O'Toole explains, is a continuum, and each person displaying traits associated with the personality disorder will fall somewhere on that continuum.[2] Dr. Robert D. Hare, Emeritus Professor of Psychology at the University of British Columbia and the author of *Without Conscience*, has dedicated his career to studying psychopathy. The recipient of numerous international awards for his four decades of work as the leading academic in the field, he developed what has become a standard of diagnosis, the *Psychopathy Checklist-Revised* (PCL-R), summarized as follows: "glib and superficial charm; grandiose sense of self-worth; need for stimulation or proneness to boredom; pathological lying; conning and manipulation; lack of remorse or guilt; shallow affect; callousness and lack of empathy; parasitic lifestyle; poor behavioral controls; promiscuous sexual behaviors; early behavioral problems; lack of realistic, long-term goals; impulsivity; irresponsibility; failure to accept responsibility for own actions; many short-term marital relationships; juvenile delinquency; revocation of conditional release; and criminal versatility."[3] The first reliable and valid interview for psychopathy, PCL is one of the best predictors of criminal offending, particularly violent offenses.

Dr. Craig S. Neumann, an internationally recognized researcher of psychopathic personality and a colleague of Dr. Hare, has analyzed the many stories of the life of John Knoll. The episode at Palisades Amusement Park first raised Dr. Neumann's suspicions.

Although he enjoyed swimming, Knoll did not go into the pool that summer day in 1931, which suggests that going for a swim was not his primary purpose for his trip across the Hudson. Easily accessible by car or subway and ferry, Palisades Park was an ideal meeting place from which three men from the Bronx could then reach the nearby estate in Englewood where the Lindberghs lived. But what sort of person with a plan to kidnap the infant son of the most famous man in the world would bring a fifteen-year-old boy along with him to such a rendezvous—then allow the boy to see him meet with his accomplices? Dr. Neumann's answer: a man with a place in that plan for the boy.

John Knoll, he suspects, had no interest in developing a friendship with my father or in sharing a hobby with someone half his age. Gene Zorn was simply an object to Knoll, just as his wife Lilly would be to him. He was using him. Knoll was grooming the boy—an innocent, hard-working student who got a paper route to help contribute to the family budget—for a specific purpose. Taking my father to Palisades Amusement Park in New Jersey was not a careless mistake on the part of a sloppy criminal. John Knoll invited the boy along that summer day to satisfy some narcissistic impulse. And after all, if he had not done so, I would not now be telling you John Knoll's story.

The trip to the amusement park, Dr. Neumann explains, was the first of several clues left behind for my father by the architect of the plot to kidnap Charlie Lindbergh. Knoll was laying out a symbolic trail of recognition that would ultimately lead back to him. And without that trail, no one would ever have found all of the evidence linking him to the crime. He needed a way to document what he was doing, and the teenage boy down the block proved a convenient target and an excellent choice to play the role of archivist. Knoll began by allowing the boy to see him meet with Hauptmann. Then, after the kidnapping had taken place, Knoll gave him an envelope with a "Lindbergh Airmail" stamp, a commemorative cover celebrating the five-year anniversary of Lindbergh's flight to Paris, several other aviation-themed cachets, and two envelopes with disguised handwriting as well as others written by someone else, all cleverly calculated to draw attention to them. And it was Knoll who had encouraged the boy to take up stamp collecting in the first place.

"John Knoll devised a way to ensure that his young neighbor Gene Zorn would never forget what he saw that day outside Palisades Park: dump him there," said Dr. Neumann. "Knoll wouldn't have chosen a man his own age to be the recorder of the images of the kidnapping. He would have used a boy—someone he could manipulate."[4]

At the time of the kidnapping, the science behind psychopathy was not strong, and Dr. Neumann commends the "impressive pioneering work" of Dr. Dudley Shoenfeld, the psychiatrist who created a psychological profile of Cemetery John. Dr. Shoenfeld believed that Cemetery John was elated by the media attention the kidnapping had attracted.

So how would John Knoll have reacted to the knowledge that his archivist would eventually figure out his role as mastermind of the Lindbergh kidnapping? "John Knoll would have been ecstatic to know that, decades after his death, his great crime would once again make headlines," Dr. Neumann said.[5] Dr. O'Toole, reviewing this theory, said, "I completely agree with [Dr. Neumann]. I think he is incredibly insightful regarding how [Gene Zorn] was used."[6]

Forensic psychiatrist Dr. Sally C. Johnson has also studied what we know of the life, behavior, and personality of John Knoll. "Knoll's marriage to his third wife Ida was far more conventional than his fast-dissolving earlier two marriages, and as he aged, his life appears to have become increasingly more conventional as well," said Dr. Johnson. "Assuming that he was involved in the Lindbergh kidnapping, I would move him toward the psychopathic end of the sociopathy/psychopathy spectrum . . . Of course, there was no way to interview him to hear his side of the many odd stories about him, but isn't it fascinating how much of his life mirrors our conception of a psychopath?"[7]

My father never lived to hear many of these stories about John Knoll's life or the expert opinions regarding the personality, behavior, and motivations of his former South Bronx neighbor. Yet until his death, many questions lingered in my father's mind, and this is one of them. When John Knoll had taken my father to the swimming pool at Tibbetts Brook Park in Yonkers one day, Knoll got off at a subway stop in the North Bronx, then told my father to go back to Jackson Avenue Station alone. The stop was not far from Hauptmann's home. Was Knoll going to a planning meeting?

My hope is that this book will open up further discussion about the case, and perhaps lead to some more startling discoveries about John Knoll's role in the crime. For the more we learn about Knoll and the life he led after the kidnapping, the more questions come to mind. Did he take any of the Lindbergh ransom money with him when he escaped to Germany before Hauptmann's murder trial? If so, what did he do with it?

Did Knoll use any of the ransom money to help him get started in his own businesses?

Did either Knoll's landlady, Emma Schaefer, or her forty-four-year-old son, Bill, who supposedly died of "acute indigestion" three weeks after her death and four months before Hauptmann's arrest, discover illegal gold certificates on the premises?[8]

How did Knoll manage to get out of the service in 1943, two years before the war ended?

Did Knoll, as Dr. Neumann further surmises, coach his younger brother and protégé Walter to leave clues regarding his own participation in the kidnapping? Or is it coincidental that Walter chose what would have been the Lindbergh baby's fifth birthday for his wedding date and Woodlawn Cemetery for his final resting place?

Do any arrest records for Knoll exist either in Germany or in one of the many places he lived in the States?

Did Knoll keep one of the gold notes as a trophy? What happened to the rest of the ransom bills?

Where is John Knoll's stamp collection that his son gave away to a postal worker in California? In these stamps and First Day Covers, do any more clues lie hidden?

# 35

# Approaching Lindbergh

I f my father was so sure of Knoll's involvement, why didn't he act sooner? As a matter of fact, he did. Despite my father's dedication to his family and work, he made diligent efforts to act on his suspicions regarding the Knoll brothers' participation in the Lindbergh kidnapping. Over the years, he recorded his observations on the case and kept them in a notebook along with folders filled with newspaper clippings. One handwritten note providing a glimpse into the leadings of his conscience reveals his primary reason for pursuing his own investigation of the case: justice.[1] If he was correct about his former neighbors on Jackson Avenue, John Knoll and his brother Walter had gone unindicted for their murder of a twenty-month-old baby. Meanwhile, their accomplice had paid with his life for the crime for which all three shared responsibility.

For years my mother worried about the attention that my father's involvement in the case might bring our family. Though he listened to her concerns, the words of Anne Morrow Lindbergh spoke to him even more strongly: "I want the truth when they find it and I will face it and Justice should be pursued."[2]

For seventy-two days, she didn't know what her baby's fate had been. There had been no release from her pain, and when release came it was to bring only more suffering. "It isn't the sorrow of last winter that stabs, it is those moments of hope—remembering those moments of hope is unbearable," she wrote in her diary.[3]

For Anne, who would live to age ninety-four, the grief would never stop. During a television interview toward the end of her life, she began to cry when asked about her murdered infant son: not a day had gone by since the kidnapping that she had not questioned what she and her husband could have done to protect her baby and prevent the crime.[4]

Described by Reeve Lindbergh as "by far the strongest" of her parents, Anne would suffer from dementia in her nineties. A "shadowy dream of loss"—a reference to the death of her baby, according to her youngest daughter—would never stop haunting Anne. "For a few days this winter, she asked her caregivers anxiously about a child she believed to be in her house," wrote Reeve more than sixty-five years after the kidnapping. "Could they see him? Was he all right? Was he hungry?"[5]

Anne's mother, too, had been inconsolable. "I keep living that nightmare over again," wrote Betty Morrow in a letter to her friend Robert Thayer after Hauptmann's capture. "It is so vivid. It is different from anything in my whole life. It is as if we had all of us been on a desert island together."[6]

John Knoll and his accomplices had also robbed the Lindberghs' other children—Jon, Land, Anne, Scott, and Reeve—of the opportunity to know their brother Charlie. The baby had lived but six hundred and eighteen days. His gentle spirit, funny antics, and happy disposition left an indelible impression on those who knew and loved him. The injustice angered my father and he decided to act.

On March 1, 1972, after much contemplation, my father composed a handwritten letter to Charles Lindbergh. He did not intentionally write on the fortieth anniversary of the kidnapping, but the timing of the letter was not the coincidence it might seem. The newspapers had revisited the story as the anniversary approached, and a particular item had spurred him to write.

My father had just read Samuel G. Blackman's AP article "Lindbergh Case Unshaken" in the February 27 edition of the *Dallas Morning News*. The first reporter to arrive at the crime scene on the night of the kidnapping, Blackman had recently interviewed Samuel S. Leibowitz, a recently retired New York Supreme Court justice. Leibowitz was the attorney whom Evalyn Walsh McLean had hired to head up her own investigation of the case. On three occasions he had visited Hauptmann at the New Jersey State Prison, trying to no avail to elicit information about his accomplices. "I was convinced then and am still convinced that he did not act alone," Leibowitz said in the interview.[7]

During his tenure as an economist with the American Bankers Association in the 1950s, my father served as Secretary of the Committee on Government Borrowing. In this role, he worked closely with Secretary of the Treasury Robert B. Anderson. Three or four times a year, my father traveled to Washington, where the committee met to discuss the oncoming financing requirements of the times.

In the early 1970s, Anderson and Charles Lindbergh sat on the Board of Directors of Pan American Airways, a position the aviator had held since 1965. My father telephoned Anderson at his offices in Radio City. Anderson listened as my father, beginning with the story about the day at Palisades Park, described the evidence implicating his former South Bronx neighbors in the kidnapping.

Though usually hesitant to request favors, he asked Anderson to consider hand-delivering his letter to Lindbergh. The willingness of a former high-ranking presidential appointee to convey the letter might just convince Lindbergh to take it seriously. For the conservative Gene Zorn, the move was risky: Anderson, a man with enough influence in the banking community to damage my father's reputation, might have concluded that he had departed his senses.

But Anderson believed the story had merit and handed Lindbergh the letter at the next Pan Am Board of Directors meeting in New York. The letter read:

March 1, 1972

Col. Charles A. Lindbergh
Darien, Conn.
Dear Col. Lindbergh,
My boyhood years were spent in a German neighborhood in the Bronx. Without realizing it, since early 1932 I have had in my personal possession tangible and convincing evidence pointing to the identity of John and another man as accomplices of Bruno Hauptmann in the kidnapping of your son. I realize that the passing of 40 years makes this appear incredible, but please distinguish this letter from the many you have received.

The enclosed biographical notes will help to indicate that this is not a crank letter. Indeed, I am known to some of your distinguished

Pan Am associates. The late Robert V. Fleming was a devoted friend who did much to further my career.

I expect to be in New York again sometime in the next few weeks and would like to visit with you to show you the evidence and relate personal knowledge bearing on the case that has had meaning to me only since my recent reading of George Waller's book and other articles. As a boy, I observed the case and trial only casually as one exposed to press reports, but certain facts that relate to the evidence in my pos-' session somehow became indelibly imprinted in my memory.

During the years after the crime I cast aside my suspicions on the presumption that the case had been settled and justice served, but Waller's book and such reports as this week's Associated Press story now convince me that this presumption was not correct. Against the background of so many years since the crime, I find it difficult to explain the persistence with which the case has come to mind. Even now I write with consider- able hesitancy, but am motivated by a haunting and compelling conviction that justice will be served if my suspicions are proved correct.

My concern for your viewpoint, as well as possible implications for my work and family, will explain why I am writing to you directly rather than contacting legal authorities at this time. I shall much appreciate a confidential telephone call to my office indicating your interest in dis- cussing the matter.

Sincerely yours,
Eugene C. Zorn, Jr.

My father provided the telephone number of his office at Republic National Bank of Dallas, where he served as Chief Economist from 1960 until his retirement in 1981. Mentioned in the letter were Robert V. Fleming, who had served as a chairman of Riggs National Bank and as a Board of Directors member of Pan Am, and George Waller, author of the 1961 bestseller *Kidnap*. Waller also wrote the article in the December 1963 issue of *True* that had sparked my father's interest in the Lindbergh case.

When my father called to follow up, Anderson informed him that Lindbergh had read the letter, folded it up dismissively, and stuffed it into his pocket. A few days after Lindbergh had received the letter, a man who claimed to represent the State Department appeared at my father's office and launched into a series of odd questions.

"He wanted to know what I might be able to do in trying to help [the government] on some international financial matters. It was just a ruse," recalled my father. "He wanted to know whether I was all there—whether I was a good citizen or a screwball. And that was the last I heard of it."[8]

My father saw Anderson at an American Bankers Association cocktail party at The Pierre three years later. As they discussed Lindbergh's reaction to the letter, Anderson sensed his friend's disappointment and offered a few consoling words. The aviator had died the previous year at age seventy-two.

One day in the late 1990s, my father received a telephone call from biographer A. Scott Berg, who had come across his letter to Lindbergh in an archive collection. My father was unfamiliar at the time with the biographer's brilliant body of work. They had but this one brief conversation, and my father concluded that Berg was likely "so well advanced in his preparation of his biography" that he decided not to follow up with another call.[9]

Discouraged by Lindbergh's indifference to his letter, my father phoned his best friend from college, Manhattan attorney Herman V. Traub. When he contacted Traub in early 1973, my father described the evidence that had convinced him that the Lindbergh kidnapping had not been solved. Fluent in German, Traub had served as an Army Air Forces Intelligence officer during the Second World War and interviewed dozens of Germans overseas. The experience made him the ideal candidate to investigate John Knoll. The two CCNY fraternity brothers teamed up to work on the case and code-named it "Project Jackson."

Walter Knoll had died in 1962, Traub reported, but his sixty-eight-year-old brother was still alive. Traub had spoken to John Knoll and summarized his findings in a letter to my father that read:

3/21/73

Dear Gene,
The following facts have been established without doubt:
    (1) John Knoll now lives in Tom's River, N.J. on Mt. Matterhorn Lane (Silverton area).
    He sold his business in Scarsdale about 5 years ago. The telephone company kept printing his old numbers in error.

His brother Walter died about 10 years ago in Yonkers. He had lived in Detroit for about 3 years (1934-7?—dates uncertain). He was a butcher by profession and worked at that trade in Detroit. When he came back East—he had his own delicatessen shop on Lake Street in Yonkers.

This John did work for Woltman's [sic] in The Bronx. He states that he came to the Bronx in 1932. [Since the event we are interested in took place on March 1, 1932, it does not seem likely that there was enough time in 1932 before that date for him to have been involved in the planning. Also, it would not have been possible for him to have taken you swimming in 1931. It could be that his memory is faulty—but the question of accuracy becomes important.]

I will tell you in person how this information was obtained when next we meet.

I have not yet finished Waller's book. When I have done so—and analyzed its contents—I am going to try to talk to him about the case without giving my reasons for a general interest in some of its legal aspects [created?] by the book. The fly leaf of the book states that he lives in Manhattan—and there is a listing under his name in the telephone book. My objective is to obtain his views as to whether or not Bruno had accomplices and his supporting data for such views.

I'll keep in touch.

All the best,
Herman

How is it possible for a man to be off by six years when recalling the timing of his move to the Bronx? Knoll's Petition for Citizenship shows his arrival in the borough in 1926. In addition, an unopened letter in my father's stamp collection addressed to Knoll's home address in the Bronx was postmarked on July 31, 1929. As a final proof that Knoll had lied, the 1930 U.S. Federal Census lists him as a lodger at 738 Jackson Avenue.[10] Perhaps a sixty-eight-year-old might miss by a year or two in remembering when he had made a major move early in his adulthood, but to be off by six years? Why might a man be so misleading in answering a simple question? Even forty-one years after the kidnapping, Knoll was acting like a man with something to hide.

By the time my father reached his retirement years, the first eight of which were consumed with caring for a wife suffering from depression and agoraphobia, he had an interesting theory about the case that would be difficult to prove. An editor at a university press that publishes books on true crime scoffed at his story about having seen two German immigrant brothers meet with a man named Bruno. To amplify his skepticism, he pointed out that Hauptmann's wife and friends in the States had called him "Richard."[11] Yet John Knoll was constantly tagging people with nicknames like *Stadtslottel* ("city bum"), *Honigplatz* ("honey seat"), and "Blondie," which, for some reason, he reserved only for dark-haired women. Once you know the man, it's not hard at all to imagine him deciding that Hauptmann would be *Bruno*—particularly because it is a tough-sounding and fitting name for a criminal accomplice.

After my mother died in December 1989 when he was seventy-three, my father no longer possessed the energy to pursue the additional evidence required to prove that John Knoll had perpetrated the "Crime of the Century" and seal the case. He would appoint me to carry on where he left off. Not until after his death, however, did I take on the assignment full-time and conduct my own investigation. For eighty years, certain details in the Lindbergh kidnapping just never added up; though justice was done, it remained incomplete. "The most important equation to solve in life is the human equation," my father used to tell me. It was his insight and integrity that completed the story and finally solved that equation.

# Epilogue

O n March 29, 1973, a few days after he had received Herman
Traub's letter updating him on Project Jackson, my father met in
Washington, D.C., with the acting Comptroller of the Currency.
That afternoon, he visited the Library of Congress and ordered a few
titles on the Lindbergh case in the Main Reading Room of the Jefferson Building. My father gazed about the octagonal room, whose 23-
carat gold-plated dome soars to 160 feet. The symbolic and portrait
statues, stucco figures, sculptures, paintings, Algerian and Italian marble,
and ornamentation unite with architectural design of genius to create
one of the most magnificent interior spaces in the country. The round
mural set inside the sky blue lantern of the dome—a painting of a
female figure removing the veil of ignorance—represents Human
Understanding.[1]

My father took six pages of notes about his experience at the Library
of Congress that day. "My selection of Desk 219 was quite by accident," he
wrote, "as there were available reading places all around the circle. I was
almost directly opposite the marble column over which the statue depicting the subject of philosophy is centered. Each of the eight columns of the
rotunda is similarly topped with a statue symbolizing different aspects of
civilized life and above each one is an inscription on a gold plaque. The one
devoted to philosophy was first to catch my eye. It reads: 'The inquiry,
knowledge, and belief of truth is the sovereign good of human nature.'[2]

"Its meaning gave me a tingling sensation—a feeling that God again
had taken me by the hand and led me there," he continued. Because the

books he had selected would take nearly an hour to arrive, he walked around the perimeter of the room and read the inscriptions above the statues devoted to Art, History, Commerce, Religion, Science, Law, and Poetry. "Having completed the circle and finding no others with the significance of the first one, I believed that some power beyond my comprehension had guided me to Desk 219, and that I was being encouraged once more to search out the truth."[3]

Just the week before, he had read Anne Morrow Lindbergh's recently published *Hour of Gold, Hour of Lead;* to help others struggling to cope with grief, Anne had described to her legions of readers her "long way out" as she had searched for inner peace in the midst of suffering.[4] "She more than anyone else in the world was the one I wanted to talk to," wrote my father, "especially since Colonel Lindbergh just a year earlier had rebuffed my efforts through a mutual and distinguished friend to contact him regarding my suspicions in the case. Her thoughts were indelibly imprinted in my mind as I recounted the introduction to the portion of the book devoted to the letters she had written while suffering the anguish of the crime—the Hour of Lead . . . And as if she were writing for me personally, Anne concluded: 'Truth that is locked up in the heart—or in a diary—is sterile. It must be given back to life so that the "hour of lead"—of others—may be transmuted.'[5] Yet there I was, seeking to unlock the truth, which for so many years had been hidden in my own diary of sorts and which, as Anne so pointedly stated, was sterile. While her phrases were so fresh in my mind, it was easy for me to understand, as I sat in the library waiting for my books, why I found sudden and renewed inspiration from the inscription."[6]

On December 22, 2006, twenty-six years after he had first told me his story about John Knoll, my ninety-year-old father lay dying in an intensive care unit. He was tired and gaunt. I sat down at the edge of his hospital bed, held his hand, and thanked him for the final time for the blessing of his presence in my life. He had sacrificed more for me than any son could imagine. Not until I had reached my mid-forties did I realize that no one had ever loved me more—nor likely ever would. A burning desire to honor what would soon become his memory came over me. As my father looked up into my eyes, I made him a promise to tell the world his story about John Knoll and the Lindbergh kidnapping.

My father was failing rapidly and he didn't have the strength to respond in words; but I could tell by the faint trace of a smile on his face that he was happy. He knew that the sterile truth that had been locked up in his "diary of sorts" for seventy-five years would someday be "given back to life" as he believed Anne Morrow Lindbergh would have wanted. And just as Anne had believed that something good could come from her irrecoverable loss, my father was convinced that something good could come from the resurrected truth. I am certain he was right.

# List of Experts

**DR. MICHAEL M. BADEN**
Forensic pathologist and former Chief Medical Examiner, New York City

**DR. JEFFREY BARNARD**
Professor of Pathology, UT Southwestern School of Medicine

**DR. WILLIAM M. BASS III**
Forensic anthropologist and founder of the University of Tennessee Anthropological Research Facility, more popularly known as "The Body Farm"; conducted study of the bones of the feet and hands of Charles A. Lindbergh, Jr., in 1983

**GOVERNOR BRENDAN T. BYRNE**
Former governor of New Jersey, longtime student of the Lindbergh case, and respected friend of the attorney general who served as prosecutor in the trial of Bruno Hauptmann; signer of the executive order releasing 250,000 files on the Lindbergh case to the public

**DR. MARY CASE**
Forensic and neuropathologist and Professor of Pathology at Saint Louis University School of Medicine; forensic expert on crimes against children and in pediatric head trauma; chief medical examiner in four Missouri counties

**JOHN DOUGLAS**
The retired FBI special agent who pioneered the Bureau's behavioral profiling program and served as chief of the Investigative Support Unit at the National Center for the Analysis of Violent Crime; the model for the character Jack Crawford in *The Silence of the Lambs*

**DR. SALLY C. JOHNSON**
Professor of Forensic Psychiatry at the University of North Carolina at Chapel Hill; the court-appointed forensic psychiatrist who interviewed Theodore J. Kaczynski, better known as the Unabomber

**KELVIN KERAGA**
An independent researcher who conducted an intensive forensic study of the wood used to make the kidnap ladder and of the floorboard in Bruno Hauptmann's attic, completed in 2005

**KEVIN KLEIN**
Master carpenter and owner of Klein Construction in Chester, New Jersey. A keen student of the Lindbergh case, he has built and performed stress tests of replicas of the kidnap ladder.

**DR. ROBERT A. LEONARD**
Internationally renowned forensic linguist; Professor of Linguistics, Head of the Hofstra University Graduate Program in Forensic Linguistics, and Director of its Institute for Forensic Linguistics, Threat Assessment and Strategic Analysis

**Dr. Craig S. Neumann**
Internationally renowned researcher of psychopathic personality and Professor of Psychology at the University of North Texas

**Mark Olshaker**
Emmy Award–winning documentary filmmaker, crime novelist, and co-author with John Douglas of several books on criminal profiling, including *Mindhunter* and *Broken Wings*

**Dr. Mary Ellen O'Toole**
Retired FBI criminal profiler and a leading expert on child abduction, psychopathy, and targeted violence; author of *Dangerous Instincts: How Gut Feelings Betray Us*

**Dr. Kathy J. Reichs**
Generally recognized as the world's most well-known forensic anthropologist; best-selling novelist, producer of the television series *Bones,* and the model for its character Temperance "Bones" Brennan

**Dr. Kim Rossmo**
Innovator and developer of the methodology of geographic profiling, now used worldwide as a crime-fighting tool; Research Professor at Texas State University and director of the university's Center for Geospatial Intelligence and Investigation

**Dr. Sargur N. Srihari**
Innovator and developer of optical handwriting recognition (OHR) and an expert in software-based pattern recognition; SUNY Distinguished Professor in the Faculty of Engineering and Applied Sciences at the University at Buffalo

**Catherine J. Sporer**
Research Information Specialist for Stepan Company, a specialty surfactant and polyol producer; former Senior Commodity Manager specializing in fats and oils for the company; has over twenty years of experience in chemistries related to surfactants

**Edward F. Sulzbach**
Retired FBI special agent and recipient of the FBI Medal of Valor; taught criminal profiling at the FBI Academy; the model for novelist Patricia Cornwell's character Wesley Benton

**Dr. Emanuel Tanay**
Clinical Professor of Psychiatry at the Wayne State University Medical School; Holocaust survivor and, at one time, one of only two full-time forensic psychiatrists in the country; author of the 1983 *Journal of Forensic Sciences* article "The Lindbergh Kidnapping—A Psychiatric View" presented at the Plenary Session at the 35th Annual Meeting of the American Academy of Forensic Sciences

**Dr. Arpad A. Vass**
Forensic anthropologist and research scientist at the Life Science Division at Oak Ridge National Laboratory; co-inventor of the Lightweight Analyzer for Buried Remains and Decomposition Odor Recognition (LABRADOR)

# Acknowledgments

For the steadfast, irreplaceable part he played in the research, analysis, and development of this book, I wish to express my deep appreciation first of all to Gregory F. Hamm. Sharing my father's desire to see justice served in the Lindbergh case, Greg has walked alongside me every step of the way on this long journey, and it was he who encouraged me to pursue the examination of the kidnapping and my father's story from the perspective of modern criminal investigative analysis. Also to Greg's wife, Mireille, and their daughters Monique, Madeleine, Theresa, and Catherine, I offer my thanks for their good cheer and gracious hospitality during my many research trips to the Washington, D.C., area.

Andrew Mailer, my favorite teacher during my eleven years at St. Mark's School of Texas, dedicated hundreds of hours to helping me edit this book. His wisdom, experience, and precision were indispensable throughout the process. I am honored to have this gifted writer in my life as a devoted friend and mentor. Matthew Scully, a former presidential speechwriter and the author of *Dominion*, was tireless in contributing his masterful editing skills to this work. Greg, Andrew, and Matthew brought constant encouragement and a sense of camaraderie to the work, and I'm very fortunate to have such friends. While this book is formally dedicated solely to the memory of my father, in a sense it also honors the three great friends who made it possible. I can't mention best friends without also including the ones who stayed close by all the time, including even on long treks across country. For the wonderful companionship they provided me over the years as I wrote this book, I'll always appreciate the role of my beloved border collie mixes: the late Brigitta, Gatsby, and Gretl as well as Friedrich and Bunkie. They're the best. Family members of John Knoll and of his second wife, Lilly, were instrumental to my research. My very deep heartfelt thanks go to Rudy Breiling, the son of John's sister Agnes, and to Rudy's wife, Sharon. The Breilings have become beloved friends and have extended me an open invitation to their annual family reunions and to stay as a guest in their home. Indeed, they are two of the most wonderful people I've ever met. I will never forget Sharon's comment to me after she had seen all the evidence presented in this book: "This story *must* be told, and the truth must come out." While there are many family members I've dealt with, I'd also like to thank John's daughter-in-law, Adrienne Knoll, and Lilly Knoll's niece Brigitte Geiger in Germany.

My editor, Dan Crissman, whose keen insights and support have proved invaluable, demonstrated that the spirit of Max Perkins is alive and well in New York. My agent, William Callahan, showed enthusiasm for this story right from the start and offered sage advice. I thank them both for their patience with a first-time author and for their excellent editorial guidance. My thanks to Peter Mayer and his whole team at Overlook Press for their great skill and their confidence in me, and especially to Amanda Bartlett for her artistry in creating the book's perfect cover. I'm also indebted to Kurt Eichenwald, Becky Ebner Hoag, Nancy Sauer, and Charles R. Helms for their editorial assistance and George H. Jones for his original artwork.

I am much indebted to Susan Vicarisi, the assistant to former New Jersey Governor Brendan T. Byrne and a paralegal with Carrella Byrne. It is only after she listened to some fellow call up out of the blue to talk about how his late father may have uncovered important new evidence regarding the Lindbergh case that she agreed to set up a meeting with the very busy former governor. Not only did Governor Byrne treat me to lunch and devote his entire afternoon to me during our first meeting (which Susan later told me *never* happens), but as I was leaving, he offered to write testimonial letters and offer his ongoing help. Governor Byrne's letters opened the door to other influential people, and before long, to my amazement, the support for my father's now eighty-year-old story grew and grew, earning more testimonials and attracting offers from some of the most highly renowned experts in criminology, forensic science, and law to contribute to his "Project Jackson." And, of course, Governor Byrne himself has my heartfelt appreciation, as does one of his partners in his law firm, Arthur T. Vanderbilt II, who has also become a good friend and wonderful advisor.

The experts listed in the previous section have exerted an influence on their respective professions that will last long beyond their retirements. Many have devoted their careers—in some cases, risking their lives—to putting violent criminals out of business. In a world obsessed with the meaningless celebrity that Charles Lindbergh himself disdained, these men and women stand out as true heroes. My thanks go to all of them. For the many hours they spent helping me understand the criminal mind and for their insights into the personality and behavior of John Knoll, I'd like to express my gratitude to John Douglas, Mark Olshaker, Dr. Craig S. Neumann, Dr. Mary Ellen O'Toole, Edward F. Sulzbach, and Dr. Sally C. Johnson. During our very first phone conversation, Ed invited me to come stay at his lovely home in Virginia and talk to him about the case; what a thrill that was for me, and what a terrific friend he has become.

Dr. Kim Rossmo was extremely generous with his time and personally created a geographic profile using the data points associated with the Lindbergh case. Legendary forensic psychiatrist Dr. Emanuel Tanay—at one time one of only two full-time forensic psychiatrists in the country—was extremely gracious and helpful. A survivor of the Holocaust and a brilliant thinker, he is an inspiration. Forensic pathologist and neuropathologist Dr. Mary Case was immensely kind in answering questions regarding head trauma to young children. Dr. Robert A. Leonard shared insights about the ransom letters and helped me understand how forensic linguistics and criminal profiling can work hand-in-hand to create a big picture—in this case, of a criminal who may have been a game-player. Kevin Klein shared incredible insights about the kidnap ladder, and his help in my writing of Chapters 6 and 33 was invaluable.

My childhood friends Marshall Payne and Robert M. Edsel, author of *The Monuments Men*, have been wonderfully supportive. Robert has been a great inspiration as well. For his help and for his enthusiasm for this project, I thank Jay Heiler—and also former Vice President Dan Quayle, to whom Jay introduced me, and who was kind enough to offer to explore the book's potential as a major motion picture. For the time they spent with me describing their experiences in the mid-1930s aboard the SS *Manhattan*, Julia Ruth Stephens (the daughter of Babe Ruth), who sailed to New York on the ship in February 1935 (John Knoll was a fellow passenger), and famed U.S. Olympic distance runner and World War II prisoner of war Louis S. Zamperini (the subject of Laura Hillenbrand's book *Unbroken*); for his untiring assistance on my fifteen or so trips to the New Jersey State Police Museum and for the hundreds of questions he answered for me over the course of a decade, archivist Mark Falzini; for the use of many photos in this book, to the New Jersey State Police Museum and the Library of Congress; for her assistance with my researching of U.S. Army military records, Susan Nash of the National Archives At St. Louis; for their helpfulness on my trip to Bruno Richard Hauptmann's home town, Thomas Binder, *Stadtarchivar* (City Archivist), Kamenz, Germany, and his assistant Odette Küntsler, who showed me the homes where Hauptmann and my grandparents' landlord, Oscar Rietschel, lived.

For their time and effort to apply Optical Handwriting Recognition (OHR) analysis to the Lindbergh case, I'd like to thank Dr. Sargur N. Srihari of University of Buffalo's Center of Excellence for Document Analysis and Recognition (CEDAR) as well as Gregory Ball and Krishnanand Das. I also appreciate the helpfulness of forensic anthropologists Dr. William M. Bass, Dr. Arpad Vass, and Dr. Kathy J. Reichs; forensic pathologists Dr. Michael M. Baden and Dr. Jeffrey Barnard; independent researcher Kelvin Keraga, who helped teach me about wood science; chemist Catherine J. Sporer; and hand surgeon Dr. J. Daniel Labs.

It's important to acknowledge how helpful various books on Lindbergh and the kidnapping have been in the writing of this book. A. Scott Berg's *Lindbergh* is a brilliant work; he belongs in the short list of America's finest biographers today. I wish to thank historian Lloyd Gardner, the author of *The Case That Never Dies,* for the insights he shared with me. In *The Ghosts of Hopewell,* Jim Fisher did a thorough job refuting the various theories suggesting that Hauptmann was innocent. Incidentally, the book you're reading wouldn't exist were it not for the *True* magazine article by the late George Waller, who also wrote the bestseller *Kidnap.* Also, for his input on design-related issues, I'd like to thank Erik Larson, author of the true crime classic *The Devil In the White City*.

My cousin Philip J. Orban and his wife, Joanne, always provided me a wonderful place to stay on my research trips to New York and New Jersey. George E. Koehler, son of the pioneering wood scientist Arthur Koehler), provided me with a treasure trove of information about his father's work. I'd also like to express my appreciation to Jorge del Cid; Thomas Dinneny; Herman and Barbara Traub; Joan Dixon (the step-granddaughter of Oscar Rietschel); Sister Mary Anthony, C. S. F. N.; Paul Carluccio and Vanessa Graham of the Albert Elias Residential Group Center at Highfields; Kathy Campbell and Shelley Hughes of the Family Research Center of the Church of Jesus Christ of Latter-Day Saints in McKinney, Texas; Matt Pinkston of ancestry.com; Jacque Schwerin; Deb Cornwell; Dr. Sandra Swain; the late Thelma Miller (an attendee of the Hauptmann trial); Jim Foote of postalhistory.com; Thomas J. Allen of the Wineburgh Philatelic Research Library of the University of Texas at Dallas; Jaime Bourassa and Molly Kodner of the Missouri Historical Museum Library and Research Center; Alexia Shows, Carolyn Blackman Jacoby and Ann Blackman Putzel (daughters of Samuel G. Blackman, the first reporter to arrive at the crime scene); Jim Koslovski at the Rosedale and Rosehill Cemetery Association; Jan Keshishian and Evan Brown of the Elisabeth Morrow School; Margaret Dakin and Mariah Sakrejda-Leavitt of the Archives and Special Collections of the Amherst College Library; Tom Adams; Vince Gargiulo of the Palisades Amusement Park Historical Society; Laura Tosi of the Bronx County Historical Society; John Favareau of the Yonkers Historical Society; Sonia Paulino of Woodlawn Cemetery; and Felix Shaulov. For the fascinating tour of Herxheimweyher, Germany, and for their hospitality, I'd like to thank Herbert Eck, Tilla Schneider, Leo and Waltraub Knoll, Lia Bullinger, Richard Knoll, and Karl Knoll; and for the tour of the Lutheran cemetery where Lilly Knoll's ashes are buried in Kempten im Allgäu, Germany, Brigitte Geiger and her daughter Kathrin. A thank you also goes to Jim Deibel; Michael L. Grace; Valoise Armstrong of the Eisenhower Library; Larry Klein; Dr. Matthew D. Lippas; John Currin; Joe Van Nostrand of the Division of Old Records, New York County Clerk; Peter Johannknecht; David Lejeune; Mandy Vicary; Robert H. Thayer, Jr.; Matthew A. Knutzen, Assistant Chief, The Lionel Pincus and Princess Firyal Map Division of the New York Public Library; Bryan Cornell, Reference Librarian, Motion Picture, Broadcasting and Recorded Sound Division, Library of Congress; Josie Walters-Johnston and Zoran Sindbad, Film and Television Reference Librarians of the Library of Congress; James Sweany, Local History and Genealogy Reading Room, Library of Congress; Bruce Kirby and Lewis Wyman, Jr., Manuscript Division, Library of Congress; Ed Redmond and John Hessler, Reference Librarians in the Geography and Map Reading Room, Library of Congress; Mark Nusenbaum and Jazmin Santini of the Bronx County Clerk's Office; Rowan Baker; Bruce Latimer of the Superior Court of New Jersey Records Center; Colleen Goode and Linda Barnes of the Ocean County Library in Toms River, New Jersey; Kathleen Short of the Broward County Main Library in Ft. Lauderdale, Florida; Susan Stepek of the Mt. Clemens Library in Mt. Clemens, Michigan; Jean Allen of the Immaculate Conception Catholic Church of Washington, D.C.; Claudette Gassler and Judith Reinfeld of the Scarsdale Public Library; Eric Rothschild; Cassandra Troini, Reference Librarian of the Warner Library in Tarrytown, New York; Philip J. Page; Susan Abbey; Rick Carrell; Richard Drummond Davis; Anita Andrews; Jean-Michel Boers; Charlie Bahr; Philip A. Smith; Lamar Hunt, Jr.; Bonnie and David Philson; and Richie Wolfheim.

# Notes

**INTRODUCTION**

[1] George Waller, "New Evidence in the Lindbergh Mystery," *True Magazine*, December 1963, 43.

[2] Then called the Hudson River Bridge.

[3] After a weekend together in the Hamptons, Eugene C. Zorn, Jr., told the author his story about John Knoll as they were driving on the Long Island Expressway. The author was on his way back to the University of Pennsylvania, where he was going to business school.

[4] Phone conversation between Edward F. Sulzbach and the author, October 20, 2011. Crime novelist Patricia Cornwell used a variation of this quote in her book *Portrait of a Killer*.

**1: THE CRIME**

[1] Temperature data from National Weather Service Daily Maps, http://docs.lib.noaa .gov/rescue/dwm/data_rescue_daily_weather_maps.html. Weather for New York City for 24-hour period beginning 8 a.m., March 1, 1932: "high of 44, low of 36." Wind "32mph" on March 1, 1932. "30mph" on March 2, 1932.

[2] The number of acres of the Lindbergh estate is from A. Scott Berg, *Lindbergh* (New York: G. P. Putnam's Sons, 1998), 219.

[3] Anne Morrow Lindbergh, handwritten notes, March 1932. Lindbergh Papers, Missouri Historical Museum, St. Louis, MO.

[4] Anne Morrow Lindbergh, *Hour of Gold, Hour of Lead* (New York: Harcourt, Brace Jovanovich, 1973), 227.

[5] From Charles Lindbergh's 79 pages of typewritten comments on the 1959 book "The Hero" by Kenneth S. Davis. This comment is dated August 16, 1969, and the quote is on p. 56, Library of Congress, *Spirit of St. Louis* Papers Box 34, Comments on Davis Biography Folder.

[6] Timing of Anne Morrow Lindbergh's coming into the room, her activities on the night of the kidnapping, and the description of the "flannel petticoat for an infant" is from her testimony: Trial Transcript, State vs. Hauptmann, in Sidney B. Whipple, *This special edition of The Trial of Bruno Richard Hauptmann* (Birmingham, Alabama: The Notable Trials Library, 1989), 106.

[7] Dimensions of the nursery from architectural plans of Delano and Aldrich Architects dated February 3, 1931. Blueprints for the home reside at Avery Drawings and Archives, Columbia University. The width of the windows on the eastern wall and the distance from the window ledges to the ground were measured by the author on September 3, 2009, on a tour of Highfields conducted by Paul Carluccio of the Albert Elias Residential Group Center.

[8] "The Lindbergh Case: An Amazing Chronicle," *The New York Times*, September 30, 1934.

[9] Anne Morrow Lindbergh, handritten notes, March 1932.

[10] A. Scott Berg, *Lindbergh* (New York: G. P. Putnam's Sons, 1998), 238. Pursuing a passion for science instilled in him by his maternal grandfather, Lindbergh was working on medical research with his mentor, Dr. Alexis Carrel, at the Rockefeller Institute in New York. They were collaborating on the design of an artificial heart.

[11] John Knoll was born on Olly Whateley's twentieth birthday.

[12] Summary report of Robert L. Thayer, March 3, 1932, pp. 6-7, The Papers of Robert H. Thayer, Library of Congress.

[13] The February 27, 1932, issue of *The Saturday Evening Post* also featured a short story by William Faulkner, who received eighth billing among the eight writers listed on the cover.

[14] Research on the location of the dog Wahgoosh in the house is from Lloyd C. Gardner, *The Case That Never Dies*, (New Brunswick, New Jersey: Rutgers University Press, 2004), 21.

[15] Precise timing of Betty Gow's excusing herself to tend to the baby is from Gardner, 22.

[16] A description of Betty Gow's actions as she entered the nursery are from Gardner, 22, and from Jim Fisher. *The Lindbergh Case* (New Brunswick, New Jersey: Rutgers University Press, 1994), 11.

[17] Conversation in this section is from Berg, 239-240 and from Anne Morrow Lindbergh, handwritten notes, March 1932.

### 2: CITIZEN OF THE WORLD

[1] *The American Experience: Lindbergh*, (PBS Video, 1990); second part of sentence in Noel Behn, *Lindbergh: The Crime*, (New York: ONYX, 1994), 18.

[2] Charles A. Lindbergh, *The Spirit of St. Louis* (New York: Charles Scribner's Sons, 1953), 18.

[3] C. Lindbergh, *Spirit*, 61.

[4] Discussion of the raising of subscriptions for the flight to Paris and the subsequent repayment of the loan is from Ron Chernow, *The House of Morgan: An American Banking Dynasty and the Rise of Modern Finance* (New York: The Atlantic Monthly Press, 1990), 291.

[5] A. Scott Berg, *Lindbergh* (New York: G.P. Putnam's Sons, 1998), 98.

[6] From Charles Lindbergh's 79 pages of typewritten comments on the 1959 book "The Hero" by Kenneth S. Davis. This comment is dated August 9, 1969, and the quote is on p. 30, Library of Congress, *Spirit of St. Louis* Papers Box 34, Comments on Davis Biography Folder.

[7] http://www.famousquotes.com/author/saint-exupery/3

[8] C. Lindbergh, *Spirit*, 162.

[9] A. Scott Berg, *Lindbergh*, 108.

[10] C. Lindbergh, *Spirit*, 185.

[11] Ibid., 187.

[12] The precise time of Lindbergh's landing in Paris varies in differing accounts of the flight. The 10:22 p.m. noted herein coincides with the aviator's account in: Lindbergh, *Spirit*, 504.

[13] Jennifer Kaylin, "Lindbergh Lands in New Haven," *Yale Alumni Magazine*, May 2002.

[14] Letter from Michel Détroyat to Charles Lindbergh, December 20, 1951, p. 2, Library of Congress *Spirit of St. Louis* Papers, Box 22, Folder 00124. The author of the letter describes the Renault as "shabby."

[15] In a letter to Lindbergh dated December 4, 1951, Détroyat referred to him as "dear Charley." From Library of Congress *Spirit of St. Louis* Papers, Box 22, Folder 00124.

[16] Before the Second World War, Lindbergh and Détroyat toured German aircraft factories together in the three-engine plane of General Ernst Udet, the Great War flying ace who played a major role in the development of the Luftwaffe. Letter from Détroyat to Lindbergh, December 20, 1951, Library of Congress, *Spirit of St. Louis* Papers, Box 22.

[17] In *Lindbergh*, p. 188, A. Scott Berg notes that "Celebrity without purpose seemed pointless to Lindbergh..."

[18] Charles A. Lindbergh, *Autobiography of Values*, (San Diego: Harvest, 1978), 310.

[19] Letter from Michel Détroyat to Charles Lindbergh, December 20, 1951, pp. 3-4, Library of Congress *Spirit of St. Louis* Papers, Box 22, Folder 00124.

[20] Charles A. Lindbergh, *We* (New York: G. P. Putnam's Sons), 251.

[21] Lindbergh's description of the crate in which the *Spirit of St. Louis* was shipped as a "coffin" is from Lindbergh, *Autobiography*, 315.

### 3: RECONNAISSANCE

[1] From Charles Lindbergh's 79 pages of typewritten comments on the 1959 book "The Hero" by Kenneth S. Davis. This comment is dated August 12, 1969, and the information regarding Lindbergh's decision to wear the dark suit is on p. 39, Library of Congress, *Spirit of St. Louis* Papers, Box 34, Comments on Davis Biography Folder.

[2] From Prologue of Ron Chernow, *The House of Morgan: An American Banking Dynasty and the Rise of Modern Finance* (New York: The Atlantic Monthly Press, 1990), xi.

[3] The quote "studying the application of airplanes to national defense" is from Chernow, p. 291. The name of the board chaired by Morrow is from Kathleen C. Winters, *Anne Morrow Lindbergh: First Lady of the Air* (New York: Palgrace MacMillan, 2006), p. 22. The phrase "wonderful raconteur" is one used by Chernow in a description of another person.

[4] Francis Trevelyan Miller, *Lindbergh: His Story in Pictures* (New York: G. P. Putnam's Sons, 1929), 18.

[5] "Lindbergh luncheon" hosted in Washington, D.C., by Daniel Boorstin, 1977-05-20, Rack Numbers RYA 1379 and RYA 1380, Recorded Sound Collection, Library of Congress. General Ira C. Eaker recalled Lindbergh's words during a speech at the luncheon.

[6] Brendan Gill, *Lindbergh Alone*, (New York: Harcourt Brace Jovanovich, 1977), 182.

[7] Charles A. Lindbergh, *Autobiography of Values*, (San Diego: Harvest, 1978), 318.

[8] Ibid., 14.

[9] Alden Whitman, "The Price of Fame," *The New York Times Magazine*, May 8, 1977, 14

[10] Letter from Charles Lindbergh to Harold Bixby, June 6, 1952, p. 1 of 2. Library of Congress, *Spirit of St. Louis* Papers, Box 22, Folder 00124.

[11] Donald E. Keyhoe, *Flying With Lindbergh* (New York: Grosset & Dunlap Publishers, 1928), 17-18.

[12] Financing mechanism for Lindbergh's flight to Paris is from Ron Chernow, *The House of Morgan: An American Banking Dynasty and the Rise of Modern Finance,* (New York: The Atlantic Monthly Press, 1990), 291.

[13] Letter from Charles A. Lindbergh to Dwight W. Morrow, September 19, 1927, Dwight W. Morrow Papers, Archives and Special Collection of the Amherst College Library, Series I, Box 31, Folder 47.

[14] Walter Lippman, "A New Ambassador to Mexico: Mr. Coolidge's Sagacity in Appointing Dwight W. Morrow Receiver of a Bankrupt Democracy," *Vanity Fair*, December 1927.

[15] Letter from Dwight W. Morrow to Charles Lindbergh, October 4, 1927. Box 28, Folder 11, Lindbergh Collection, Missouri History Museum, St. Louis, MO.

[16] Letter from Dwight W. Morrow to Charles Lindbergh, November 18, 1927. Dwight W. Morrow Papers, Archives and Special Collections of the Amherst College Library, Box 3, Folder 18.

[17] Anne Morrow Lindbergh, *Bring Me a Unicorn: Diaries and Letters of Anne Morrow Lindbergh 1922-1928*, (New York: Harcourt Brace Jovanovich, Inc., 1971), 103. Anne uses the word "odious" to describe her envy for her sister Elisabeth.

[18] Ibid., 89.

[19] Ibid., 101.

[20] Anne Morrow Lindbergh, *The Flower and the Nettle: Diaries and Letters of Anne Morrow Lindbergh 1936-1939*, (New York: Harcourt Brace Jovanovich, 1976), xiii.

[21] Anne Morrow Lindbergh, *Bring Me a Unicorn*, back cover.

[22] From Charles Lindbergh's 79 pages of typewritten comments on the 1959 book "The Hero" by Kenneth S. Davis. This comment is dated August 22, 1969, and the quote is on p. 77, Library of Congress, *Spirit of St. Louis* Papers, Box 34, Comments on Davis Biography Folder.

[23] Anne Morrow Lindbergh, *Bring Me a Unicorn*. 191.

[24] A. Scott Berg, *Lindbergh* (New York: G.P. Putnam's Sons, 1998), 195.

[25] Interview comment of Reeve Lindbergh in *The American Experience: Lindbergh*, a PBS Video, 1990.

[26] Berg, 194. The author states that Anne Morrow had won "the Jordan Prize" and that she had had "a poem published in *Scribner's.*"

[27] Observation made by Lindbergh biographer A. Scott Berg on *The Charlie Rose Show*, September 25, 1998.

[28] "A Walled Garden" is the title of chapter one of Kathleen C. Winters, *Anne Morrow Lindbergh: First Lady of the Air*, (New York: Palgrace MacMillan, 2006), 7. Original reference to "walled garden" is from Anne Morrow Lindbergh, *Bring Me a Unicorn*, xxi.

[29] Anne Morrow Lindbergh, *Bring Me a Unicorn*, 131.

[30] Anne's comment about wanting to marry a hero is from Winters, 20.

[31] From written comments by Charles Lindbergh about the book *The Last Hero: Charles A. Lindbergh* by Walter S. Ross. This is from a comment dated August 5, 1968, and the quote is on p. 31, Library of Congress, *Spirit of St. Louis* Papers Box 34, Comments on Ross Biography Folder.

[32] Marlen Pew, "Shop Talk At Thirty," Editor and publisher *The Fourth Estate*, July 26, 1930. Box 3, Folder 19, Dwight W. Morrow Papers, Archives and Special Collections of the Amherst College Library.

[33] From written comments by Charles Lindbergh about the book *The Last Hero: Charles A. Lindbergh* by Walter S. Ross. This is from a comment dated August 5, 1968, and the reference to Lindbergh's having his plane flown to Rochester is on p. 33, Library of Congress, *Spirit of St. Louis* Papers, Box 34, Comments on Ross Biography Folder.

[34] The scene of the wedding is drawn with help from Berg, 101-02.

[35] Information in this section is from written comments by Charles Lindbergh about the book *The Last Hero: Charles A. Lindbergh* by Walter S. Ross. This is from a comment dated August 5, 1968, and the quote is on p. 34, Library of Congress, *Spirit of St. Louis* Papers, Box 34, Comments on Ross Biography Folder.

[36] According to the sixth article of the canons of journalism adopted by the American Society of Newspaper Editors on April 27, 1923, "A newspaper should not invade private rights or feelings without sure warrant of public right as distinguished from public curiosity."

[37] Daniel J. Boorstin, *The Image: A Guide To Pseudo-Events In America*, (First Vintage Books edition, 1992), 68.

[38] Anne Morrow Lindbergh, *Hour of Gold, Hour of Lead*, (New York: Harcourt, Brace Jovanovich, 1973). The word "sightseers" to describe the people in the car, p. 153, quote of Anne Morrow Lindbergh, 154.

[39] That Dwight Morrow's "real passion was politics" is from Chernow, 290.

[40] Letter to Constance Morrow from person threatening to kidnap her, April 1929, Dwight W. Morrow Papers, Archives and Special Collections of the Amherst College Library, Series XIII, Box 3, Folder 12.

[41] Anne Morrow Lindbergh, *Hour of Gold, Hour of Lead*, 155.

[42] Phone conversation between Edward S. Sulzbach and the author, September 3, 2011.

### 4: JOHANNES

[1] Lindbergh conceived his attempt to fly to Paris in September 1926.

[2] From research conducted by Laura Tosi of the Bronx Historical Society. Information conveyed to the author in a phone conversation on October 9, 2011.

[3] William March's quote serves as an epigraph for Robert D. Hare, *Without Conscience* (New York: The Guilford Press, 1993).

[4] Celia Applegate, *A Nation of Provincials: The German Idea of Heimat*, (Berkeley: University of California Press, 1990), 108.

[5] Interview of Dr. Craig Neumann by the author, March 13, 2012.

[6] Interview of Rudolf Breiling, a nephew of John and Walter Knoll, by the author at Mr. Breiling's home, September 10, 2009. Historical context in this paragraph supplied by Dr. Jay Winter, Professor of History at Yale University, in an email to the author, December 22, 2011.

[7] Source Citation: Year: *1925*; Microfilm Serial: *T715*; Microfilm Roll: *T715_3599*; Line: *4*; Page Number: *22*. Source Information: Ancestry.com. New York Passenger Lists, 1820-1957 [database online]. Provo, UT, USA: Ancestry.com Operations, Inc., 2010.

Original data: Passenger Lists of Vessels Arriving at New York, New York, 1820-1897; (National Archives Microfilm Publication M237, 675 rolls); Records of the U.S. Customs Service, Record Group 36; National Archives, Washington, D.C. Passenger and Crew Lists of Vessels Arriving at New York, New York, 1897-1957; (National Archives Microfilm Publication T715, 8892 rolls); Records of the Immigration and Naturalization Service; National Archives, Washington, D.C.

[8] Oscar Rietschel, Petition for Naturalization, Certificate of Naturalization No. 264644, issued on March 12, 1912.

[9] Remembrance of Eugene C. Zorn, Jr., told to the author.

[10] From an interview of Odette Küntsler of the Kamenz City Archives by the author in Kamenz, Germany, on July 2, 2010.

[11] That Hauptmann traveled to New Jersey to meet fellow former Kamenz resident Otto Heyne is from Ludovic Kennedy, *The Airman and the Carpenter: The Lindbergh Kidnapping and the Framing of Richard Hauptmann*, (New York: Viking Penguin, Inc., 1985), 164.

### 5: THE STAMP COLLECTOR

[1] That Walter was called "Lazy Walter" came from a conversation between the author and Adrienne Knoll (daughter-in-law of John Knoll) at her home, September 18, 2009. In the early 1960s, an elderly woman in Herxheimweyher made the comment about "Lazy Walter" to Adrienne's new husband, Bob Knoll, while they were visiting the village.

[2] Ages of Alice and William J. (Bill) Schaefer are from a letter dated July 7, 2010, from Daniel C. Austin of All Faiths Cemetery, Middle Village, New York, to the author. The Schaefers are buried in this cemetery, as is the father of Donald Trump.

[3] Names of residents on Jackson Avenue from personal files and recollections of Eugene C. Zorn, Jr., and from the 1930 U.S. Census. Professions of people in the neighborhood from the 1930 U.S. Census. Source: Ancestry.com.

[4] One day, after his friend Larry Dick bought a fake pile of dog waste at the novelty shop, Gene Zorn raced to the high school chemistry laboratory to concoct a bottle of hydrogen sulfide, a mixture that smelled like rotten eggs. Gene laid the phony excrement on the floor of the delicatessen and poured the pungent formulation over it, whereupon Larry held his nose and yowled, "Peeeeeeeee Yewwww!" John grabbed his broom and chased the boys out of the store.

[5] State of New York, Certificate and Record of Marriage No. 28706, of John Knoll (groom) and Paula Trauth (bride), October 13, 1927. Paula's occupation as a showgirl does not appear on the document.

[6] Source Citation: Year: 1926; Microfilm Serial: T715; Microfilm Roll: T715_3957; Line: 1; Page Number: 47. Source Information: Ancestry.com. New York Passenger Lists, 1820-1957 [database online]. Provo, UT, USA: Ancestry.com Operations, Inc., 2010.

[7] Having searched divorce records both in New York and New Jersey, the author was unable to find evidence that John Knoll and Paula Trauth obtained a divorce. Because one had to prove adultery to obtain a divorce in New York in those days, it was easier to obtain a divorce in New Jersey.

[8] Meeting between Sharon Breiling and the author, February 15, 2012.

[9] Source Citation: Year: 1930; Census Place: St. Louis, St Louis (Independent City), Missouri; Roll: 1241; Page: 2B; Enumeration District: 174; Image: 1065.0.

Source Information: Ancestry.com. 1930 United States Federal Census [database online]. Provo, UT, USA: Ancestry.com Operations Inc, 2002. Original data: United States of America, Bureau of the Census. *Fifteenth Census of the United States, 1930.* Washington, D.C.: National Archives and Records Administration, 1930. T626, 2,667 rolls.; Phone interview of Richard J. "Richie" Wolfheim by the author, September 21, 2011. Mr. Wolfsheim attributes his longevity to whiskey.

[10] Petition for Citizenship No. 97404 of John Knoll, October 31, 1931.

[11] Source Citation: Year: 1933; Microfilm Serial: T715; Microfilm Roll: T715_5397; Line: 6; Page Number: 142. Source Information: Ancestry.com. New York Passenger Lists, 1820-1957 [database online]. Provo, UT, USA: Ancestry.com Operations, Inc., 2010.

Original data: Passenger Lists of Vessels Arriving at New York, New York, 1820-1897; (National Archives Microfilm Publication M237, 675 rolls); Records of the U.S. Customs Service, Record Group 36; National Archives, Washington, D.C.; Passenger and Crew Lists of Vessels Arriving at New York, New York, 1897-1957; (National Archives Microfilm Publication T715, 8892 rolls); Records of the Immigration and Naturalization Service; National Archives, Washington, D.C.

[12] Karoline Lilly (née Karg) Knoll is a member of the List or Manifest of Alien Passengers list sailing on the SS *Manhattan* from Hamburg, Germany, and arriving in New York on June 5, 1935. Her last permanent residence is listed as Mt. Clemens, Michigan.

[13] In-person interview of Brigitte Geiger, niece of Lilly Knoll, by the author, July 4, 2010.

[14] Viewpoint of Edward F. Sulzbach expressed to the author, September 3, 2011.

[15] http://www.bartleby.com/104/3.html, January 24, 2012.

[16] A teacher and church organist, John Knoll's brother-in-law Ernst Schlachter is said to have observed, "Honor will always be around because it's so little used." After the priest at his church had forbidden him to play certain hymns in his repertoire, Schlachter surprised the congregation with a rendition of the popular folk song *"Muss i denn zum Städtele hinaus"* ("Got To Go Leave This Town"). Then the organist stormed out, never

to walk through the doors of the church again. From in-person interview withRudolf Breiling, nephew of John and Walter Knoll, and his wife, Sharon Breiling, by the author, September 10, 2009. Mr. Breiling is the son of Agnes Knoll Breiling, a sister of John and Walter Knoll.

[17] Calculation of value of $1.15 in 1932 in 2011 dollars (a multiple of 15.01) is derived from http://www.dollartimes.com/calculators/inflation.htm, December 26, 2011. All such calculations in this book use this multiple.

[18] The ball was hit by the notoriously hot-tempered ballplayer Ben Chapman.

### 6: THE SINGNATURE

[1] The description of how the sections of the ladder "nest" together is from George Waller, *Kidnap*, (New York: The Dial Press, 1961), 12.

[2] New Jersey State Police Teletype announcing the kidnapping, March 1, 1932.

[3] N.Y. File 62-3057: Physical Evidence.

[4] Phone conversation between the author and Dr. Mary Ellen O'Toole, January 10, 2012.

[5] The dust jacket of *The Anatomy of Motive*, (New York: A Lisa Drew Book/Scribner, 1999), by John Douglas and Mark Olshaker, refers to Douglas as "the pioneer of modern criminal investigative analysis during his remarkable twenty-five-year career with the FBI."

[6] John Douglas and Mark Olshaker, *The Crimes That Haunt Us*, (New York: A Lisa Drew Book/Scribner, 2000), 180.

[7] Ibid., 162.

[8] Major Initial Report by Corporal Joseph A. Wolf #371, Section A: DESCRIPTION OF CRIME, March 1, 1932.

[9] Corporal Joseph A. Wolf's report states that the ladder was found seventy-five feet from the house; reports vary regarding the ladder's distance from the house from fifty to seventy-five feet. [Major Initial Report by Corporal Joseph A. Wolf #371, March 1, 1932.

[10] Summary report of Robert Thayer, March 3, 1932, 16, The Papers of Robert H. Thayer, Library of Congress, Box 7, The Lindbergh Case Report and Photographs Folder.

[11] Lloyd C. Gardner notes that Anne Morrow Lindbergh could not remember which window she had hit with the pebble. From the historian's December 1, 2011, blog "Pebbles and Mud" blog http://www.caseneverdies.blogspot.com/ (January 9, 2012).

[12] General H. Norman Schwarzkopf, *It Doesn't Take a Hero*, (New York: Bantam Books, 1992), 1. General Schwarzkopf's father was the superintendent of the New Jersey State Police who investigated the Lindbergh case.

[13] The Hall-Mills case involved the 1922 murder of an Episcopal priest and his married lover, whose corpses were discovered by a fifteen-year-old girl. The priest's wife and her brothers were acquitted of murder four years later.

[14] Sometimes in the ransom notes the word is spelled "Polise" and at other times it is spelled "Police." In this first ransom note, the end of the word is made illegible by a smudge, a point made in Gardner, 27. Gardner also interprets that the last word in the ransom note may be "hohls"—or possibly "holds." Gardner, 27. The kidnappers *do* spell the word "holes" correctly in a later ransom letter.

[15] Phone conversations between Dr. Mary Ellen O'Toole and the author, December 14, 2001.

[16] From "Our Missions" on the homepage of the National Security Agency website, http://www.nsa.gov/index.shtml

[17] From allgov.com website, http://www.allgov.com/agency/National_Security_Agency _Central_Security_Service__NSA_.

[18] Former National Security Agency (NSA) analyst Ken Scarborough interpreted the

kidnappers' signature-symbol during a meeting with the author in Dallas, Texas, in December 2003.

### 7: BUTTERFLIES

[1] Emanuel Tanay, M.D., "The Lindbergh Kidnapping—A Psychiatric View," *Journal of Forensic Sciences*, JFSCA, Vol. 28, No. 4, Oct. 1983, 1076-1082. Presented at the Plenary Session, 35th Annual Meeting of the American Academy of Forensic Sciences, Cincinnati, OH, 15-19 Feb. 1983.

[2] From phone interview of Carolyn Blackman Jacoby, daughter of AP reporter Samuel G. Blackman, by the author, September 5, 2011.

[3] Jargon of newspaper reporters of the day from "Walter Winchell On Broadway" column, *Daily Mirror*, November 27, 1934.

[4] *New York Times*, March 3, 1932.

[5] *New York Evening Post* editorial, March 3, 1932.

[6] Adela Rogers St. John, *The Honeycomb*, (Garden City, New York: Doubleday & Company, Inc., 1969), 295.

[7] *The Wit and Wisdom of Will Rogers*, edited by Alex Ayres (New York: A Meridian Book, 1993), 135.

[8] "I needed press cooperation, and therefore tried to cooperate with the press in return. I asked the police not to close our property to reporters and photographers," Lindbergh wrote. From Charles Lindbergh's comments on the book *The Last Hero: Charles A. Lindbergh* by Walter S. Ross. This comment was dated August 6, 1968, and the quote is on p. 39, Library of Congress, *Spirit of St. Louis* Papers, Box 34, Comments on Ross Biography Folder.

[9] Memo of Colonel H. Norman Schwarzkopf dated April 7, 1932, Personal File Folder of Colonel Schwarzkopf in the New Jersey State Police Museum archives.

[10] Anne Morrow Lindbergh, *Hour of Gold, Hour of Lead* (New York: Harcourt, Brace Jovanovich 1973), 245.

[11] Elmer R. Irey, *The Tax Dodgers: The Inside Story of the T-Men's War with America's Political and Underworld Hoodlums* (New York: Greenberg Publisher, 1949), 73.

[12] Ibid., 72-73.

[13] Anne Morrow Lindbergh, *Hour of Gold, Hour of Lead*, 212.

[14] A. Scott Berg, *Lindbergh* (New York: G. P. Putnam's Sons, 1998), 251.

[15] Ibid., 231.

### 8: UNDERWORLD

[1] Anne Morrow Lindbergh, *Hour of Gold, Hour of Lead* (New York: Harcourt, Brace Jovanovich 1973), 228.

[2] Ibid., p. 237.

[3] *Detroit Free Press*, March 4, 1932, 3.

[4] Anne Morrow Lindbergh, *Hour of Gold, Hour of Lead*, 228.

[5] The Lindberghs' letter appears on the front page of the *New York Daily News*, March 5, 1932 (and in other newspapers).

[6] "Anxious City Awaits News: Rumors Feed on Fear for Baby, Each Parent Sharing Pain of Lindy and Anne," *Detroit Free Press*, March 5, 1932.

[7] Barbara Goldsmith, *Little Gloria: Happy At Last*, (New York: Alfred A. Knopf, 1980), xi.

[8] Ibid., xii.

[9] Summary report of Robert Thayer, March 3, 1932, p. 10, The Papers of Robert H. Thayer, Library of Congress, Box 7, The Lindbergh Case Report and Photographs Folder.

[10] References to people who wrote to share their dreams and to demand money from the Lindberghs is from Anne Morrow Lindbergh, *Hour of Gold, Hour of Lead*, 239.

[11] Anne Morrow Lindbergh, *Hour of Gold, Hour of Lead*, 235. The crank letters fill four folders in the Charles A. Lindbergh Papers at the Missouri History Museum Library and Research Center.

[12] Summary Report: Kidnaping and Murder of Charles A. Lindbergh, Jr. (N.Y. File 62-3057), Preface, 10.

[13] U.S. Bureau of Investigation "Memorandum for the Attorney General" from J. Edgar Hoover, Director, to Attorney General Homer S. Cummings, June 8, 1934, 1.

[14] One of Schwarzkopf's letters to "My dear Director Hoover" is dated September 25, 1933. From New Jersey State Police Museum files.

[15] From letter from Colonel Schwarzkopf to Hoover, May 1, 1934, FBI Archives in College Park, MD.

[16] Elmer R. Irey, *The Tax Dodgers: The Inside Story of the T-Men's War with America's Political and Underworld Hoodlums* (New York: Greenberg Publisher, 1949), 80.

[17] Phone conversation between Dr. Robert A. Leonard and the author, January 16, 2012.

[18] Thomas Fensch, *FBI Files On the Lindbergh Kidnapping*, (The Woodlands, Texas: New Century Books, 2001), p. 177. "The sheet of paper upon which [this letter #2] is written is the opposite half of the sheet upon which the first ransom note was written," wrote Osborn. "When the torn edges of these papers are placed together, it may be seen that the figure work in the paper as examined by transmitted light, indicates that the two edges were originally attached."

[19] Ibid.. 177

[20] Analysis of Mark Olshaker. From phone interview of Olshaker by the author, February 6, 2012.

[21] Thomas Fensch, *FBI Files On the Lindbergh Kidnapping*, 221.

[22] Thayer's relationship as a friend of the Lindberghs was mentioned during a phone interview of his son, Robert H. Thayer, Jr., by the author, August 15, 2011.

[23] Summary report of Robert Thayer, March 3, 1932, p. 1, The Papers of Robert H. Thayer, Library of Congress, Box 7, The Lindbergh Case Report and Photographs Folder.

[24] Ibid.

[25] Timing of the 6:30 a.m. meeting is from summary report of Robert Thayer, March 3, 1932, p. 5, The Papers of Robert H. Thayer, Library of Congress, Box 7, The Lindbergh Case Report and Photographs Folder.

[26] Ibid., 2.

[27] *Detroit Free Press*, March 7, 1932, 1.

[28] "Spurred By Racket King, Underword Hunts Baby," *New York Daily News*, March 7, 1932, 4.

[29] Banner headline, front page of *New York Daily News*, March 7, 1932. Text of letter from Charles A. Lindbergh and Anne Lindbergh also appears on the front page along with their signatures.

[30] Anne Morrow Lindbergh, *Hour of Gold, Hour of Lead*, 232.

[31] "Spurred By Racket King, Underword Hunts Baby," *New York Daily News*, March 7, 1932, 3. From a quote of "a Police Inspector, who asked to keep his name secret" on the trustworthiness of Spitale and Bitz.

[32] Daniel J. Boorstin, *The Image: A Guide To Pseudo-Events In America*, (First Vintage Books edition, 1992), 71.

[33] Handwritten notes of Robert Thayer dated 11 a.m. on Saturday, March 12, 1932, page 6 of 6 of unnumbered pages. The Papers of Robert H. Thayer, Library of Congress, Box 7,

The Lindbergh Case Miscellaneous: Notes, Photostats, Newspaper Clippings Folder.

[34] Anne Morrow Lindbergh, *Hour of Gold, Hour of Lead*, 231.

[35] Ibid., 252.

[36] The draft of Lindbergh's book *The Spirit of St. Louis* is housed at the Library of Congress in the *Spirit of St. Louis* Papers.

### 9: THE GO-BETWEEN

[1] Ritual For Initiation, Bronx Old Timers Association Handbook (provided by Bronx County Historical Society).

[2] Reference to Charles Lindbergh as "the greatest hero of this age" is made in a letter from John F. Condon to Henry Breckinridge, March 3, 1938, The Papers of the Breckinridge Family in the Library of Congress, Container 524, Henry Breckinridge General Correspondence Folder, 1937-38.

[3] John F. Condon, *Jafsie Tells All*, (New York: Jonathan Lee Publishing Corp., 1936), 16.

[4] Ibid., 18.

[5] *Bronx Home News*, March 8, 1932, 1.

[6] From "Walter Winchell On Broadway" column, *Daily Mirror,* October 2, 1934.

[7] Thomas Fensch, *FBI Files On the Lindbergh Kidnapping*, (The Woodlands, Texas: New Century Books, 2001), 221. (Although NY Police File 62-3057 incorrectly states that Station "T" was near Condon's home, it was right in John Knoll's South Bronx neighborhood.)

[8] John F. Condon, *Jafsie Tells All*, 23.

[9] Analysis of Mark Olshaker. From meeting of the author with Olshaker and John Douglas, October 12, 2011.

[10] Description of Condon's trip to Max Rosenhain's restaurant is created with the help of Jim Fisher, *The Lindbergh Case,* (New Brunswick, NJ: Rutgers University Press, 1999), 42-43.

[11] John F. Condon, *Jafsie Tells All*, 32-33.

[12] Anne Morrow Lindbergh, *Hour of Gold, Hour of Lead*, (New York: Harcourt, Brace Jovanovich, 1973), 234.

### 10: THE CEMETERY

[1] John F. Condon, *Jafsie Tells All*, (New York: Jonathan Lee Publishing Corp., 1936), 55-56.

[2] Dialogue from the conversation above and description of the events pertaining to the phone call are primarily from John F. Condon, *Jafsie Tells All*, 57-61.

[3] Phone interview of Dr. Robert A. Leonard by the author, January 16, 2012.

[4] From a brochure produced by Woodlawn Cemetery.

[5] John F. Condon, *Jafsie Tells All*, 72.

[6] Ibid., 75.

[7] Ibid., 77 and 80.

[8] *The New York Times*, "Dr. J. F. Condon Dies; In Lindbergh Case," January 3, 1945.

[9] Thomas Fensch, *FBI Files On the Lindbergh Kidnapping*, (The Woodlands, Texas: New Century Books, 2001), 251-52.

[10] John F. Condon, *Jafsie Tells All*, 83.

[11] Ibid., 87.

[12] Analysis of Dr. Mary Ellen O'Toole. From a phone conversation with the author on December 14, 2011.

[13] According to Cemetery John, the kidnappers had added another member of the gang, a fact that gave the gang justification for raising the ransom amount from $50,000

to $70,000. With five members in the gang, $50,000 wouldn't have resulted in nice, even round numbers for the gang members, assuming "Number One" received a higher share than his accomplices.

[14] Conversation between Cemetery John and Condon is from *Jafsie Tells All*, 78-79.

[15] Ibid., 91-92.

[16] Cemetery John's not wanting others to get credit for the kidnapping is the analysis of profiler John Douglas. From meeting between John Douglas and the author, Washington, D.C., October 12, 2011.

[17] Douglas and Olshaker, *The Anatomy of Motive* (New York: A Lisa Drew Book/Scribner, 1999), 110.

[18] Comment about being Scandanavian is from *Jafsie Tells All*, 84. Comment about the letter left in the crib from *Jafsie Tells All*, 80.

[19] Ibid., 95.

### 11: The Little Package

[1] Walter Winchell radio broadcast, January 13, 1935, from Walter Winchell Papers, 1920-1967, The New York Public Library For the Performing Arts, Billy Rose Theatre Collection, Box 3, Jergens, Jan. 3, 1934–Dec. 27, 1936.

[2] Decades later, both the Zodiac killer in California and Ted Kaczinski, better known as the Unabomber, would intentionally leave clues on packages by placing more postage on them than was required.

[3] John F. Condon, *Jafsie Tells All*, (New York: Jonathan Lee Publishing Corp., 1936), 109.

[4] Elmer R. Irey, *The Tax Dodgers: The Inside Story of the T-Men's War with America's Political and Underworld Hoodlums* (New York: Greenberg Publisher, 1949), 75.

[5] Both women's seeing the thumb guard at the same time is from the testimony at the Hauptmann trial of Elsie Whateley. From Trial Transcript, State vs. Hauptmann, in Sidney B. Whipple, *This special edition of The Trial of Bruno Richard Hauptmann*, (Birmingham, Alabama: The Notable Trials Library, 1989), 323.

[6] Lloyd C. Gardner, from December 24, 2011, blog "Give 'Em Hell, Harry!" blog http://www.caseneverdies.blogspot.com/ (January 9, 2012).

[7] From comment of John Douglas in meeting with the author, December 29, 2011.

### 12: Payment

[1] Conversation in this section is from John F. Condon, *Jafsie Tells All*, (New York: Jonathan Lee Publishing Corp., 1936), 151-56.

[2] It is difficult to determine how the name of the island is spelled in the note: *Elisabeth* or *Elizabeth*. John Knoll's mother and one of his sisters were both named *Elisabetha*. The correct spelling of the island is *Elizabeth*.

[3] Elmer R. Irey, *The Tax Dodgers*, (New York: Greenberg, 1949), 36.

[4] Ibid., 79.

[5] Ibid., 71.

[6] A. Scott Berg, *Lindbergh*, 267.

[7] Anne Morrow Lindbergh, *Hour of Gold, Hour of Lead,* (New York: Harcourt, Brace Jovanovich, 1973), 244.

### 13: Hand of the Kidnapper

[1] From a filmed interview of the author speaking to his father, Eugene C. Zorn, Jr., on May 3, 2004, in Valley View, Texas. Filming done by Charlie Bahr.

[2] John Knoll's signature on his marriage license is from State of New York, Certificate and Record of Marriage No. 28706, of John Knoll (groom) and Paula Trauth (bride), October 13,

1927. John Knoll married Paula Trauth at St. Thomas the Apostle Church in Manhattan on October 13, 1927, just less than a year after her arrival in the States on October 31, 1926.

[3] Certified Document Examiner Susan Abbey said that changing the first letter of a name or word is a way that people use to disguise their handwriting. Meeting between Ms. Abbey and the author, January 27, 2010.

[4] Dr. Sargur N. Srihari, "Computational Methods for Handwritten Questioned Document Examination," submitted to U.S. Department of Justice, August 12, 2010, pages 3 and 9 of 46. Document No. 232745. Award No. 2004-IJ-CX-K050.

[5] Lee Dye, "Computer Tests Proves Handwriting Analysis Is Legitimate," ABC News Internet Ventures, June 5, 2010.

[6] Results of the CEDAR-FOX test conveyed by Dr. Sargur N. Srihari of CEDAR on March 18, 2012, in email to the author.

[7] Thomas Fensch, *FBI Files On the Lindbergh Kidnapping*, (The Woodlands, Texas: New Century Books, 2001), 251.

[8] Ibid., 251-52.

[9] Declaration of Intention No 216665 of John Knoll, September 20, 1926.

[10] Source Information: National Archives and Records Administration. *U.S. World War II Army Enlistment Records, 1938-1946* [database online]. Provo, UT, USA: Ancestry .com Operations Inc, 2005. Original data: Electronic Army Serial Number Merged File, 1938-1946 [Archival Database]; World War II Army Enlistment Records; Records of the National Archives and Records Administration, Record Group 64; National Archives at College Park, College Park, MD.

[11] Meeting between Sharon Breiling and the author, February 15, 2012.

[12] If Gene Zorn had ever remembered noticing this defect, he never mentioned it to the author. Because he never complained about being blind in one eye, he probably wouldn't have given much thought to a strange-looking thumb. The author doesn't believe his father ever knew about the lump at the base of Cemetery John's thumb. Or if Gene Zorn did come across this piece of information at some point, he didn't draw any connection regarding the thumb to Knoll.

### 14: The Victim

[1] That the body was likely scavenged by these types of animals was a comment made by forensic anthropologist Dr. William M. Bass. Renowned for his research on human osteology and human decomposition, Dr. Bass authored the 1991 article "Skeletal Materials Associated With the Lindbergh Case" in the *American Journal of Human Biology* (Vol. 3, pp. 613-16). From a phone conversation between the author and Dr. Bass, November 7, 2011.

[2] "William J. Allen Is Dead At 76," *New York Times*, December 22, 1965.

[3] Phone conversation between Dr. Kathy J. Reichs and the author, November 14, 2011.

[4] Analysis of Dr. William M. Bass. From a phone conversation between the author and Dr. Bass, November 7, 2011.

[5] Phone conversation between the author and Dr. Arpad Vass, December 13, 2011.

[6] Analysis of crime victims dumped casually on the side of a road comes from John Douglas and Mark Olshaker, *The Anatomy of Motive*, (New York: A Lisa Drew Book/Scribner, 1999), 32.

[7] In *Dangerous Instincts: How Gut Feelings Betray Us*, (New York: Hudson Street Press, 2011), 62, Dr. Mary Ellen O'Toole writes, "A psychopath feels about as guilty about destroying your peace of mind, reputation, financial livelihood, and life as you do when your blow your nose into a tissue and toss it in the trash."

[8] Opinion regarding the rate of decomposition made by forensic anthropologist

Dr. William M. Bass. From a phone conversation between the author and Dr. Bass, November 7, 2011.

[9] Forensic anthropologist Dr. William M. Bass examined the bones in 1982. He noted that they were so well preserved that they looked "about a week old—and still greasy." Information in this section is from a phone conversation between the author and Dr. Bass, November 7, 2011 and from his article, 615.

[10] Dr. William M. Bass, "Skeletal Materials Associated With the Lindbergh Case."

[11] Anne Morrow Lindbergh, *Hour of Gold, Hour of Lead,* (New York: Harcourt, Brace Jovanovich, 1973), 248.

[12] Response of Anne Morrow Lindbergh is from Berg, *Lindbergh*, 272. The author drew on Berg's biography here regarding Anne's reaction to her mother's words and regarding her belief that the baby had been dead since the night of the kidnapping.

[13] Anne Morrow Lindbergh, *Hour of Gold, Hour of Lead,* 248-49.

[14] "Sympathy Pours In From All Over the World," *The New York Times*, May 13, 1932, 1.

[15] That Dr. Mitchell's directing the coroner when and how to make incisions was "improper" came from a comment made by forensic pathologist Dr. Michael M. Baden. From a phone conversation between the author and Dr. Baden, November 6, 2011.

[16] Autopsy "Report on Unknown baby" signed by Dr. Charles H. Mitchell, on letterhead of WALTER H. SWAYZE, TRENTON, NEW JERSEY, May 12, 1932. From the files of the New Jersey State Police Museum.

[17] Email from Dr. Mary Case to the author, January 16, 2012.

[18] Meeting of the author with John Douglas and Mark Olshaker, December 29, 2011.

[19] Douglas and Olshaker, *The Anatomy of Motive,* 34.

[20] Email from Dr. Mary Case to the author, January 16, 2012.

[21] Anne Morrow Lindbergh, *Hour of Gold, Hour of Lead,* 249.

[22] Anne Morrow Lindbergh's never having seen her husband cry is from Berg, 275.

[23] From Charles Lindbergh's 79 pages of typewritten comments on the 1959 book *The Hero* by Kenneth S. Davis. This comment is dated August 16, 1969, and the quote is on p. 57, Library of Congress, *Spirit of St. Louis* Papers, Box 34, Comments on Davis Biography Folder.

[24] From a comment made by Charles Lindbergh regarding the book *The Last Hero: Charles A. Lindbergh* by Walter S. Ross. The comment is dated August 6, 1968, and the quote is on p. 40, Library of Congress, *Spirit of St. Louis* Papers, Box 34, Comments on Ross Biography Folder.

[25] Opinion of Dr. Mary Ellen O'Toole. From phone conversation between Dr. O'Toole and the author, January 31, 2012.

[26] "Stolen In the Night," an ABC documentary hosted by Peter Jennings, 1999.

[27] *The Lindberghs: Alone Together*, an A&E Biography video, 2005.

[28] Opinion of Dr. Mary Ellen O'Toole. From phone conversation between Dr. O'Toole and the author, January 31, 2012.

[29] From Charles Lindbergh's 79 pages of typewritten comments on the 1959 book *The Hero* by Kenneth S. Davis. This comment is dated August 4, 1969, and the quote is on p. 2, Library of Congress, *Spirit of St. Louis* Papers, Box 34, Comments on Davis Biography Folder.

[30] Anne Morrow Lindbergh, *Hour of Gold, Hour of Lead,* 250.

[31] Charles A. Lindbergh, *The Wartime Journals of Charles A. Lindbergh* (New York: Harcourt Brace Jovanovich, Inc., 1970), 187.

[32] Anne Morrow Lindbergh, *Hour of Gold, Hour of Lead,* 250.

[33] Ibid., 204.

[34] Lindbergh biographer A. Scott Berg has spoken of the great joy that Charlie Lindbergh brought his father.

[35] In many accounts of the Lindbergh kidnapping, the child was said to have overlapping toes, a feature that Lindbergh himself looked for as he sought to determine the identity of the corpse in the morgue. Yet, as Lindbergh would write, "Charles's toes did not overlap, but turned in slightly—not enough to be described as a deformity. Anne mentioned this in a description of the child that covered everything she felt might be used in identification. The press siezed [sic] on this item and built it up as a physical deformity." From Charles Lindbergh's typewritten comments on the book *The Last Hero: Charles A. Lindbergh* by Walter S. Ross. This comment is dated August 6, 1968, and the quote is on pp. 38-39, Library of Congress, *Spirit of St. Louis* Papers ,Box 34, Comments on Ross Biography Folder.

[36] This is from a comment made by Charles Lindbergh regarding the book *The Last Hero: Charles A. Lindbergh* by Walter S. Ross. The comment is dated August 6, 1968, and the quote is on p. 39, Library of Congress, *Spirit of St. Louis* Papers, Box 34, Comments on Ross Biography Folder.

### 15: A NEW LIFE

[1] Anne Morrow Lindbergh, *Hour of Gold, Hour of Lead* (New York: Harcourt, Brace Jovanovich, 1973), 248.

[2] Ibid., 263.

[3] Anne Morrow Lindbergh, *Locked Rooms and Open Doors* (San Diego: A Harvest Book, Harcourt Brace & Company, 1974), 4.

[4] From Charles Lindbergh's 79 pages of typewritten comments on the 1959 book *The Hero* by Kenneth S. Davis. The information about Anne Morrow Lindbergh's having become the first woman in the United States to be issued a glider-pilot's license is dated August 15, 1969, and comes on p. 51, Library of Congress, *Spirit of St. Louis* Papers, Box 34, Comments on Davis Biography Folder. The designation of the license as "first-class" is from Kathleen C. Winters, *Anne Morrow Lindbergh: First Lady of the Air* (New York: Palgrace MacMillan, 2006), 80.

[5] Anne Morrow Lindbergh, *Locked Rooms and Open Doors*, 4-5.

[6] Anne Morrow Lindbergh, *Hour of Gold, Hour of Lead*. Uses word *"un*-happen" on p. 215.

[7] Ibid., 252.

[8] http://thinkexist.com/quotation/there_is_no_greater_sorrow_than_to_recall/159374 .html, January 22, 2012; used on "The Genius" episode of *Criminal Minds,* January 18, 2012.

[9] Telegram from Paramount Sound News to Colonel Schwartkopf [sic], May 17, 1932; from Personal Files of Colonel Schwarzkopf in the New Jersey State Police Museum archives

[10] Anne Morrow Lindbergh, *Hour of Gold, Hour of Lead*, 282.

[11] Ibid., 283.

[12] Lloyd C. Gardner, from December 24, 2011, blog "Give 'Em Hell, Harry!" blog http://www.caseneverdies.blogspot.com/ (January 9, 2012)

[13] J. E. Seykora, U.S. Department of Justice memo dated May 10, 1934. New Jersey State Police Lindbergh Files, F-447.

[14] "Servant, 28, Takes Poison: Was Awaiting Police For Fourth Questioning in Lindbergh Case," *New York Times*, June 11, 1932.

[15] Report of Inspector Harry Walsh of the Jersey City Police regarding the questioning of Violet Sharp, May 23, 1932, p. 2. In files of the New Jersey State Police Museum.

[16] George Waller, *Kidnap,* (New York: The Dial Press, 1961), 150.

[17] What happens when a person ingests cyanide is described by John Douglas and Mark Olshaker in *The Anatomy of Motive,* (New York: A Lisa Drew Book/Scribner, 1999), 104. Additional insights in this section into the body's reaction to cyanide were provided by Dr. Jeffrey Barnard, Professor of Pathology at UT Southwestern Medical School. Emails from Dr. Barnard to the author, January 11, 2012.

[18] Sebastian Junger, *The Perfect Storm,* (New York: W. W. Norton & Company, 1997), 142.

[19] "Servant, 28, Takes Poison: Was Awaiting Police For Fourth Questioning in Lindbergh Case," *New York Times,* June 11, 1932.

[20] "Sister Denies Maid Aided Kidnapping," *New York Times,* June 12, 1932.

[21] "British Rage Over the Violet Sharpe [sic] Suicide," *Literary Digest,* June 25, 1932, 12.

[22] From e-mail from Mark Olshaker to the author, Februaary 10, 2012, and another from John Douglas to Olshaker, February 11, 2012.

[23] From Charles Lindbergh's 79 pages of typewritten comments on the 1959 book *The Hero* by Kenneth S. Davis. This comment is dated August 19, 1969, and the quote is on p. 58, Library of Congress, *Spirit of St. Louis* Papers, Box 34, Comments on Davis Biography Folder.

[24] The story of Skean's death and the quote are from Charles A. Lindbergh, *The Wartime Journals of Charles A. Lindbergh* (New York: Harcourt Brace Jovanovich, Inc., 1970), 417.

[25] Description of the Morrow apartment is from Winters, 18.

[26] Anne Morrow Lindbergh, *Hour of Gold, Hour of Lead,* 299.

[27] Ibid., 320.

[28] This is from a comment made by Charles Lindbergh regarding the book *The Last Hero: Charles A. Lindbergh* by Walter S. Ross. The comment is dated August 6, 1968, and the quote is on p. 40, Library of Congress, *Spirit of St. Louis* Papers, Box 34, Comments on Ross Biography Folder.

[29] Anne Morrow Lindbergh, *Hour of Gold, Hour of Lead,* 257.

[30] The phrase "feelings of joy" and a description of the details of the delivery come from Berg, 281.

[31] "A Son For Colonel Lindbergh," *The London Times*, August 16, 1932. Also in Berg, 281-82.

### 16: "THE KILLERS"

[1] "Police Intensify Hunt," *New York Times,* May 13, 1932.

[2] "Sympathy Pours In From All the World," *New York Times,* May 13, 1932, 3.

[3] Public Papers of the Presidents of the United States, Herbert Hoover: Containing the Public Messages, Speeches, and Statements of the President, January 1, 1932 to March 4, 1933 (United States Government Printing Office, Washington, 1977), p. 215.

[4] George Waller, *Kidnap*, (New York: The Dial Press, 1961), 105.

[5] *The New York Times,* "Schwarzkopf 'Bungling' Charged," May 20, 1932.

[6] Major Schoeffel, "Report of trip to Europe from March 28 to April 27, 1932," from the New Jersey State Police Museum.

[7] Ibid.

[8] Memorandum dated June 1, 1932, Captain Lamb Personal File, New Jersey State Police Museum.

[9] Letter from Albert S. Osborn to Colonel H. Norman Schwarzkopf, July 14, 1932. New Jersey State Police Museum.

[10] Leon G. Turrou, *Where My Shadow Falls: Two Decades of Crime Detection*, (Garden City, New York: Doubleday & Company, Inc., 1949), 118.

[11] George E. Koehler, *Our Koehler Ancestry*, April 2006, Chapter 4, 12. George Koehler is the son of Arthur Koehler.

[12] Opinion of C. P. Winslow, director of the United States Forest Products Laboratory, quoted in *New York Times*, "Wood His Life Study," January 24, 1935.

### 17: CAPTURE

[1] Dr. Kim Rossmo, *Geographic Profiling* (2000), CRC Press.

[2] Email from Dr. Kim Rossmo to the author, November 16, 2011.

[3] The author supplied Dr. Rossmo with the data for the geographic profile on the Lindbergh case. The resulting analysis was discussed in a conference call among Dr. Rossmo, Zorn, and Gregory F. Hamm on October 8, 2011. The image contained herein was generated by the software program *Rigel*, developed by ECRI, Vancouver, BC, Canada. This section was edited and approved by Dr. Rossmo.

[4] Thomas Fensch, *FBI Files On the Lindbergh Kidnapping* (The Woodlands, Texas: New Century Books, 2001), 285.

[5] George Waller, *Kidnap,* (The Dial Press, 1961: New York), 213.

[6] Leon G. Turrou, *Where My Shadow Falls: Two Decades of Crime Detection* (Garden City, New York: Doubleday & Company, Inc., 1949), 119.

[7] Biographical Note on Walter Winchell accompanying the Walter Winchell Papers, 1920-1967, The New York Public Library For the Performing Arts, Billy Rose Theatre Collection, 1-2.

[8] *Liberty Magazine* article by Lt. James J. Finn and D. Thomas Curtin, November 9, 1935.

[9] "$10 Bill Trapped Lindy Kidnapper," *New York Daily News,* September 21, 1934.

[10] *Liberty Magazine* article by Lt. James J. Finn and D. Thomas Curtin, November 9, 1935, 43.

### 18: INTERROGATION

[1] Dialogue beginning "Richard, what is this?" from Waller, *Kidnap,* (The Dial Press, 1961: New York), 223.

[2] "Hauptmann Slow To Pay His Rent," *New York Times*, September 23, 1934.

[3] Film interview of Pauline Rauch, shown in Monster All-Star Midnight Show, Film and Television Reference, Library of Congress.

[4] Sgt. Thomas J. Ritchie, New Jersey State Police Trial Transcripts, 865.

[5] Description of the ranch is from Betty Rogers, *Will Rogers: His Wife's Story* (Indianapolis: The Bobbs-Merrill Company, 1941), 266-67.

[6] Ludovic Kennedy, *The Airman and the Carpenter* (New York: Viking, 1985), Prologue.

[7] Anne Morrow Lindbergh's 1973 book *Hour of Gold, Hour of Lead* contains her diaries and letters during the time of the kidnapping and its aftermath.

[8] From Charles Lindbergh's 79 pages of typewritten comments on the 1959 book "The Hero" by Kenneth S. Davis. This comment is dated August 4, 1969, and the quote is on p. 2, Library of Congress, *Spirit of St. Louis* Papers, Box 34, Comments on Davis Biography Folder.

[9] Analysis of Dr. Mary Ellen O'Toole is from phone conversation between the author and Dr. O'Toole, January 31, 2011.

[10] Anne Morrow Lindbergh, *Locked Rooms and Open Doors* (San Diego: Harcourt Brace & Company, 1974), 202.

[11] *Harold Nicolson: Diaries and Letters 1930-1964*, Collins (London: St. James Place, 1980), 70.

### 19: NOT THE MAN

[1] "Arrest of Hauptmann in Bronx Street Described by New Jersey State Trooper," *New York Times*, January 19, 1935.

[2] Division of Investigation document entitled "Isidor [sic] Fisch," September 24, 1934, Declassified FBI Headquarters Files, Lindbergh Case 7-1, FBI Archives, College Park, Maryland.

[3] The author's father recalled an afternoon when John Knoll had taken him to the pool at Tibbetts Brook Park in Yonkers. On the way home, when they were in the north Bronx not far from Hauptmann's home, John told Eugene Zorn to go the rest of the way home by himself, then went off by himself.

[4] "$10 Bill Trapped Lindy Kidnapper," *New York Daily News*, September 21, 1934, 6.

[5] Lloyd C. Gardner, *The Case that Never Dies* (New Brunswick, NJ: Rutgers University Press, 2004), 167.

[6] Ibid., 167.

[7] Ibid., 169.

[8] "Files Show Hoover Continued To Believe Hauptmann Guilty," *New York Times*, October 23, 1977.

[9] Gardner, 171.

[10] *New York Daily News*, September 22, 1934, 9.

[11] A. Scott Berg, *Lindbergh* (New York: G.P. Putnam's Sons, 1998), 302.

[12] Phone interview of George Koehler, son of Arthur Koehler, by the author, November 16, 2010.

[13] "My father was never satisfied with a job that would be judged merely acceptable," recalled Koehler's son George. "He was determined to do things *right*. In 1948, when we were getting our home in tip-top shape in preparation to sell it, he made me climb up an extension ladder to paint the trim of an attic window—a detail no buyer ever would have noticed." From a phone interview of George Koehler by the author, November 29, 2010.

[14] Arthur Koehler, "Technique Used In Tracing the Lindbergh Kidnapping Ladder," United States Department of Agriculture – Forest Products Laboratory publication No. D1420, Reissued September 1952, p. 6. This paragraph also contains the analysis of independent researcher Kelvin Keraga. From Keraga's email to the author, February 5, 2012.

[15] At the time, the average annual family income in America was less than two thousand dollars.

[16] Letter from Bruno Richard Hauptmann to his mother, Pauline Hauptmann, December 27, 1935. The letter was never mailed.

[17] Gardner, 165.

### 20: HOMECOMING

[1] Transcript of Charles A. Lindbergh's grand jury testimony at Bronx County Courthouse, September 26, 1934, 4-6.

[2] Curt Gentry, *J. Edgar Hoover: The Man and His Secrets* (New York: W. W. Norton & Company, Inc, 1991), 163.

[3] Standard Certificate of Death #4858 May 25, 1934 for William J. Schaefer, State of New York—Department of Health of the City of New York, Bureau of Records. Cause of death stated as "angina factors," contributory (secondary) cause of death stated as "acute gastritis."

[4] Source Citation: Year: 1934; Microfilm Serial: T715; Microfilm Roll: T715_5567; Line: 9; Page Number: 116. Source Information: Ancestry.com. New York Passenger Lists, 1820-1957 [database online]. Provo, UT, USA: Ancestry.com Operations, Inc., 2010.

[5] From the author's meeting with John Douglas and Mark Olshaker on December 29, 2011.

[6] The author's search for any other records pertaining to foreign travel for John Knoll between 1925 and 1980 resulted in just this one trip to Germany near the time of the Hauptmann trial.

[7] Phone interview of Louis Zamperini by the author, August 7, 2011.

[8] Typical menu items for Hauptmann in the Flemington jail were liver pudding, liverwurst sandwiches, onion sandwiches, green tomato chow-chow, and scrapple. Source: "Report of Hauptmann's Meals," New Jersey State Police Museum.

### 21: TRIAL OF THE CENTURY

[1] History on Samuel Fleming from George Waller, *Kidnap* (New York: The Dial Press, 1961), 251.

[2] Flemington is classified as a borough is according to the *American Places Dictionary* (Detroit: Omnigraphics, Inc., Frederick G. Ruffner, Jr., *Publisher*, 1994), 201.

[3] Anthony Scaduto, *Scapegoat: The Lonesome Death of Bruno Richard Hauptmann* (New York: G. P. Putnam's Sons, 1976), 119.

[4] Story from phone interview of Carolyn Blackman Jacoby, daughter of AP reporter Samuel G. Blackman, by the author, September 5, 2011.

[5] Gabriel Heatter, *There's Good News Tonight* (Garden City, New York: Doubleday & Company, Inc., 1960).

[6] Adela Rogers St. John, *The Honeycomb* (Garden City, New York: Doubleday & Company, Inc., 1969), 288.

[7] Walter Winchell Papers, 1920-1967, The New York Public Library For the Performing Arts, Billy Rose Theatre Collection, Box 3 Jergens Jan. 3, 1934 – Dec. 27, 1936.

[8] *Daily Mirror*, October 23, 1934.

[9] Reference to "frinstance" (for instance) is from "Winchell On Broadway" column, *Daily Mirror*, November 8, 1934. References to "slanguage" and "Cupiding" from Biographical Note about Winchell in the Walter Winchell Papers, 1920-1967, The New York Public Library For the Performing Arts, Billy Rose Theatre Collection.

[10] Walter Winchell, "Winchell On Broadway" column, *Daily Mirror*, October 3, 1934.

### 22: THE STATE'S CASE

[1] Walter Winchell Jergens radio program, January 13, 1935. Walter Winchell Papers, 1920-1967, The New York Public Library For the Performing Arts, Billy Rose Theatre Collection, Box 3, Jergens, Jan. 3, 1934 – Dec. 27, 1936.

[2] Berg, 304.

[3] Walter Winchell, "Winchell On Broadway" column, *Daily Mirror*, November 8, 1934.

[4] *The New York Times*, "Digest of the Opening Session of the Hauptmann Trial," January 3, 1935.

[5] Quote from Attorney General Wilentz's opening is from Trial Transcript, State vs. Hauptmann, in Sidney B. Whipple, *This special edition of The Trial of Bruno Richard Hauptmann*, (Birmingham, Alabama: The Notable Trials Library, 1989), 96.

[6] Ibid., 103.

### 23: SWORN TO TRUTH

[1] From Trial Transcript, State vs. Hauptmann, in Sidney B. Whipple, *This special edition of The Trial of Bruno Richard Hauptmann* (Birmingham, Alabama: The Notable Trials Library, 1989), 103.

[2] Dialogue from Anne Morrow Lindbergh's testimony is from Trial Transcript, State vs. Hauptmann, in Whipple, 108.

[3] Dialogue from Charles Lindbergh's testimony is from Trial Transcript, State vs. Hauptmann, in Whipple,125.

[4] Adela Rogers St. John, *The Honeycomb* (Garden City, New York: Doubleday & Company, Inc., 1969), 321.

[5] Dialogue from Lindbergh's testimony is from Trial Transcript, State vs. Hauptmann, in Whipple, 125. The author also draws from A. Scott Berg, *Lindbergh* (New York: G. P. Putnam's Sons), 314.

[6] "Why the Jury Voted To Put Him In Chair," *The Detroit News*, February 15, 1935.

[7] Leon G. Turrou, *Where My Shadow Falls: Two Decades of Crime Detection* (Garden City, New York: Doubleday & Company, Inc., 1949), 127-28.

[8] Berg, 315.

### 24: "Who Is John?"

[1] "Breckinridge Backs Condon Who Acted On His Orders But Opposed Ransom Deal," *New York Times*, January 11, 1935.

[2] John F. Condon, *Jafsie Tells All* (New York: Jonathan Lee Publishing Corp., 1936), 238.

[3] Condon's letter to Henry Breckinridge dated October 29, 1933, is in The Papers of the Breckinridge Family in the Library of Congress, Container 523, Henry Breckinridge General Correspondence Folder, July-Dec. 1933.

[4] Walter Winchell Jergens radio program, January 13, 1935. Walter Winchell Papers, 1920-1967, The New York Public Library For the Performing Arts, Billy Rose Theatre Collection, Box 3, Jergens, Jan. 3, 1934–Dec. 27, 1936.

[5] Copy of the program for the May 14, 1935, Bronx Chamber of Commerce event is found in The Papers of the Breckinridge Family in the Library of Congress, Container 524, Henry Breckinridge General Correspondence Folder, 1937-38.

[6] Bob E. Lype, "The Handwriting on the the the Wall: The State & Handwriting Expert Testimony in Tennessee," *Tennessee Bar Journal*, Vol. 34, No. 5, September/October 1998.

[7] From Trial Transcript, State vs. Hauptmann, in Sidney B. Whipple, *This special edition of The Trial of Bruno Richard Hauptmann* (Birmingham, Alabama: The Notable Trials Library, 1989), 337-38

[8] An in-depth forensic study conducted by Kelvin Keraga three-quarters of a century later incorporated the findings of twenty of the country's leading wood scientists and professionals. The results validated Koehler's conclusion that the wood from Rail 16 had come from a floorboard in Hauptmann's attic.

[9] Lloyd C. Gardner, *The Case that Never Dies* (New Brunswick, NJ: Rutgers University Press, 2004), 298.

### 25: The Carpenter

[1] Phone interview of Kevin Klein by the author, March 3, 2012.

[2] *Star Ledger*, "Wilentz vividly recalls Lindbergh kidnap case," February 26, 1976.

[3] From Trial Transcript, State vs. Hauptmann, in Sidney B. Whipple, *This special edition of The Trial of Bruno Richard Hauptmann* (Birmingham, Alabama: The Notable Trials Library, 1989), 401-02.

[4] Ibid., 407.

[5] State of New Jersey, Department of State Police, Special Report of Investigation of Trooper Hugo Stockburger, October 24, 1934.

[6] A. Scott Berg, *Lindbergh* (New York: G. P. Putnam's Sons, 1998), 327.

### 26: THE VERDICT

[1] A. Scott Berg, *Lindbergh* (New York: G. P. Putnam's Sons, 1998), 335.

[2] Summary of Attorney General David T. Wilentz for the prosecution, State of New Jersey vs. Bruno Richard Hauptmann, February 12, 1935.

[3] Ibid.

[4] George Waller, *Kidnap,* (New York: The Dial Press, 1961), 485.

[5] "Stolen In the Night," an ABC documentary hosted by Peter Jennings, 1999.

[6] Neal Gabler, *Winchell: Gossip, Power and the Culture of Celebrity* (Alfred A. Knopf: New York, 1994), 212.

[7] Harold Nicolson, *Harold Nicolson: Diaries and Letters 1930-1964*, Collins (London: St. James Place, 1980), 73.

[8] Ibid., 73.

[9] Anne Morrow Lindbergh, *Locked Rooms and Open Doors* (San Diego: A Harvest Book, Harcourt Brace & Company, 1974), 249.

[10] Adela Rogers St. John, *The Honeycomb,* (Garden City, New York: Doubleday & Company, Inc., 1969), 340.

### 27: ARRIVAL AND DEPARTURE

[1] Dr. Mary Ellen O'Toole, *Dangerous Instincts: How Gut Feelings Betray Us* (New York: Hudson Street Press, 2010, 165.

[2] During the Second World War, Kamenz was the site of a massive extermination of Jews. The town is currently building a memorial to the people who lost their lives there.

[3] John Knoll is a member of the passenger list of United States Citizens sailing from Hamburg, Germany, on the SS *Manhattan* and arriving at the Port of New York on February 20, 1935. His address in the United States is listed as 51 Cherry Street, Mt. Clemens, Michigan, the address of his sister and brother-in-law Agnes and Ludwig Breiling. This address coincides with Agnes and Ludwig Breilings' address listed in the 1930 U.S. Federal Census. See source citation below.

[4] The following is the source citation and information for John Knoll's voyage from Hamburg to Southampton to New York. The SS *Manhattan* sailed from Southampton on February 13, 1935. Source Citation: Year: *1935*; Arrival: New York, United States; Microfilm Serial: T715; Microfilm Roll: T715_5609; Line: 8; Page Number: 25. Source Information: Ancestry.com. New York Passenger Lists, 1820-1957 [database online]. Provo, UT, USA: Ancestry.com Operations, Inc., 2010.

[5] The following is the source citation and information for Babe Ruth's voyage from Southampton to New York. Source Citation: Year: *1935*; Arrival: *New York, United States*; Microfilm Serial: *T715*; Microfilm Roll: *T715_5609*; Line: 27; Page Number: *14*.

Source Information: Ancestry.com. *New York Passenger Lists, 1820-1957* [database on-line]. Provo, UT, USA: Ancestry.com Operations, Inc., 2010. Babe Ruth went to Mt. Clemens, Michigan, to visit the town's famed mineral baths. John Knoll lived in Mt. Clemens for a period with his sister and brother-in-law Agnes and Ludwig Breiling.

[6] Phone interview of Julia Ruth Stephens by the author, July 19, 2011.

[7] Karoline Lilly (née Karg) Knoll is a member of the List or Manifest of Alien Passengers sailing on the SS *Manhattan* from Hamburg, Germany, and arriving in New York on June 5, 1935. Her last permanent residence is listed as Mt. Clemens, Michigan.

[8] The headstone of Lilly Knoll's grandmother, Margarethe Zorn Karg, is in the Lutheran Cemetery in Kempten im Allgäu, Germany. Observed by the author on July 4, 2010.

[9] Estimate of the cost of the investigation and trial is from "Hauptmann Case Marches

To a Climax," *The Literary Digest,* January 18, 1936, 9. Calculation of value of $1,2000,000 in 1932 in 2011 dollars (a multiple of 15.01) is derived from http://www.dol-lartimes.com/calculators/inflation.htm, December 26, 2011.

[10] Interview of C. Lloyd Fisher by George G. Hawke, quoted in "Trial By Fury: The Hauptmann Trial," a Princeton University senior thesis of George G. Hawke, April 27, 1951, 9.

[11] State of the Case: State of New Jersey vs. Hauptmann, p. 4507, New Jersey State Police Museum archives.

[12] "Governor Orders New Kidnap Hunt," *New York Times,* January 30, 1936, p. 1, 6.

[13] "Anthony Hauck Jr., Prosecutor in Lindbergh Kidnap Case, Dies," *New York Times,* September 15, 1972.

[14] "Reflections On an Execution," *Ft. Lauderdale News and Sun Sentinel,* February 22, 1976.

[15] Letter from Amelia Earhart to Governor Harold G. Hoffman, April 1, 1936, from the Hoffman Collection, New Jersey State Police Museum, Box 20, Miscellaneous file. Letter found on website http://www.lindberghkidnappinghoax.com/amelia.jpg.

[16] "Lindberghs' Exile from Country Stirs Demand for Kidnap Purge," *Detroit Free Press,* December 24, 1935, 1.

[17] "Englewood Voices Regret and Relief," *New York Times,* December 24, 1935.

[18] This comment was made by Charles Lindbergh regarding the book *The Last Hero: Charles A. Lindbergh* by Walter S. Ross. The comment is dated August 6, 1968, and the quote is on p. 40, Library of Congress, *Spirit of St. Louis* Papers, Box 34, Comments on Ross Biography Folder.

[19] Anne Morrow Lindbergh, *Locked Rooms and Open Doors* (San Diego: A Harvest Book, Harcourt Brace & Company, 1974), 335.

[20] New York passenger list for Charles, Anne, and Jon Lindbergh, arriving in Liverpool on the SS *American Importer* on December 31, 1935.

[21] "Lindbergh Wants 'Even Name Forgotten,'" article from unnamed newspaper, Thelma Miller Collection, New Jersey State Police Museum, January 14, 1935.

[22] Alden Whitman, "The Price of Fame," *The New York Times Magazine,* May 8, 1977, 18.

[23] Charles A. Lindbergh, *Autobiography of Values* (San Diego: Harvest, 1978), 18.

[24] "How Now, Col. Lindbergh?", *New York Daily News,* January 1, 1936.

[25] "Englewood Voices Regret and Relief," *New York Times,* December 24, 1935.

[26] Anne Morrow Lindbergh, *Hour of Gold, Hour of Lead* (New York: Harcourt, Brace Jovanovich, 1973), 255.

[27] "Lindberghs' Exile from Country Stirs Demand for Kidnap Purge," *Detroit Free Press,* December 24, 1935, 1.

[28] "Hoffman To Order New Investigation," *New York Times,* January 19, 1936.

[29] Lloyd C. Gardner, from December 24, 2011, blog "Give 'Em Hell, Harry!" blog http://www.caseneverdies.blogspot.com/ (January 9, 2012)

[30] Transcript of interview with John F. Condon by Harry Walsh and others, June 2, 1932. From Box 24, Folder 6, Lindbergh Collection, Missouri History Museum, St. Louis, MO.

[31] George Waller, *Kidnap,* (New York: The Dial Press, 1961), 534.

[32] Letter from John F. Condon to Henry Breckinridge, March 3, 1938, The Papers of the Breckinridge Family in the Library of Congress, Container 524, Henry Breckinridge General Correspondence Folder, 1937-38.

[33] "Files Show Hoover Continued To Believe Hauptmann Guilty," *New York Times,* October 23, 1977.

**28: SILENCE**

[1] Robert G. Elliott, *Agent of Death*, (New York: E. P. Dutton & Co., 1940), 193.

[2] Ibid., 196.

[3] Ibid., 269.

[4] Ibid.

[5] Phone interview of Carolyn Blackman Jacoby by the author, September 5, 2011.

[6] Charles A. Lindbergh, *The Wartime Journals of Charles A. Lindbergh* (New York: Harcourt Brace Jovanovich, Inc., 1970), xiv.

[7] Letter from Charles Lindbergh to Harold Bixby. Library of Congress files.

[8] Charles A. Lindbergh, *The Wartime Journals of Charles A. Lindbergh*, 193.

[9] From newspaper clipping in the Hauptmann files, Kamenz City Archives.

[10] "The Case Hauptmann," *Kamenzer Tageblatt*, April 6, 1936, in German, Kamenz file, New Jersey State Police Museum.

[11] "Hoffman Rebukes State Police Head," *New York Times*, March 1, 1936.

[12] Catherine Davidson, "Trial of the Century," *Columbia Magazine*, Summer 1995, 37.

**29: LAST CHANCE**

[1] Sam Leibowitz, "The Lindbergh Kidnapping Case," *TV Guide*, February 21, 1976, 16.

[2] "Bruno's Death House Story," *Daily Mirror*, February 21, 1936.

[3] Quote from Edward W. Sulzbach and description of how Leibowitz's strategy became one commonly used by the FBI came from a phone conversation between Sulzbach and the author, September 3, 2011.

[4] Sam Leibowitz, "The Lindbergh Kidnapping Case," 17.

[5] Lloyd C. Gardner, *The Case That Never Dies*, (New Brunswick, New Jersey: Rutgers University Press, 2004), 210-11.

[6] Letter written from the New Jersey State Prison in Trenton, New Jersey by Bruno Richard Hauptmann to his mother, Pauline Hauptmann, December 27, 1935. The warden, Colonel Mark Kimberling, never mailed the letter.

[7] Meeting between Mark Olshaker and the author, Washington, D.C., October 12, 2011.

[8] Phone interview of Dr. Sally C. Johnson by the author, February 17, 2011.

[9] Lunch meeting among the author, Barry H. Evenchick, Esq., and Governor Brendan T. Byrne in Roseland, New Jersey, August 25, 2011.

[10] Meeting between the author and Governor Brendan T. Byrne in the former governor's offices at Carella Byrne in Roseland, New Jersey, October 6, 2010.

[11] Conference call among the author and Governor Brendan T. Byrne in the former governor's offices at Carella Byrne in Roseland, New Jersey, and Don Linky, October 6, 2010.

[12] Phyllis Plitch, "Widow Comes Back to Flemington to Say Again that Bruno Was Innocent," *Hunterdon County Democrat*, October 10, 1991.

[13] Ibid.

**30: JUSTICE DELAYED**

[1] U.S. World War II Army Enlistment Records, 1938-1946 dated 22 Sep 1942 for John Knoll. Source Information: National Archives and Records Administration. *U.S. World War II Army Enlistment Records, 1938-1946* [database online]. Provo, UT, USA: Ancestry.com Operations Inc, 2005. Original data: Electronic Army Serial Number Merged File, 1938-1946 [Archival Database]; World War II Army Enlistment Records; Records of the National Archives and Records Administration, Record Group 64; National Archives at Col-

lege Park, College Park, MD.

[2] Letter of condolence from Ida Knoll to Agnes Breiling following the death in 1965 of Agnes's husband, Lud.

[3] The animal he was holding was identified by a staff member of the San Diego Zoo as a monkey.

[4] Meeting of the author with Mark Olshaker and John Douglas, Washington, D.C., October 12, 2011.

[5] From conversation between the author and John Knoll's daughter-in-law, Adrienne Knoll, in her home, September 18, 2009.

[6] Bob Knoll was Adrienne's devoted husband for forty-six years, a loving father of their only child (a daughter), and a man known for his faithfulness to friends. He died in 2009 before the author had the privilege to meet him.

[7] According to his Declaration of Intention No. 107559, July 27, 1931, Bronx County, New York, Walter Knoll was five-foot-eleven and 149 pounds.

[8] According to Sharon, her father had fixed motorcycles in Detroit with Charles Lindbergh before the aviator became famous.

[9] Dinner table comment noted by the author at the home of Sharon and Rudolf Breiling, September 10, 2009.

[10] Car ride conversation between the author and Eugene C. Zorn, Jr., on way from Remsenburg, New York, to Philadelphia, Pennsylvania, March 1980.

### 31: CEMETERY JOHN KNOLL

[1] Opinion of Dr. Mary Ellen O'Toole that the Lindbergh kidnapping was "not a one-man crime" is from a phone conversation with the author on December 14, 2011.

[2] Phone conversation between retired criminal profiler Edward F. Sulzbach, a recipient of the FBI Medal of Valor, and the author, October 20, 2011. Crime novelist Patricia Cornwell used a variation of Sulzbach's quote in her book *Portrait of a Killer*.

[3] Phone interview of Catherine J. Sporer by the author, November 29, 2009.

[4] State of the Case: State of New Jersey vs. Hauptmann, p. 2431 ("*mit* two friends"), p. 2432 ("*farder vest*"), p. 2515 ("*slippy*"), p. 2447 ("*cardon*"), p. 2438 ("Bronx Park subway"), New Jersey State Police Museum archives; Whipple, p. 387 ("*dem* bundles"), p. 411 ("like *dat*"), p. 424 ("I don't *tink* so"), p. 434 ("*mitout*").

[5] Petition for Citizenship No. 97404 of John Knoll, October 31, 1931.

[6] The author's search on ancestry.com for foreign travel records for John Knoll after his voyage on the SS *Manhattan* in February 1935 yielded no results.

### 32: AN UNCOMMON CRIMINAL

[1] John Douglas and Mark Olshaker, *Mindhunter* (New York/London/Toronto/Sydney/Tokyo: Scribner, A Lisa Drew Book, 1995), 151.

[2] John Douglas's view of Hauptmann as a "common criminal" was verified in a phone conversation between the author and Mark Olshaker, February 6, 2012.

[3] Phone conversation between Edward S. Sulzbach and the author, September 3, 2011.

[4] John Douglas and Mark Olshaker, *The Anatomy of Motive* (New York: A Lisa Drew Book/Scribner, 1999), 15. Analysis in this paragraph that follows Douglas's quote is the author's.

[5] From the kidnappers' ransom notes. Source: New Jersey State Police Museum. Specific quotes from the ransom notes selected by the author, not by Dr. O'Toole.

[6] Phone interview of Dr. O'Toole by the author, January 10, 2012. Dr. O'Toole said that "thrill-seeking" was one of the "high points" of the crime.

[7] Phone interview of Dr. Mary Ellen O'Toole by the author, January 10, 2012.

[8] George Waller, *Kidnap*, (New York: The Dial Press, 1961), 171.

[9] The concept of the $50,000 ransom demand's being twice the $25,000 awarded for the Orteig Prize comes from the author, not from Dr. Shoenfeld.

[10] John Douglas and Mark Olshaker, *The Anatomy of Motive*, 33.

[11] From phone conversation of the author with Mark Olshaker, February 6, 2012.

[12] Interview of Dr. Mary Ellen O'Toole by the author, January 31, 2012.

### 33: MARCH 1, 1932

[1] This section on Dr. Lane's 1977 analysis is from Jim Fisher, *The Ghosts of Hopewell: Setting the Record Straight In the Lindbergh Kidnapping*, (Carbondale, Illinois: Southern Illinois University Press, 1999), 44.

[2] Anthony Scaduto, *Scapegoat* (New York: G. P. Putnam's Sons, 1976), 180.

[3] Ibid., 178.

[4] Kelvin Keraga, "Testimony in Wood: Analysis of the Rail 16 evidence in the Lindbergh Kidnapping," Summary Report 1.2, 2005, 1.

[5] Ibid., 3.

[6] Ibid., 10.

[7] Phone conversation between Kelvin Keraga and the author, December 11, 2011.

[8] Phone conversation between Eugene C. Zorn, Jr., and Anthony Scaduto, October 28, 1980.

[9] Former FBI agent Jim Fisher does a thorough job refuting the theories suggesting that Hauptmann had no role in the kidnapping in his books *The Lindbergh Case* and *The Ghosts of Hopewell*.

[10] A repeated quote from Ed Sulzbach's conversations with the author.

[11] Phone conversation between Mark Olshaker and the author, December 14, 2011.

[12] John Douglas and Mark Olshaker, *The Cases That Haunt Us*, (New York: A Lisa Drew Book/Scribner, 2000), 182.

[13] Analysis of Hauptmann's being a good partner for the job is from John Douglas. From meeting between John Douglas and the author, December 29, 2011.

[14] Possibility of John Knoll's having shown up at the Lindberghs' house during the construction phase looking for work is the analysis of John Douglas. From meeting between John Douglas and the author, December 29, 2011.

[15] Email from Kevin Klein to author, March 7, 2012.

[16] Analysis of Dr. Mary Ellen O'Toole. From phone interview of Dr. O'Toole by the author, January 31, 2012.

### 34: THE ARCHIVIST

[1] John Douglas and Mark Olshaker, *The Anatomy of Motive*, (New York: A Lisa Drew Book/Scribner, 1999), 29.

[2] Phone conversation between the author and Dr. Mary Ellen O'Toole, January 10, 2012.

[3] PCL-R: Psychopathy Checklist—Revised. Includes 20 items, developed by Dr. Robert D. Hare to assess psychopathy (Widiger & Lynam, 1998, 173-178), as quoted in http://www.criminalmindsfanwiki.com.
Robert D. Hare's Psychopathy Checklist-Revised (PCL-R)
1. Glib and Superficial Charm
2. Grandiose Sense of Self-Worth
3. Need for Stimulation or Proneness to Boredom

4. Pathological Lying

5. Conning and Manipulativeness

6. Lack of Remorse or Guilt

7. Shallow Affect

8. Callousness and Lack of Empathy

9. Parasitic Lifestyle

10. Poor Behavioral Controls

11. Promiscuous Sexual Behaviors

12. Early Behavioral Problems

13. Lack of Realistic, Long-Term Goals

14. Impulsivity

15. Irresponsibility

16. Failure to Accept Responsibility for Own Actions

17. Many Short-Term Marital Relationships

18. Juvenile Delinquency

19. Revocation of Conditional Release

20. Criminal Versatility

[4] Opinion of Dr. Craig S. Neumann, internationally recognized researcher of psychopathic personality and Professor of Psychology at the University of North Texas. Opinions of Dr. Neumann expressed in this chapter are from an interview by the author, February 22, 2011.

[5] From the interview of Dr. Neumann by the author, February 22, 2011.

[6] Email from Dr. Mary Ellen O'Toole to the author, January 26, 2012.

[7] Phone interview of Dr. Sally C. Johnson by the author, February 17, 2011.

[8] Forensic pathologist Dr. Mary Case was asked if it's possible that someone had poisoned Schaefer. "As far as the death certificate, you can't tell much from that as heart disease is sort of the default diagnosis put down when one doesn't really know—it is the most likely," said Dr. Case. "However, the deaths could have been poisoning but there is no way to know that." From email from Dr. Case to the author, January 29, 2012.

### 35: APPROACHING LINDBERGH

[1] Personal notes on the Lindbergh case of Eugene C. Zorn, Jr.

[2] Anne Morrow Lindbergh, *Hour of Gold, Hour of Lead* (New York: Harcourt, Brace Jovanovich 1973), 253.

[3] Anne Morrow Lindbergh, *Locked Rooms and Open Doors* (San Diego: A Harvest Book, Harcourt Brace & Company, 1974), 14.

[4] Arthur T. Vanderbilt II recalled the details of this PBS interview of Anne Morrow Lindbergh during a meeting with the author on August 26, 2011. The author of *Fortune's Children: The Fall of the House of Vanderbilt* and many other nonfiction books, Mr. Vanderbilt is Counselor At Law with Governor Brendan T. Byrne's law firm, Carella, Byrne, Cecchi, Olstein, Brody & Agnello.

[5] Reeve Lindbergh, *No More Words* (New York: Touchstone, 2001), 71.

[6] Letter from Elizabeth C. Morrow to Robert H. Thayer, Esq., October 8, 1934, The Papers of Robert H. Thayer, Library of Congress, Box 7, The Lindbergh Case Correspondence Folder.

[7] Samuel G. Blackman, "Lindbergh Case Unshaken," *The Dallas Morning News*, February 27, 1972.

[8] From a filmed interview of the author speaking to his father, Eugene C. Zorn, Jr., on May 3, 2004, in Valley View, Texas. Filming done by Charlie Bahr.

[9] From a filmed interview of the author speaking to his father, Eugene C. Zorn, Jr., on May 3, 2004, in Valley View, Texas. Filming done by Charlie Bahr.

[10] Source Citation: Year: 1930; Census Place: Bronx, Bronx, New York; Roll: 1471; Page: 1B; Enumeration District: 262; Image: 558.0. Source Information: Ancestry.com. *1930 United States Federal Census* [database on-line]. Provo, UT, USA: Ancestry.com Operations Inc., 2002. Original data: United States of America, Bureau of the Census. *Fifteenth Census of the United States, 1930.* Washington, D.C.: National Archives and Records Administration, 1930. T626, 2,667 rolls.

[11] The acquisitions editor at the Kent State University Press had appeared quite interested in the story of Eugene C. Zorn, Jr., but the editor in charge of the true crime publications dismissed Zorn's theory as implausible and sent a rejection letter.

### EPILOGUE

[1] Description of the Main Reading Room in the Library of Congress is from *The Library of Congress: The Art and Architecture of the Thomas Jefferson Building,* Edited by John Y. Cole and Henry Hope Reed, (New York: W. W. Norton & Company, 1997), 121 and 135.

[2] The quote comes from "Of Truth" in Francis Bacon's *Essays.*

[3] Handwritten notes on the Lindbergh case of Eugene C. Zorn, Jr., March 29, 1973, 2.

[4] Anne Morrow Lindbergh, *Hour of Gold, Hour of Lead,* (New York: Harcourt, Brace Jovanovich 1973), 216.

[5] Ibid., 217.

[6] Handwritten notes on the Lindbergh case of Eugene C. Zorn, Jr., March 29, 1973, 4.

# Index